For Ever and Ever,
Eamonn

For Ever and Ever, Eamonn

*The Public and Private Life
of Eamonn Andrews*

*EAMONN AND GRAINNE
ANDREWS*

with Robin McGibbon

GRAFTON BOOKS
A Division of the Collins Publishing Group

**LONDON GLASGOW
TORONTO SYDNEY AUCKLAND**

Grafton Books
A Division of the Collins Publishing Group
8 Grafton Street, London W1X 3LA

Published by Grafton Books 1989

British Library Cataloguing in Publication Data

Andrews, Eamonn
  For ever and ever, Eamonn: the public and private
  life of Eamonn Andrews.
  1. Great Britain. Television programmes.
  Broadcasting. Andrews, Eamonn
  I. Title II. Andrews, Grainne   III. McGibbon, Robin
  791.45'092'4

ISBN 0–246–13491–7

Photoset by Deltatype Ltd, Ellesmere Port, Cheshire
Printed in Great Britain by Mackays of Chatham plc, Kent

For Hymie

CONTENTS

AUTHOR'S NOTE

For several years before his death in November 1987, Eamonn wrote 50,000 words of a proposed autobiography, which he wanted to supersede a previous memoir – *This is My Life*, published in 1963. In trying to tell the story of his career, as Eamonn would have wished it told, his wife, Grainne, and I combined all he was writing in the eighties with that first publication. Certain events, however, were described differently in Eamonn's more recent manuscript and this posed a problem: was he right or wrong first time around? And, strict accuracy apart, would he have wanted the benefit of twenty years' hindsight to take precedence over what he had written earlier? In the end, Grainne decided that the story Eamonn was desperately trying to finish was the one he would have wanted in this book, and I have done my best to interpolate it into the general account of his career without being too unfaithful to what was published in 1963.

How and when to tell her own story of their life together without confusing the reader was also a problem for Grainne. If Eamonn had lived, she would not have needed someone to help her put her memories and views on paper; they could have been expressed through *his* pen. As it is, her story is separate and set in italics to make it clear when she, not Eamonn, is speaking.

Sadly, Grainne died in April 1989, shortly after completing this book. She had never got over her husband's death, and her sadness was deepened when a former colleague wrote a less than complimentary book about Eamonn which tarnished the memory of the man she adored. Coming at a time when she was still reeling from her husband's death, it broke her heart.

With the information she had, Grainne must have been tempted to hit back with an equally hurtful attack. It says much about her integrity and loyalty to Eamonn that she chose not to, preferring instead to let her husband's words, and her own contribution about his private life, speak for themselves.

It meant everything to Grainne to finish her story and so set the record straight. Her devotion to Eamonn was such that everything else – even, tragically, her health – took second place. She was forever saying what emotional torture this book was. But, like Eamonn, she had fierce determination which, coupled with enviable self-discipline, resilience, and not a little courage, saw her through. She turned out a true professional. Eamonn would have been proud of her.

Robin McGibbon
April 1989

ACKNOWLEDGEMENT

I would like to thank my children, Emma, Fergal and Niamh for their love and support and help in recalling our family's memories; and Sue McGibbon for the weeks spent transcribing those memories on to paper so that the book could be written.

PROLOGUE

He had been crying that day. He had been told he'd never do anything any more: he'd never play golf again; he'd have to do his shows in a wheelchair. The news had destroyed him. He'd always been mentally alert, physically strong, and the thought of being an invalid broke his heart. He knew he couldn't live like that.

I looked at him in the hospital bed, the once strong giant of a man now so gaunt and weak, the once bright blue, sparkling eyes dulled in defeat. My poor, poor darling. How I wished I could ease his suffering, take away that terrible pain of knowing he would never be the same again.

It was a Wednesday and he wanted to watch This is Your Life, *recorded the previous Friday. I couldn't take in what was on the screen; I just looked at him watching himself in the familiar role, and all I could think was: Did he know how dreadful he looked? Was he aware how much he had faded in the last few months?*

After the programme, he looked tired. I hoped he wanted to sleep, and I got up to leave. I leaned over and kissed him and told him I'd see him in the morning.

'Goodbye, darling,' he said. 'Don't forget to bring the script.'

I forced a smile. How typical of him. Weak and tired and slipping away, but still thinking of work; still the professional.

'I won't forget. Goodbye, darling.'

And then I was gone, fighting to convince myself that sleep would help him feel fresher and stronger in the morning.

I was woken by a phone call at about 3 A.M.; I must have been in a deep sleep, for I took a long time to hear the ringing. It was the ward sister from Cromwell Road Hospital; she said she'd been trying to reach me for ages. It was necessary for me to go to the hospital, she said. I didn't ask why, just agreed. She said she would send a car and I gave her the address of the flat in Chiswick. I got out of bed and tried to dress. But suddenly my whole body started to shudder and I found it hard to get my clothes on. It was a cold November night all right, but my shuddering was due to some inner emotion: apprehension or fear, perhaps; maybe even dread. I knew the question I should have asked the sister. And I knew I hadn't asked it because I didn't want to hear the answer.

I had to make two phone calls: one to my elder daughter, Emma, in Dublin; the other to Malcolm Morris, the This is Your Life *producer, one of our closest friends.*

Emma seemed to be half-expecting me to ring. I had phoned her seven hours earlier when I'd got back from the hospital and I'd sounded so miserable she offered to fly over immediately. I'd told her not to worry; she had her job to do and, anyway, there was nothing she could do. Now, shuddering in the early hours, I wasn't sure. I was so frightened I felt I needed her.

'Darling,' I said. 'I have to go back to the hospital. They're sending a car for me.'

'Mummy, I'm coming,' Emma said immediately. 'We can be there in a couple of hours.'

I can't understand why, but I heard myself telling her not to come; to wait until I'd been to the hospital. For some wild reason, born out of desperate optimism, I was still hoping everything would be all right.

'Darling,' I said tenderly, fighting to conceal my anxiety, 'stay there with Niamh. I'll phone you when I get back from the hospital.'

Reluctantly, Emma agreed. Still shuddering, I put the phone down and rang Malcolm Morris. He had left his answering machine off so that I could speak to him. I told him I was going to the hospital. He said he would meet me there.

My phone call to Emma woke Niamh, my younger daughter, and she got up, wanting to know what was going on. She stood shivering in the kitchen, looking to Emma, as the eldest and captain of the ship, to decide what they should do. They were both tired, but sleep was out of the question: they were worried sick about their Daddy and concerned that I was on my own. Finally, Emma decided that they should fly to join me and she rang to find out the next Aer Lingus flight: there wasn't one until 8 A.M. They packed a suitcase, made cups of tea and rang Fergal, their brother, who was staying at a friend's house. He seemed to think Emma was over-reacting and said he wouldn't be joining them on the flight.

After that, Emma and Niamh drank more tea and prowled around the house, not knowing what to do with themselves, just trying to make the time go quicker.

Emma, I knew, had been expecting her Daddy to die. When she had seen him so sick just eight months before, she felt something was dreadfully wrong and, in her own way, had been preparing herself for the worst. And, I learned later, that when she'd waved goodbye to us in Dublin, she felt sure it would be the last time she saw him alive. Only yesterday, she had rung me from her office in Dublin, sobbing: 'Dadda is going to die, Mummy, I know it.'

I had consoled her, of course. 'Don't be ridiculous, darling,' I said. 'Don't upset yourself. He's going to be all right.'

And I had believed it.

Why shouldn't I? He'd had three bad attacks before and I'd watched him recover from them all. That first one, in March 1986, when he was taken from the house by ambulance, at 3 A.M., unable to breathe, was particularly bad. He'd spent five days in intensive care, but he'd recovered, hadn't he? He had got better — in time for Niamh's eighteenth birthday. Then two more attacks, in the following January and March, had left him woefully weak, but alive, at least. This time would be no different, I told myself. He was brave, a real fighter; he didn't know what it meant to give up.

If I felt, deep down, that I was fooling myself, I didn't tell anyone. Yes, it had concerned me to see him so hyperactive with business the previous day — dictating letter after letter to his secretary, Margaret Ritchie, faster and faster, as though he were in some race and running out of time. But that was him — always had been. Hadn't I watched him, throughout thirty-five years of marriage, always doing more than he had to — replying to this enquiry here, offering that bit of advice there, always being courteous and helpful, always giving his time, forever thinking of others, not himself? And hadn't I listened to him telling me over the weekend about the surprise This is Your Life *they were to spring at a celebrity boxing dinner? That was typical of him, too: no sooner had he been confined to bed than he was making plans to get out of it, to work. That was not the mentality of a man who was going to die, was it?*

Oh, yes, he was a great actor, for sure: I'd seen that side of him in three-dimensional Technicolor over the past twenty months. When he had been so ill he could hardly breathe, let alone speak, he had performed the greatest cover-up since Watergate to keep the seriousness of his condition from the children. He fooled me at times, too. He was so heroic, so uncomplaining, even in the dark times, that I began to think I was imagining he was worse than he was. But I felt sure he was not putting on a performance this time. His mind was still so active, his voice still so clear and commanding, his determination still so fierce, that I truly believed he would recover a fourth time.

So, when Emma was crying that her Dadda was going to die, I meant it when I told her not to be ridiculous; of course he was going to get better.

But when I went to the hospital the next evening, the Wednesday, and learned what he'd been told I wasn't so sure.

In a few cruel seconds, a piece of plain-speaking from an unsympathetic man of medicine, who had not even consulted me, had brought home the terrible reality of his condition. And from the moment I saw his eyes, red-rimmed from his tears, I knew, deep down in my aching heart, that he wasn't going to make it. He was a man who never asked much out of life: he had money, but wanted only enough to know the future was secure; he had friends in high places, but never used them to further his own ends, his own ambitions; he had power, but never abused it.

All he wanted was to work on television shows and play golf and be a good husband and see his children happy. And when he heard his life would never be the same again, it took away the will to live. Whoever decided that hospital bed was the place to tell him that he would have to spend his remaining years inactive, being nursed like a handicapped child, should have his premature death on his conscience. For those callously blunt words snuffed out that light of hope still flickering faintly in his faltering heart.

I was still shuddering in my flat when the nurse tapped lightly on a rear window. I could hear a taxi ticking over noisily in the stillness of the night. I motioned the nurse round to the front and was waiting at the entrance for her. Since the phone call my mind had been filled with images of my big, strong giant looking so weak, so vulnerable, of him weeping in despair at the hopelessness of it all, and I knew I had to find an inner strength to take what the nurse had come to tell me. I stared at her. I steeled myself.

'Is he dead?'

'Yes,' she said, and went to put her arm round me. Instinctively, I withdrew. I wanted to be in control of myself; I didn't want a stranger's comfort. In the taxi, though, I felt an arm go round me, and a hand holding mine, and I didn't object, although I didn't like it. I was in shock, my mind numbed by the suddenness of his death and what the loss would mean to me, to us all. All my emotions seemed frozen, deathly still inside me. My tears would come later.

At the hospital, I went in to him. He lay there lifeless, the eyes that had been so despairing now closed, the pain-racked face now peaceful. I sat and looked lovingly at him, holding his hand. He wasn't even cold. And then Malcolm arrived and got some sedatives from a nurse and took me home. It was 4 A.M. I had to break the news to Emma. And to close friends who were concerned about him.

Emma answered the phone quickly; she had been worrying too much to go back to sleep.

'Darling' was all I could say, 'your Daddy is dead.' Trembling, I handed the phone to Malcolm. He spoke to Emma for a few moments. Then he rang a few other people and gave me a sedative. Before the drug drowsed me into welcome sleep, I started to shudder again and felt the first pangs of grief tighten ever so slightly in my stomach.

It must be true because I had seen his body in his bed, but I couldn't believe it, didn't want to. Life without him was unthinkable; he had been so strong and reliable, like an oak door, Emma said. What were we all going to do: me and Emma and Fergal and Niamh and Mairead and Jack and Margaret and Sheelagh and all the others who had loved him so much?

It hit my poor darlings differently. Niamh, I learned later, burst into tears immediately and started to bawl. Emma was shocked, but calm at first: she had felt her Daddy was dying, but she had been praying that they would get to the hospital in time and honestly thought they would. Niamh, now hysterical, wanted comforting; she tried to throw her arms around Emma. But when she is upset, Emma cannot bear to be touched and she pushed her sister away. Fighting to be strong like her Daddy would have wanted, Emma made the important phone calls – to Fergal and to other close relatives – and then, wanting to be alone, she stood under a hot shower and stamped her feet and shouted and screamed and sobbed in heartbreak.

She, more than anyone, had known how it was going to be. When we'd left for London the previous Wednesday, she'd written in her diary about things never being the same again; looking at a step she'd sat on as a child, she'd thought: 'The next time I look at it, I'll be heartbroken.'

Sadly, knowing that your heart is going to be broken does nothing to ease the pain when it happens.

Under sedation in Chiswick, I could only pray that Emma, and the rest of us, would be able to handle what was ahead of us with the strength and dignity the big man had shown throughout his life.

My darlings arrived around 9 A.M. with my sister, Susan. The children looked pale and tired, but had dressed smartly because they knew the press would make the death a very public affair. The flat was in darkness; the sedation had left me heavy-eyed and I hadn't got around to opening the curtains. I was wearing a black skirt and a blouse as white as my face. I wasn't wearing any shoes, and Emma was to say later that she saw me for the first time without her Daddy, and I looked so tiny, so vulnerable. She thought: This woman is on her own now and she is going to die like Daddy. He was so strong, so much the centre of our tiny world, that she will be unable to exist without him.

We talked and cried together as more people arrived: Malcolm, our housekeeper Mrs Lehart, Margaret and Bunny France, a close family friend. News of the death had been on the radio, and by half past nine the entrance to the flat was packed with reporters wanting to know what I had to say about it and photographers wanting pictures of me saying it. Emma, still in the role of ship's captain, refused to subject me to photographers; instead, she and Fergal and Niamh went outside and had pictures taken there. Then she arranged for reporters to come into the house, three at a time, to talk to me for a few minutes. The children were marvellous. Their Daddy had lived such a public life, with the press second nature to him, and I know he would have been proud of the courageous, courteous and dignified way they conducted themselves that mournful Thursday morning.

I had to get out, though. And when the last newsman had left, I walked into the dank Chiswick air with my sister, not knowing where I was going, but glad to be away from all the people and the claustrophobia of the flat, and actually doing something. In the event, we went to Marks and Spencer. That sounds kind of bizarre and, I suppose, it was. But, that morning, I needed to get something for lunch for eight people and Marks was the ideal place to go. Not that I can remember much about it: I just walked along with Susan, like a zombie, buying this and that without really being aware of what I was doing. I do remember Susan trying her best to divert my eyes from a newspaper placard outside a newsagent's. But I saw it anyway, and looking at his name and the word DEAD *underneath sent a chill through me and I was glad to have my beloved sister with me. Thoughts about him, and how we were going to miss him, kept going in and out of my head as we walked around; and then, almost before I knew it, we were back home again and I was helping to prepare lunch, glad to have something to do.*

We were lucky, if that is the word, to have Bunny France: he was an undertaker and had been a loyal, trusted friend for thirty years or so. He went with the children to register the death, and then to the hospital so that they could see their Daddy for the last time. It was traumatic for them, but it was something they were prepared to experience, and I'm sure having Bunny with them helped them through it.

By evening, everyone except the children and Susan had left. I was pleased about that: I knew I would watch the Thames Television tribute, but I wanted to be alone with my family. It was going to be agonizing watching the man I adored so full of life, but knowing he was dead in a mortuary just up the road, and it was an ordeal I could not have shared with anyone except the children and close relatives. I'm told the tribute was touching, a fitting accolade to one of the nation's best loved, most respected, broadcasters. I have to accept that, but I cannot judge. I sat staring at the TV in a sort of trance, and cannot remember one thing about it.

We took him home to Dublin on a plane the next evening. It was by far the worst part. The tears, never far away, started again as the plane took off and we thought of him beneath us, lifeless in a coffin, making the familiar journey for the last time. Fergal, never one to make a show of affection, was wonderful, and had his arm round Emma most of the time as shock gave way to grief and she wept quietly. We didn't speak much on that flight, just sat there, alone in our thoughts, but bonded tightly in sorrow that nothing would ever be the same again; that our tiny world would be unbearably dark now that the light of our lives had gone out.

To our surprise, there were many people waiting to greet us at the airport; a touching, much appreciated, show of support. I felt like crawling into a corner and sobbing for a week, but his life had been public and I couldn't suddenly make it private. He would not have wanted me to display my emotions, to break down and cry, so I put myself on Hold and vowed to keep myself together, at least until I was safe in the sanctuary of our home in Portmarnock. It was going to be awful and I didn't know whether I could do it. I hadn't been tested before; my parents' deaths were traumatic, of course, but they were old and ill, and their passing was played out in private. But I was determined to ensure that this final homecoming, and all that would go with it, would have the dignity he deserved.

It took nearly three hours to release the coffin. We had left everything to other people and it horrified me when I saw a picture of it in the paper: it was bare, without a single flower on it; a stark, friendless coffin that could have been carrying a total stranger. It looked so pathetic.

It was a relief to reach the rambling house in Carrick Hill he had loved so much. Mairead, our housekeeper and friend, was there, of course, devoted and caring as usual, and she had lit a candle beneath the statue of Our Lady in the hall. It must have been awful for her, staying alone in the house, unable to do anything, except, like us, think about what a terrible loss we would all have to bear.

No sooner had we got inside the door than we started thinking about the removal service – when the body is taken from the house or parlour to the church for the funeral the next morning. After the service that evening about forty people came back to the house for drinks and food, delivered by Roche's, our favourite restaurant in the village of Malahide. The children, particularly Emma, would have preferred his body to have been brought to the house, not taken to the funeral parlour, but I think it would have been too much anguish for us. It was impractical anyhow: we could not have handled the number of people who would want to see him and pay their last respects. Hundreds went to Stafford's Funeral Parlour, in the North Strand. It was like he was lying in state and many of the people who stared at him did not know him, had never met him, but nevertheless found themselves crying. I went with the children to see him one last time. It was harrowing and heart-rending, but it was something we had to do. He looked at peace, but he was very pale and his face was not as we wanted to remember it.

And then it was the funeral, and the whole town, it seemed, turned out that cold, damp Tuesday morning to say goodbye to him. He'd spent so much of his life in London, but there was no question his last resting place would be St Anne's church in Portmarnock, where he'd gone to Mass so many Sunday mornings over twenty years. For Dublin had always been special to him. He had battled, with unquenchable self-belief and dogged determination, to break out of the city and display his talents on a bigger broadcasting stage; but he'd always loved coming back. It was where his roots were: where that overwhelming desire to make something of himself had manifested itself; where that raw, self-conscious teenager had overcome his suffocating shyness;

where he'd met the man who gave him that golden chance to make his mark in England.

And it was Dublin where we had met and fallen in love and returned to, with our three darling children, after twenty gloriously happy, roller-coasting years, in which he became the most famous face and voice on television; loved not only by the thousands who had met him, but by many millions who never did.

But that is making a mess of the story, and one of the many things he taught me was that storytelling, like any job, was only worth doing if you did it well. For a man who told the story of so many people's lives, he was remarkably reticent about telling his own: perhaps that embarrassing childhood shyness never really left him. But he did put pen to paper before his premature death, and it is his own writings that form the basis of this book.

Like all the television stories for which he became renowned, he starts at the beginning. In that beginning, the five-year-old could not know what destiny had in store, but that childhood does hold a clue to why he chose the path he did; why he enjoyed This is Your Life *so much for so long.*

For it was as a wide-eyed little boy that he experienced the magical effect of surprise – the ingredient that was to play such an important part in the life of the man I affectionately called Hymie, but who the world knew as . . . Eamonn Andrews.

Part I

1 CANARY BIRD OF SYNGE STREET

I never thought of ourselves as poor; broke, and waiting for the wage-packet to turn up, but never poor. If you've had first-hand encounters with an outside loaf, you'll know what I mean. The loaves carried by the baker into retail shops on a wooden tray were brown and crispy on top and bottom, warm and doughy inside. One side of the outer edges, or maybe two, would have a deeper colour and a tougher texture, presumably from being exposed directly to the heat of the oven. These were known as outside loaves and they came one farthing cheaper.

As a child, my mother would tell me to get an outside loaf from the shop at the end of Synge Street where we could buy groceries on tick. The trick about the outside loaves, of course, was to pretend you preferred them to the virgins they surrounded. Indeed, I *did* come to like the outside of the outside loaf. It was a better chew.

My father often said he hadn't tuppence to rattle on a tombstone and one Christmas was filled with great tension waiting to hear if he was going to get the traditional hand-out from a mysterious boss-like figure called Mr Kettle.

L. J. Kettle was part of top management of the Electricity Supply Board which employed my father as a carpenter. In his spare time, Dad would go to Mr Kettle's home in Rathmines to do odd jobs. If he did get paid, it was small enough for him to expect a present at holiday-time, but this particular Christmas Mr Kettle seemed to have forgotten.

I heard my mother whisper: 'Well, did he give you anything yet?'

A negative shake of the head.

'Maybe you should find some excuse to call in again tomorrow.'

A turkey, or the contents of a Christmas stocking, it seemed, was hanging in the balance of Mr Kettle's generosity and memory. It came out all right in the end as it did always, although once we did have to settle for a goose. The experience with Mr Kettle taught me that no matter how well informed people 'up there' think they are, they never really know the fears, the uncertainties, the little hopes of those 'down there'.

He was a small, slight, sensitive man, my father, and he had grey hair, which he was losing. He was serious, too, and could be quite stern when necessary. He was the ultimate court and if a row needed settling, it was reported to him. My mother's severest threat was: 'Wait till Daddy comes home.' He had a razor strop with which my brother and sisters and myself were sometimes threatened. We never experienced it, but its very existence kept mutinies under control.

Although he smoked heavily, he rarely drank and lived only for his family and work. Much of his early working life was spent cycling the long distance from our home in Synge Street to The Pigeon House, on that promontory stretching out by the side of the Liffey. He would have to make a very early start to be there by eight o'clock and my mother would get up and make his breakfast and lunch-time sandwiches. He would seldom be home before 7.30 P.M. and if the wind had been in his face he would drop into a chair exhausted. By the time he'd recovered enough for a chat I was in bed asleep.

And then he bought a motorbike, and his life became easier. He didn't have to leave so early in the morning and he was always home by six o'clock in the evening. There would be a knock at the door and he would be standing outside in his blue overalls, holding the huge Rudge Whitworth, a carbide-lamp flickering on the handlebars. He would lug the bike into the tiny hall, and as soon as he had settled it against the wall, I'd run to him.

He would take his carpenter's spirit-level from his toolbox and hand it to me. 'Where's the mouse, Eamonn?' he'd say. 'Find the mouse.'

It was a game I loved. The 'mouse' was the 'bubble' and I was to call it a 'mouse' for years after I learned its real name.

My mother swore the motorbike was too big for my father. She may have been right, because he was always having skids on it, but her judgement was swayed by the vast amount of space it took up in the hall every night.

To me, however, the monster machine was a source of wonder, for it took me on mystery tours around Dublin that never failed to excite me. Sitting on the pillion, I would duck under my father's great oilskin cape and pull its generous folds around my shoulders. Then I'd be whisked off in blackness, trying hard to count the turns and guess where we were going. What a feeling of wonder it was, when the cape was removed, to find myself magically in Phoenix Park, or by a river or halfway up a mountain. I always thought life should be full of surprises.

Other memories lingered on from childhood: running down the mountainside from the ruins of the Hell Fire Club so fast we had to fling ourselves on the grass to avoid crashing into the hedge and then exaggerating the dangers to mother when we got home . . . visiting Dublin Zoo, where even the most forlorn creature was dangerous and mysterious . . . and, of course, going to the circus in Rotunda Gardens.

Way up on the wooden seats, I heard a clown call out the raffle-ticket numbers.

'Daddy, Daddy,' I shouted. 'We've won. We've won.'

We'd won all right: a massively made pottery tea-set that must have been fine Belleek china to my child's eyes. How we carried it home on the bus, and walked the last mile or two, bit by balanced bit, was always a mystery.

In 1927, when I was five, with a baby sister, Peggy, my parents moved from that flat in Synge Street to a corporation house in St Thomas's Road, Fairbrothers Fields. I only vaguely sensed the importance and excitement of getting a house, but it must have meant the world to a young couple with two children. Certainly the drop in rent from eighteen shillings to fourteen would have been very welcome. It was a small, simple house, with a kitchen, scullery and sitting room – we called it the parlour – downstairs and three bedrooms upstairs. We were one up on the pack because we had a *bathroom*, but soon enough this had to give way to a bedroom when my brother, Noel, and two other sisters, Kathleen and Treasa, arrived.

Fairbrothers Fields seemed to be full of houses which had just been built or were being built and for me everything at that time seemed to centre around planks of wood and muck. To a five-year-old, it was a sort of heaven, but I quickly got into trouble for sneaking into one nearly completed house with some pals and climbing into an inviting empty bath. A watchman chased us, and when I got home, my mother scolded me for disappearing and making her heart go crossways with worry.

When the time came for me to go to school, I was taken to the Holy Faith Convent and taught catechism by a seemingly seven-foot nun named Sister Bonaventure. First Holy Communion Day was very important and I was taken to church wearing new shoes, stockings, shirt and short pants and a new top coat. Afterwards I, with other boys and girls, trooped out into the sunshine to be admired and congratulated and hugged by proud parents weeping tears of happiness.

That day was an important milestone – a sign that a child is no longer an infant and that its babyhood has gone for ever – and it should have been my greatest and tenderest memory of those years. But it wasn't. The most exciting experience was sitting at Sister Bonaventure's feet, being coaxed to read. Suddenly, like discovering you are swimming unaided, I realized I had tumbled down the page by myself, and that I understood what the words meant; that I recognized each individual golden key.

I was reading. My mind had wings.

My father's name was William. Everyone called or referred to him as Willie, but there were two exceptions to this: one was my mother, who called him Daddy in front of us; and the other was when his name appeared in programmes for his amateur dramatics. Then, it was Will Andrews.

He used to act in St Teresa's Hall in Clarendon Street. He would take me there after Mass, leading me by the hand through the smoky billiards-room into the hall where all the chairs were. I sat there watching him and the other players rehearsing, secretly wishing to go back into the billiards-room which was more exciting and had a sort of forbidden air about it.

My father never tried to instil a love of acting into me. I was just a child; he was an adult and what he was doing was a separate thing. I

was brought along merely to keep me out of Mother's way while she
got on with the Sunday lunch. My father was devoted to that old style
of acting that is regarded as hammy. He hated microphones.
Mumblers were anathema to him; he loved clear, loud, melodic
speech. He did not look the sort of man who would be at home on a
stage, in front of hundreds of people, declaiming the lines of
melodrama. But that is precisely what he used to do.

A shy man my father wasn't; unlike me, who would pray to be
swallowed up into invisibility when the spotlight looked like being
thrust on me. How well I remember cowering in corners on boring
tea-saturated Sundays when we'd visit my father's sister, Jennie, and
her husband Bill, in Washington Street, where the houses had long
gardens and the children didn't play marbles in the gutter. Jennie
would play and Dad would sing 'Snowy Breasted Pearl'. Then
Jennie's daughters would play, and any other chance visitors would
play or sing or both. I would feel the terror swell inside of me. As sure
as Hell, it was going to happen again.

'Come on, Eamonn, there must be something *you* can do.'

No voice would come and I would shake a beetroot-red face.

'Come on. Even a recitation.'

Somewhere along the line I was coaxed into learning some endless
poem that began or ended with: 'O, Mary go and call the cattle home
across the sands of Dee.' My parents finally wound me up after weeks
of coaching and set me off on one of their *sotto voce* Sunday soirées. I
think I got the cattle home so fast, so unintelligibly, I was never asked
again.

Aunt Jennie said she would teach me the piano. My lessons lasted two
weeks when she pronounced that I was tone-deaf. She was probably
right, although, at the time, I felt it was a slight exaggeration, and it
simply heightened my terror at the mere thought of singing with, or
near, anyone. Aunt Jennie found my sister, Kathleen, far more sensitive
and her talent persuaded my father to put down whatever small deposit
was required on a tiny, highly polished piano. One of my duties was
to call into the furniture shop in Camden Street with the weekly
instalments that seemed to go on for ever and ever. It was a worthwhile investment, for Kathleen became most proficient and would

be called on to play the five-finger exercise or, later, Chopin or one of those simple little pieces of music that never seem to emerge beyond parlours and drawing rooms and schools of music.

My brother, Noel, was next and made progress by stealth. Once, I was astonished to overhear him rattling off a current pop tune. I couldn't wait to mention my secret discovery to one of my friends. I might as well have told him I'd discovered gravity.

'You mean, you didn't know?' he said. 'I was at a party the other night and Noel was the star turn!' He had made a go of the piano, too, so maybe the family honour was saved after all.

I detested those Washington Street soirées and they caused a friendship with a pal to turn to hatred one Sunday when he sang in a clear true soprano: 'Oh, I wonder, yes, I wonder, will the angels way up yonder, will the angels play their harps for me?' The angels almost played their harps prematurely when I heard the applause that greeted his efforts, and the comments clearly intended not so much to laud his talent as to emphasize my useless non-productive untalented drone-like presence. I wanted to scream that I was brighter than he, and that I could do lots and lots of things he couldn't do, but I couldn't sing. I couldn't sing, 'O, Lord, make me invisible.'

Ironically, and to my astonishment, we both became choir boys in St Teresa's Church. The automatic assumption, it seemed, was that, if you became an altar boy, you could also sing. In my mind, of course, everybody in the world could sing, except me. Little did the choir know how loyal I was to them. On all important occasions, or if the choir master came too close, I would mouth the words all right, but no sound would come. This was by way of being a small sacrifice because I'd come to enjoy letting the vocal cords twang invisibly, as it were, tucked away among dozens of eager choir boys.

The choir must have been fairly good because we won many Feiseanna (Music Festivals) for Plainchant, and I remember the excitement when were told we were to broadcast on Radio Éireann. It was the first time we had a radio in the house. One night there was the marvel of a crystal set, my father tinkering with it and trailing a length of wire across the bedroom to the iron spring-frame of the bed. Sounds of exultation then when he claimed he heard the broadcast on a pair of headphones shared between himself and my mother. I didn't witness the achievement. I was broadcasting, mouthing quietly at the back lest the sinister dull microphone should discover what Father Valentine Burke, the priest in charge, had not – that I was more of a toneless liability than a liquid asset.

Father Burke almost certainly knew he had a ringer in me, but he kept me on, probably because he believed I would become a priest. It must have been a great blow to him when I became a junior insurance clerk. He may even have regarded it as a shape of things to come when I was transferred to the fire department!

At the convent I'd had my first experience of being bullied. What made it worse was that the bullies were . . . girls! There was a tiny play-yard with one raised section reserved for male infants and the rest of it for monster schoolgirls. When no nuns were watching, the girls organized raids into male territory and, no matter how tightly I cringed into whatever corner, under whatever seat, they prised me out and carried me, a terror-stricken trophy, into their own mysterious world from which I would scurry back through jeers in humiliation. Indeed, my humiliation became so great that some of the older girls took pity and formed a protection society.

I had the same longing for invisibility later when I went to the Christian Brothers School, in Synge Street, where we'd once lived. But it never worked. I seemed to have some inner light that beckoned the bully boys. I was a constant, but unresponsive, target. I became an even more attractive bait when I started wearing pullovers knitted by my mother – a joint product of affection and economy. It didn't help either that I'd come to the tough, all-male school from a convent and not from one of the free, earthier infant schools.

I was never fond of fighting and only got involved if I was cornered and there was no other way out. If honour demanded a fight, an all-embracing dread would build up inside me and my heart would become jittery. An awful little ritual was played out solemnly to the end: first, there was the long, heart-stopping walk up the lane outside the school, then the dropping of the satchel and coat and finally the noisy sparring, in which far more clamour was made than damage done. There was a lot of shouting, tapping on the chest, huffing and puffing, much struggling to pummel the other fellow's ribs and then one good punch and that was it. These little scraps always ended if someone was walloped in the eyes or if a nose bled. I hated and dreaded these occasions. I had a huge fear of getting one on the nose.

The excitement did help to break the tedium of school, though – as did the little old man, with soft hat and a small half-pipe sticking out of his mouth, who stood all day in the corner of the yard with his barrow full of sweets. To us, he was the sweet-man and I always thought his name *was* Sweetman! He was a source of distraction and relief; a sort of symbol of the normal life that existed outside the crushing classroom. We knew the mouth-watering things he had for sale and I would find excuses to stand up so that I could look out of the window and see him. Sometimes, in an agony of longing, I would ask to go to the lavatory. Once outside, I had to gauge whether it was possible to sneak across the yard, get some sweets, then sneak back without being seen. It was at times like these that I'd be thankful I'd walked to school and saved the penny my mother had given me for the bus or tram. This was something I often did if it was raining: I'd be so wet by the time I reached the stop that I felt it would be a shame to spend the penny. Instead, I'd trudge down the South Circular Road, sustaining myself with the thought of what that precious penny could purchase from the sweet-man. So, once safely outside the classroom, copper coin clenched tightly, I often took the chance and made a run for that symbolic barrow. Nearly always it was worth it.

At the end of the day, the old man would pull a cover over the barrow and wheel it off into the evening. When he was round the corner, I felt he vanished in a puff of smoke.

I experienced a tremendous feeling of isolation at that primary school. I was different from the other boys: I was big for my age, but I was softer than they were. I didn't know as much of the Irish language as they did and I felt I would always be behind in this subject. I was right. I was beaten many times by my first teacher, Mr Lillis. The shock and indignity of it shattered me and I began to hate school and dread being isolated by my ignorance. I invariably read the English reader right through within a few days of joining a class, and this left me bored for the rest of the year's English lessons. To relieve the tedium, I would smuggle in a comic – *Hotspur*, *Bull's-eye* or *Dandy* – or a book and read it in class. Unfortunately, I would get lost in what I was reading and not hear the master talking to me. Disaster came quickly. Silence. A shadow. Suddenly I'd be aware of the danger. But too late. A soul-searing crack on the knuckles and I'd be back in that awful, droning classroom.

I never had any good reports and was a problem pupil, both to the teachers and my parents. The only good thing about school was actually going there. Two pals, Tommy Murphy and Dermot Golfer, and I used to scrounge a lift with the milkman who had an open chariot-style, horse-drawn cart. We'd run alongside him until he'd say: 'All right, then, jump in,' and we'd take it in turns to hold the horse's reins and slap its grey, hairy rump and shout: 'Giddap.'

More and more, I began to look forward to weekends. Sunday really was the day out, but sometimes my father would work only half a day on Saturday and we would go to Sandymount. One of our favourite treats, if the tide was out, was to collect cockles and take them home for stewing. I never forgot how to find a cockle: the faint blue shadow on the sand, the tiny holes like pinpricks, the slight bump with its promise of succulence; a quick scrabble with the fingers and – click! – another cockle tossed into the handkerchief knotted at the corners.

Less often, because it was more of an expedition, we'd go to Bray, in County Wicklow; or else we'd go to the zoo on the mountains just outside the city.

Like every schoolboy, I longed for the long summer holidays. There was no question of going away anywhere, because my parents could not afford it, but it was enough not having to go to school. When my father's own holiday-time came around, it would signal the beginning of a series of day adventures and we would have marvellous picnics on the beach at Killiney and enjoyable walks along the canal and across the fields, always, it seemed, in endless sunshine.

'Going up the canal' on our own was a special sort of adventure because it was forbidden. It was only forbidden because children drowned there and parents were afraid. The canal was a sort of symbol. I never knew where it went to and where it came from. It was mysterious. It was dirty. It was brown. The tough boys from the tenements in Bride Street and Aungier Street would jump or dive from the bridge or the banks and swim around in the canal, naked. But I couldn't swim and, anyway, I was afraid: the canal was full of pinkeen – minnows – and gudgeon. Instead, I used to go to quieter parts of the canal and try to catch the pinkeen with a net.

It was great when barges came along the canal, pulled by horses. If you were daring, you'd jump aboard at the bridge where the canal narrows. But you had to make sure you jumped off before the bridge was left behind; if you didn't, the banks widened and you were trapped until the next bridge was reached and the bargee could come and clout you round the ear.

Something was always happening along that canal, even if only a stone battle from one bank to the other. It was amazing none of us lost an eye or was permanently injured. After one battle, I was inspired by a story in Bull's-eye comic to form my own gang which I called My Tong. But, quite honestly, it never struck terror in anyone's heart, particularly the fellows on the other side of the canal. If they had been on our side, we'd have run for it!

During one summer holiday, I was introduced to the cinema, thanks to a cousin called Joe Clarke. My mother wasn't keen on me going but relented when she heard that her sister, Polly, allowed Joe to go. Mum insisted I went with Joe, and I had to walk right across the city to his home in Fairview, to meet him.

I didn't understand the films I was watching, but it didn't matter. 'The pictures' had always been something other people went to, and in my new exhilaration, I paid little attention to what was on the screen. The mere fact of being there meant a great new sense of freedom to me.

When I was ten, the streets buzzed with talk of the Eucharistic Congress, which was being held in Dublin. The papers were full of it and, since the eyes of the world would be on us, our drill master, Mr Gallagher, told us we would all have to get new white flannels and white shirts and school badges. In 1932, the financial strain must have been great on my parents. What was an even greater strain for me was that whenever we went into a shop, my mother would say: 'Yes, he's very big for his age. You know, he's only ten.' I knew full well I was big and awkward, but I detested attention being drawn to it. And I disliked the 'only ten' part, too.

The day of the Eucharistic Congress ceremonies came, and as we marched to Phoenix Park, resplendent in our new uniforms, line upon line of other schoolboys called out mockingly: 'Canary Boys' – a nickname from the pronunciation of the Irish Christian Brothers' Synge Street school name. We didn't care. We felt posher than all the others and very proud of ourselves.

That sixth-year class was when we all sat the Primary Certificate – our first *real* examination. My eleven-year-old nerves were shaky as I looked at the printed paper with the questions and their correct-answer values set out and my heart sank when I realized how few of them I felt I knew. When the exam was over the summer holidays began, and with them the long, anxious wait for the results. I played by the canal and had seaside picnics and played in the fields and throughout those wonderful never-ending sunny days the only dark cloud on my horizon was the exam results. And then, one day, they arrived. Somehow I had passed.

No one was more surprised than I.

My parents' joy at my success was mixed with a certain financial worry. Secondary school would mean a lot of extra expense and now, with four other children in the house, there was not a lot of money around. It was a big decision for my parents and I knew what the answer was when I overheard: 'Well, let him go for a year and see what happens.'

2   THE BADGER

The first time I thought about trousers, long or short, was soon after I started secondary school. The principal stopped me on the steps.

'What's your name, boy?'

'Andrews, sir. Eamonn Andrews.' I flinched under his long stare.

'Don't you think it's about time you got into long trousers, Andrews?'

And he walked off without waiting for an answer, leaving me standing there, the redness of my embarrassment flushing my face and the back of my neck.

I couldn't wait to get home to ask for 'longers' as soon as possible. While waiting for them, even a distant glimpse of the principal made my neck go hot and my bare pink knees seemed to swell to gigantic proportions. When I did pull on the trousers, it was like burying two grotesque gargoyles. I never did understand how a grown man could ever wear a kilt.

I didn't like any of the new subjects we had to learn. I was still interested in English, however, and took out two new books from the library each Saturday morning, mainly on travel and animals.

We had several teachers now, and one of them, Brother Dineen, had a big thick strap called 'the leather', which he used to punish anyone who aggravated him. 'Out,' he would shout, and the offender would stand on what was called 'the line' – an invisible, but clearly defined, area of lonely isolation – until the end of class. Waiting on 'the line', thinking about the inevitable, would make the palms tingle.

When the class had emptied, he would snap: 'Hold it out,' and he would pull up the sleeve, leaving the wrist bare. I was scared stiff of the strap hitting me on the wrist and would infuriate Dineen by drawing my hand back as the strap swished down. 'Hold it out,' he would insist and then he would be up, on his toes, beads of sweat on his forehead, as he prepared to wield the strap again. You couldn't cry, not in secondary school, but the strap hurt so much that when I heard of a way to ease the pain, I grabbed it eagerly. A hair from a horse's tail laid across the palm, I was told, would break the punishing leather. It was a minute sliver of hope, a tiny solace, and I went off in search of horses who wouldn't miss a few hairs. But my pain disproved the theory. Dineen's leather never even cracked.

In those early secondary school days, I became aware of a species I had never encountered before – the eggheads. They sat on the right-hand side of the class, at the front. They always had their homework done. They always had the right answers. Nothing was ever a problem. They were a race apart.

I sat at the back, seldom had a home exercise done, and rarely had a right answer. To get over the homework problem, I started going to school half an hour early, at half past eight, to copy the answers from a pal's work. We called it 'getting a cog' and it was during one of these hurried 'cog' sessions that something happened that was to shape my life.

I was crowding close to someone's book, desperate to get down what I should have done the previous night, when I was shoved by a boy called Brennan.

'Cut it out, Brennan, or you'll be sorry,' I said.

'Who'll make me?' he said. My heart sank. But he kept on. 'Go on, who'll make me sorry? You? Eh?'

His confidence sounded a danger note, but I couldn't back out. He was looking for a fight and if I didn't take him on, I would be a coward.

Brennan was half my size. But he hit me where and when he pleased, leaving me dazed and bloodied in a matter of seconds. Washing away the blood in the toilet, I decided I'd had enough of getting the wrong end of the physical stick. I needed to learn how to take care of myself. There was no earthly use growing into a six-foot bruiser dangling its way through the community waiting to be bumped against.

There was an even smaller fellow than Brennan called Sean Tallow, who had been making a name for himself as an amateur boxer, and I asked him if I could join his boxing club. It was called St Andrew's, he said, and all I had to do was find sixpence and go to a semi-tenement building in York Street and sign on.

York Street was a street of sad, plain, gaunt houses in need of repair. To get into the St Andrew's Club, I had to go down a long, dingy corridor on the ground floor of number 42. There was a smell peculiar to such buildings, but the further along I went I got a whiff of sweat, too, and winter-green, an embrocation for aching muscles I would always find exciting.

I went down some steps and suddenly was in the middle of St Andrew's Boxing Club. It was a murky, smelly basement, but magic to me.

It was crowded with boys and men, all stripped to vests and trunks. They were all moving: skipping, shadow-boxing, punching bags, throwing medicine balls or just doing exercises. In a roped-off area representing a ring, two boys were going at it while a man at the side shouted advice. I stood there, taking it all in, mesmerized and nervous. So this was a boxing club. I found it exciting and happily signed on that night. Sixpence a week for three nights supervised training, with the occasional Sunday morning thrown in, was pretty good value, I felt.

The reaction at home, however, was quite cool. My father may have been secretly pleased, but he didn't let on. Mum certainly thought the whole business a bit odd, and not quite respectable. But they didn't stop me, and over the next couple of years I got to know every inch of the club: the skipping area, the ring, the ice-cold shower and, eventually, the tiny committee room, not quite sealed off from the odour of sweat and poverty.

All I had were a pair of canvas shoes, shorts, singlet, socks and a tattered old pair of my father's leather gloves; I wore the gloves to stop my hands getting scarred on the heavy bag or either of the punchballs.

The main room of the club was dimly lit with a low ceiling and there were cane chairs along the side for spectators when a tournament was held. When the club was doing well, some stars of the Irish amateur boxing world came along to train us and there were nights, too, when the famous Jimmy Ingle took on the juveniles, one after the other. It was good exercise for him as well as magnificent experience for us to see how a champion defended himself against our impulsiveness.

Two school pals, Joe Breen and Paddy Nolan, came to the club for a while, but for some reason they didn't stick it out as long as I. Maybe they had more sense. Gradually, therefore, school and the club became divorced: what I did at the club, and who I met there, were all part of a separate existence. To outsiders, my decision to take up boxing must have seemed strange, because I hated fighting. But boxing in the club was formalized, a prepared thing, in which gloves were worn and rules applied. I loved it and trained hard three or four times a week.

One evening, a tough, hard-punching boxer called Paddy Woodburn asked me to give him a few rounds because he needed sparring practice. He caught me with a cracker of a right hand on the chin early in the first round and that was about the last thing I remembered until I was sitting in the pub at the top of York Street with Paddy Nolan an hour or so later. I thought I'd been knocked out, but Paddy told me I hadn't. He said we had had three cracking rounds, after which I went through the usual exercise routine, had a shower and dressed, then strolled up to the pub, chatting quite normally. He was amazed when I said I remembered only the first few moments of the opening round. It was weeks before I could shake off that amnesic feeling of coming up against a blank wall.

My only injury in my fairly short boxing career happened outside the ring, and resulted in the bridge of my nose being squashed so flat that no normal-sized spectacles will fit on to it.

I was doing press-ups in the gym. Nearby was an international featherweight exercising with a medicine ball. As I was on the downward part of one press-up, the diminutive young man heaved the heavy ball to a colleague. But he misjudged his throw – and it landed on my back, burying my nose in the floor. I thought I'd have a flat nose for life.

If the boxing was going well, school wasn't. The exam at the end of my first secondary school year was a disaster for me. I 'cogged' some stuff from a close friend – and paid for it. He came last and I came second last. I was terribly embarrassed, but my father's reaction to my poor performance was one of sorrow. If he was angry too, he hid it. He was a bit mystified, because he knew I wasn't stupid. It would have been easier for him, and better for the family, if he'd simply said: 'Well, all right, I'll get you a job as an apprentice carpenter.' At least I would have been able to earn something which would have been useful at home just then. But he was thinking of me, not himself or the family, and he and Mum decided unselfishly that I should have one last fling at this studying business.

The second year was a scholarship class, which meant the bright boys had a chance of winning enough money to take care of the rest of their education. I didn't think I had the remotest chance of a scholarship, but when I returned to school that September I was determined to do better than I had in my first year.

Thanks to Brother Madden, I did.

Nobody knew anything about Brother Madden. He just arrived, transferred from somewhere else, a white-haired, long-nosed giant of a man with a fresh complexion, a precise voice and lips that were habitually pressed together. For some reason we nicknamed him the 'Badger'.

The first time he came into our class, he stared at us, a slight look of distaste on his face.

'I *know* what you fellows are thinking,' he said. 'And if you think of *anything else* but mathematics during the next hour, I will *know*.'

He must have made up his mind to teach by fear, for his range of punishments, it seemed, was enormous and terrifying: he used a leather, caught your hair over your ears and rocked the head backwards and forwards, wielded a stick and occasionally banged a recalcitrant head against the blackboard. The fear he instilled in us worked; nobody dared arrive without having learned what he'd warned us to learn or written what he warned us to write.

One day, he tried something new. He outlined a lesson he wanted us to study, then looked down at us with that all-embracing stare.

'Right, *do* that exercise,' he said. 'I am going out of the classroom for a short while, but if *anyone* does *anything* I will *know*.'

He was claiming there and then he could read our minds, that he could see through walls. And we believed him. When he went out of the room, we felt he was still there, looking at us. I knew he wasn't physically there, but it seemed just possible that he could still be looking. I was tempted to prove he wasn't, but I didn't have the courage. I didn't move from my desk the whole hour he was out.

That second year was when Brother Madden helped me 'discover' the parlour. 'Cogging' was out and I became a bit of a swot; probably a bigger swot than anyone else, because I had more catching up to do. And almost every night I retreated into that unused front room to study in peace and quiet; long after my parents had gone to bed, I would be hunched over schoolbooks, developing fierce, shiny chilblains from the small, heavy-breathing gas fire placed so conveniently in the corner of the room; hour after hour of swotting, desperately trying to protect the future and store knowledge for what my father always referred to as a 'safe, pensionable job'. In those lonely hours, the polished linoleum and the bric-à-brac of the parlour all came to know me well; and, in moments of desperation, when inspiration was lacking, I would gaze at the stuffed squirrel, unreal and stringy on its pedestal.

September dissolved into October, grey and wintry and wet, and then November darkened into December and at the end of it there was the blessed oasis of Christmas and all that went with it. Christmas was always important. I had always hung my pillow-case at the end of my bed on Christmas Eve, and still did, even though, at fourteen, I knew the answers. Year after year I asked for a bicycle and a flashlamp. I never got the bike because the family were never in a position to buy one, but I did get the flashlamp that Christmas. It was a magical sensation finding it inside the pillow-case and I ran my fingers over it in disbelief, then tried it several times under the bedclothes. I was struck dumb by the joy of getting that lamp and would keep looking at it lovingly as I got ready to go to six o'clock Mass.

We all trooped out of the house into the cold, starry, sparkling morning. 'Happy Christmas' – 'And many of them to you' – the good wishes were exchanged with other families, dim in the starlight, as they, too, made their way to Mass. All the way along those dark streets I pointed my treasured lamp at faraway walls, sweeping the beam around like a searchlight and flashing mock messages with it when I discovered how to cut the light without moving the switch.

After Mass, it was back home to inspect the rest of the presents, back to the toys and sweets and chocolates and story-books until it was time to leave for Auntie Jennie's house in Washington Street; we always went there on Christmas Day for a massive turkey dinner and all the trimmings. Afterwards, we would loll around, stuffed with food, looking at each other's toys, or go out in the garden or have fights.

Grannie was grey and bent and gentle, and her worn, knotted hands would shake with the strain of clicking open her black purse to find me a shiny new penny or, sometimes, a sixpence. She died at Christmas after what seemed like a long, long sleep. It was the first time I'd seen anyone die and I was frightened and unbelieving. We knelt around, saying the rosary for her and all the time I kept expecting to hear a long, soft sigh to prove she was still alive.

Christmas over, it was back to the hard slog under Brother Madden. At fourteen, I should have been taking more notice of relationships inside and out of the home, but I didn't. In the Badger's regime, the whole emphasis was on isolation: just a boy and his books, and the forthcoming examination hanging over the head like a suspended sentence. As the year went on, my hopes for a scholarship rose; in the beginning, I felt I had no chance, but now I felt, perhaps, I had a very slender one.

It was the summer holidays again when the results came through. It was incredible. I couldn't believe it. Surely there was a mistake. Somehow I had got through. All those days of concentration under the Badger's uncompromising discipline and my lonely nights of isolation in the parlour had paid off. I had won a scholarship. And in the matter of getting results, Brother Madden had proved himself a brilliant teacher.

The cheque for the first £20 instalment of the scholarship was made payable to me, and I went into a bank for the first time. I had to sign my name on the back of the cheque before the remote God-like cashier behind the grille would pay the money. My mother was with me – but the feeling of importance belonged to me.

3 MICHAEL MERIEL

There was no question of the scholarship turning me into an overnight hero. The family said, 'Well done,' in their own ways, and that was that. But I was aware of their pride in little ways: the picture of the winners being framed, the subject being brought up by my mother at the most casual meeting with a neighbour. I pretended to be uninterested, but, really, I loved it. Nobody's head was bigger than mine.

At school, Brother Madden had made it clear that, for those who might win a scholarship, it was only the beginning: there would be no question of resting on the oars. The prospect of going back to his teaching in September heightened my appreciation of those summer holidays, and I basked in the relief of being able to read for pleasure, not for work. I read everything I could lay my hands on and the more I read, the more I felt the urge to write myself.

What's so difficult about writing an article? I asked myself. Nothing, I answered – so I began to write, fired with a conviction that editors would only have to glance at my work before wanting to pay for it straight away. It was a miscalculation: they had a variety of rejection slips which, I was to discover, all said the same thing. I kept plugging away and then turned my hand to poetry. In our garden, there was a lilac tree and I became enamoured with its beauty so much that I decided to enshrine it for all time in my own jewelled verse. I thought it was a lovely poem, but it couldn't have been that wonderful, because I lost it.

Slightly envious of my pals who were now working and earning money, I went back to school that September dreading the prospect of another year under the Badger. But his genius for achieving good scholarship results had been rewarded with a move to a new class, and we were taken over by Brother McAuley, whose appearance was as different from Madden's as his manner and method.

McAuley, who, for some reason, we nicknamed 'Birdseed', had a great love of literature and taught me things about language, about poetry and drama, I never knew existed. And when it came to essay time, I found myself pouring out words in a way I would have shied away from before. One day, he singled me out and said: 'Andrews, that's a good essay you wrote.' He read it to the class, saying: 'This boy is using his imagination, which is what I'd like some more of you to do.' After that, he read many of my essays out loud, or got me to read them. My confidence soared and I redoubled my efforts at writing.

Poetry, particularly, appealed to me, because it could be done in secret and I didn't have to declaim it to the public or even the parlour; it was a great safety valve, a way at times of relieving the aches and pains of adolescence.

When Brother McAuley discovered I had written poetry, he gained my confidence sufficiently for me to let him see it. He said he was no judge, but he thought the poems were good and he wanted to show them to the great Francis McManus, a teacher in Synge Street primary school, who was beginning to be recognized as a novelist.

I trembled for days, waiting for a reaction. Finally, I was told to go across to Mr McManus's classroom. Nervously, I knocked on the door. Mr McManus came out and handed me my poems.

'Do you always suffer from a pain in the belly?' he said.

Over the next few days I re-read the poems and discovered they were, indeed, full of tears and dreams. I seemed to work best when I felt desolate and alone and unrecognized, with no one to pour out my troubles to, except the poem itself. I didn't want to get into a trough of artistic despondency. I decided to push poetry into second place, even though I continued to love it.

It was around this time that my mother made yet another effort to distance me from the mob by putting me down for elocution lessons, given by a statuesque disciplinarian called Ena Burke in the school music-room. There were little metal studs on the floor and the other boys and I had to stand on them, our hands at our sides, and repeat after Madam whatever Madam said.

We arranged ourselves on the floor and Miss Burke asked us to read aloud, while she stood and criticized. 'Open your mouth, don't try to talk through clenched teeth . . . pronounce your ds, the word is andeh, an-deh . . . if it were *an*, it would be spelt that way. And watch your *th* sounds. It's not turty, it's *th*, *th*irty, *th*irty . . .' When we had to recite together, it didn't bother me very much, but any solo flights filled me with the usual terror.

Inevitably, some of the boys not taking elocution mocked us, saying it was sissy to speak too correctly. But I didn't care. Those lessons were to prove the best investment my mother ever made for me.

Convinced I had the talent to earn money from writing, I spent more and more time knocking out short stories and articles. And whenever I read of a competition that had a literary flavour, I would hide myself away in the parlour and write furiously to try to win a prize. One competition concerned a certain brand of hair-oil. I wrote an essay praising it and posted it with high hopes.

Some months later, when I had forgotten about it, a boy came up to me in the playground and said: 'Your mother's outside. She wants you.'

Cheeks burning with embarrassment, I went out of the gates on to the pavement, and there she was, in an old black mac, heavily pregnant. 'You shouldn't come down here like this,' I blurted, looking over my shoulder to see if any of the boys were watching us.

'But I've got news for you – '

'I don't care,' I interrupted, with the brutal insensitivity of adolescence. 'What will the fellows say?'

'Ah, for goodness' sake, Eamonn,' she said. 'Don't worry about the fellows.' She took a letter from her purse. 'Here, look, this came for you.'

When I read the letter, I wanted to jump up and down with excitement. It said that I'd won the boy's prize in the hair-oil competition; and if I would go along on a certain date, I would be presented with one new bicycle.

'There you are, now,' Mother was saying. 'You've got your bike at last. Isn't that great?'

'I can hardly believe it,' was all I could think to say.

'Aren't you glad I came down now?'

'Yeah,' I answered. But then a sliver of embarrassment injected itself into my elation. 'But I wish you hadn't come all the same. The fellows . . .'

'Ah, the fellows!' she scoffed. 'You're too sensitive, Eamonn. Go on now, you'd better go back in, and I'll see you afterwards.'

She went off and I walked back into the playground, waving the letter. The fellows were as excited as I was and before the first class settled down that afternoon, one of the boys told a lay teacher, 'Buzzer' Ford: 'You know, sir, Andrews won a bike.'

Buzzer looked at me, with interest. 'Really? For what?'

'For an essay I wrote, sir,' I said, proudly. I handed him the envelope.

'Good, good,' he said, taking the letter out. 'What was the subject?'

'Hair-oil,' I replied.

'Hair-oil!' Buzzer froze. His lip seemed to curl and he dropped the envelope and letter on to my desk as though they were contaminated. Then he turned and walked back to the front of the class without a word.

I was so deflated, I could have cried with no trouble at all.

Boxing continued to take up a lot of my life outside school. I trained at the club every night it was open. I listened to every word of advice. And I ran round the trees in Phoenix Park until I wanted to drop. But I didn't confine myself to toil and sweat. I owned three tickets at St Kevin's public library – one more than the legal limit – and read every book that had anything remotely to do with boxing. Instruction books, autobiographies, biographies all disappeared into my brain. In the long, boring sessions of shadow-boxing, punchball and punchbag work, or simply running, I would imagine myself as Joe Louis, my current hero, or John L. Sullivan, Gene Tunney or Jack Dempsey; and, in my mind's eye, I would execute – needless to say with perfection – the moves that had made them successful and famous.

I had joined the club only to learn defensive skills. Which was why I was surprised when one of the club officials called me aside one night.

'Eamonn,' he said. 'We're going to enter you for the County Dublin Championships.'

It was my first boxing competition. I was in deep now, whether I liked it or not.

I did well in that competition and went on to win a number of tournaments held by various clubs in the Dublin area. At first, prizes were usually silver-plated trophies, medals, alarm clocks and knives and forks. But then vouchers came along – and, with them, great temptations for the amateur boxer. If someone wanted cash, not kind, it was easy for him to present a £4 voucher in a store where he was known and say: 'Give us three quid for this, will you?' All sorts of investigations went on and precautions taken to see that the voucher system was not abused. I did fairly well out of vouchers, winning enough of them to get a pair of real boxing boots, a proper pair of mitts, jockstrap, gumshield and, eventually, even headgear.

I knew I wasn't built to be a tough slugger, or even a really top-class boxer: I was too stringy for pugilistic comfort and my hands were too fragile. I soon persuaded myself that triumphing in the ring was all in the mind: not only would I *feel* superior to opponents, I would concentrate, even across the wide ring, on making *them* feel I felt superior. It seemed to work most of the time because I'm certain that some of the lads I beat were better than me.

My mother could not bring herself to watch me box in public. I didn't mind: in a way, it made me feel slightly heroic, very male, we-men-together and all that. When I reached the final of my first all-Ireland championship, however, she said she would like to be there. Uncle Jack had managed to borrow a car and he drove her and my father to Portlaoighis where the bout was being held. When she got to the entrance, my mother's apprehension got the better of her and she decided to wait outside until it was all over. The hall where the ring had been erected was in a mental asylum which she no doubt thought appropriate for the occasion.

I was not disappointed she missed the fight. I was beaten and, since I'd had some success locally, it was a shock to my ego.

The family were, no doubt, going through hard times, but I was seldom made aware of it; there were never serious talks about money or what I should do for my future. And until now, I'd rarely given it much thought myself. I still dreamt of being a writer, but, judging by the enormous collection of rejection slips, that line of country was likely to remain just a dream. Everybody looked on the Civil Service as a grand job. But it held no attractions for me; I cared nothing about the pension-for-life angle. Going back to school for my fourth and crucial year, I did begin to wonder where I was going. I was to face the terror of the Intermediate Certificate – roughly the equivalent of what was the English GCE – and it dawned on me that I had no idea where to get a job. I didn't know anyone who could fix me up.

In those early fourth-year days, I couldn't get it out of my head that writing was the only answer. I read the great authors – such as O. Henry, Conrad, Stevenson, Belloc, and even wrote essays in the style of my favourite, Chesterton. One day, I got the idea that everything would be all right if only I had a typewriter. I saw an advertisement for a second-hand one at £5 and immediately started saving up. It was well into winter when I'd reached the magic figure and I trudged through thick snow to the tenement house of a small-time junk dealer to make my purchase. The machine I carried home was a circular little thing that looked as though it had come out of Noah's Ark. But to my sixteen-year-old mind it was wonderful. I felt that if a letter was *typed*, you could write to God!

My first taste of typewritten success came when I had a poem published in the school magazine: the kick I got out of seeing my words printed – and my name there, too – was like no other feeling I knew. There was no stopping me after that. I wrote letters all over the place, wrote articles about every subject I could think of, wrote poems at the drop of a hat. Most were rejected, but I did have a few poetic essays published by obscure magazines, including one cryptically called *111* (one hundred and eleven), the staff magazine of the Hammond Lane Foundry. They were probably printed because the editor, Frank Hogan, lived near me and knew I needed some encouragement. But it was a nice kind of encouragement which paid two or three guineas every quarter when the magazine was published.

For some reason, it struck me that I should establish two separate identities and I adopted the name of Michael Meriel (the first names of Michael MacLiammoir and Meriel Moore, two theatrical people I admired enormously). My reasoning was this: I would become a great poet as Michael Meriel, but nobody would know who he was. At the same time, I would write low-brow stuff under my own name. Then, one day, there would be a sensational disclosure: Identity of Famous Poet Revealed – It's Eamonn Andrews, the Well-Known Hack.

My double literary life was short-lived. A poem about a boy in a barber's shop was published in *Hibernia* magazine under the name, Michael Meriel. But I never got paid, so I quickly went back to plain Eamonn Andrews again.

The parlour was not sacrosanct any more: school pals, such as Joe Reynolds and Mick Mawe, would come and we'd sit in there discussing literature, poetry and essays in the presence of the stuffed squirrel. Mick was a delightful, if nutty, freckled fellow who wrote weird existentialist stuff that totally baffled me. Joe was more serious, something of a sober essayist and poet. At that time, I was trying to write catchy commercial stuff, and Joe would put me down.

'You're prostituting the art of writing,' he'd say.

'I'm not prostituting anything,' I'd hit back.

'You are, you are,' Joe blazed. 'You're merely trying to catch the ear or eye, or something, with an up-beat ending.'

'Look, Joe,' I tried to explain. 'I'm more concerned with writing something that will sell. You're more concerned with something that's good. OK, so you're a much purer writer than I am.'

'Ah, don't talk nonsense – '

'No, no,' I'd cut in. 'I understand what you're criticizing about my stuff, Joe, but it's a waste of time. It's just that we're looking at it in different ways.'

And so it went on; ambitious teenagers, young and keen and eager, flexing our literary muscles in search of ourselves. Joe became a very good writer who sold a good deal more than I. Mick? I never did find out whether he kept plugging away at his existentialist writings, or whether it was just a passing fad. Certainly, in those teenage days, I used to think he was years ahead of his time.

My life was so full then that often I didn't seem to have the time to get around to all the activities in which I was involved. There was the boxing, for instance: I was doing fairly well now and went to the club to fight or train at least twice a week. Then there were the plays to be seen and talked about, which led to some pals and I forming our own little drama group. I listened to the wireless avidly, no matter what programme was on. I still pounded the ancient circular typewriter with letters and stories and poems that nobody, sadly, seemed to want. Ambition was burning the living daylights out of me.

I did find time, however, to get involved with that great organization, the St Vincent de Paul Society. The Society is broken up into cells, known as conferences, each of which takes charge of a parish or part of a parish. Some pals and I formed a junior conference at Synge Street School to assist a nearby adult conference serving slum areas and deprived bedsit-land around Aungier Street, Whitefriar Street and Bride Street. I was president of the St Brendan's Conference, and I have no doubt it was all more part of my push-forward process than from any inspiration from on high to help the poor. It was also part of my belief that if you wanted something to happen you had better do it yourself.

I couldn't rest easy. I formed the Christmas Carol Singing Group to raise funds which St Brendan's would distribute. But I am equally certain that the desire to take on so much of the administration was not unconnected with the assumption that this would preclude me from getting too involved with the actual singing. Carol singing and collecting on cold winter nights on fairly busy street corners had other compensations too: girls. 'Angels We Have Heard on High' would hardly be high enough without a soprano or two – so we were a mixed group.

Visiting the poor was sometimes depressing, frequently embarrassing, and very often rewarding, especially dealing with the very old who somehow made you feel that they had visited you. We took them vouchers for food or fuel, or both, since we were not allowed to distribute money. The amounts involved were quite pathetic, but I suppose filled some sort of gap. We went around in pairs and we must have looked pretty gauche, moving from one foot to the other, making conversation, trying to time the moment for leaving the voucher and end the conversation, or make a note to look for something they needed – an old bedstead, a reference, a letter written. The vouchers caused me agonies of embarrassment and if I was the one distributing, I would try to slip it on the mantelpiece or the dresser, believing this would save the recipient's dignity – a bit like putting a tip under a plate for a waiter you know too well. The hardest thing to do was to forgive the ones who told you lies and made you feel foolish for believing them. This, of course, was the great test. It is so easy to forgive the charmer, the joker, the good looker. This is what social service bureaucrats forget so often under the pressure of heartless rules and endless efforts to avoid them. It's like a kitten trying to steal a ball of wool out of your pocket. You may have to take the wool back, but you don't hit the kitten with a hammer. Besides, I felt I understood most of those poor people and they me. I lived only a few parishes away and I know some of my neighbours had been born in slums. There was no spare cash where I came from either, and wouldn't be for years. We were pulling ourselves up by our bootstraps and these folk just hadn't got bootstraps.

That near-sabbatical fourth year was almost a pleasure: I'd got over most of my complexes about people and was far more confident. Brother McAuley called on me more and more frequently to read my essays to the class, and I found myself beginning to enjoy the spotlight. I appeared in school plays, too. Vocal expression, it appeared, was not so terrifying after all.

I still dreamed of being a writer but the people on the radio were making a living from their voice and I thought – why shouldn't I have a try? I'd read a book that said the best way into broadcasting was to offer to speak about a subject on which you were expert, rather than make a vague request just to sit in front of a microphone.

That was sound advice. But I had a major problem. I reckoned I was an expert on – *nothing*. I thought long and hard and finally decided that boxing was the only subject on which I could produce credentials. But, even then, how could I persuade anyone to give me a crack at broadcasting about it?

The fact that I'd got to an all-Ireland final would carry some weight, I felt. But it wasn't enough. I thought hard about what broadcasting entailed: it was a speaking job, not a writing one. Suddenly I remembered Miss Burke and all those elocution lessons standing on the studs in the music room. It would not prove to anyone I was a good broadcaster, but it was worth a try. That day, I wrote to Radio Éireann, saying: 'I am an expert on boxing and have studied elocution. Please give me an audition.'

What I chose not to say was that I was only sixteen.

It seemed ages before I got a reply, but finally a short, official letter with the exciting words, 'Radio Éireann', on the heading dropped through the letterbox at St Thomas's Road. Broadcasting auditions were being held at the boxing stadium in a week or two. I was on the list.

Eight hopefuls were there, all more knowledgeable than I. The only one I can remember is a charming fellow named Dick Hearne, who had been in the international class as a cruiserweight. When I recognized him, my heart sank: how could I possibly do better than him? But I didn't have time to dwell on it because someone was telling me to go into the glass-fronted box overlooking the ring and suddenly my audition was about to start.

I had no preconceived ideas other than to describe what I was looking at as quickly and as accurately as possible. What I hadn't bargained for was being confronted with two obscure juvenile scrappers I'd never heard of, one of whom had – the commentator's nightmare – an almost unpronounceable name. No time to dwell on that, either. The noise of the crowd rose up to me. The bell sounded. I had to start speaking into the microphone for the first of three one-and-a-half-minute rounds.

The verdict on my performance took somewhat longer to be announced than the referee's that night. Days turned into weeks . . . and then months.

And then, one wonderful day, another 'Radio Éireann' letter arrived: I was to get a try-out on a live broadcast. I held the letter and read it over and over, tingling with excitement and the anticipation of it all.

That flashlamp, the scholarship, the bicycle . . . they all faded into insignificance. This was it. This was the key to radio.

Three weeks later I was back at the stadium, broadcasting for real. I wasn't nervous at all: after all, I was practically invisible in that glass-fronted box on the balcony. Radio, I knew, was perfect for me.

If my head was filled with dreams of becoming a famous broadcaster, my feet were firmly on the ground – and being made to run around fetching what seemed like millions of files for the Hibernian Insurance Company. The salary of £60 a year (less deductions) wasn't exactly champagne and caviare, especially as the fellows who had left school before me were probably earning five times that. But at least it was a job – if a very formal one. The advertisement I'd answered had been short and *formal*; the office in Dame Street was about the most *formal-looking* place I'd set foot in; my interview with the general manager was conducted with stiff *formality*. And even though I was only seventeen and a very junior clerk, I was called 'mister', like everyone else. Not that the 'mister' bit fooled me: the designation junior clerk was merely a polite alternative for dogsbody and I was under no illusions that, as far as everyone in that office was concerned, I was just about the lowest form of animal life.

Those files were the bane of my life: they were kept downstairs in a gloomy basement, in dozens of cabinets, most of which wouldn't shut properly. It was my job to look after those files, tend them, know where each one was, and find any requested number of them at a moment's notice.

'I want this file in a hurry,' someone would say, waving a piece of paper at me. I'd bend away in a scurrying run towards the basement, only to hear another voice shout: 'Hey, where's this one? This one's missing.' American screenwriter Budd Schulberg wrote a fine book in the fifties called *What Makes Sammy Run?* Nobody in the Hibernian Insurance office in 1939 needed to ask what made Eamonn run – it was the never-ending stream of requests for those damn files.

Only in that gloomy basement did I feel free, and it wasn't long before I found that the furnace room was the ideal spot for a secret smoke or a quiet uninterrupted read. After a blissful fifteen-minute escape, I would take the lift to the second floor and walk down, to confuse the trail for a possibly suspicious chief clerk. The downward journey was meant to imply I'd been delivering a message to the accounts department on the third floor, or even to the typists twittering away like caged birds on the fourth. I devised a system to warn me if any of the top brass were approaching my smoky furnace room, but it is one I refuse to disclose to any but bored junior clerks who have to do filing.

At the far end of the basement were several empty cabinets and one day it occurred to me that a magnificent solution to my filing nightmare was at my fingertips; it was so easy, and so devoid of trouble. The next time I trundled downstairs with my mountain of documents I walked past the in-use cabinets and dumped them unceremoniously in one of the empty ones. The relief was exquisite.

It was great while it lasted: once a file had been dealt with, the odds were that it would not be asked for again for, perhaps, a year. However, time and files crept up on me. What had once been empty cabinets started filling up with documents in no particular order. Almost before I knew where I was, they started advancing towards the cabinets with proper files.

When I received the inevitable request, 'Mr Andrews, get this file for me,' I would first search the correctly filed cabinets. If there was no sign of the required documents, I would lock the basement and scrabble through the chaotic mess at the other end. Predictably, the one I needed was nearly always the last one I looked at.

Upstairs, the dialogue became familiar: 'You've been long enough. Where've you been? Timbuktu?'

Red-faced, I would laugh in embarrassment. 'No, no, it was, eh, slightly misfiled.'

'Huh,' would come the disbelieving or despairing response.

Eventually, the inevitable happened. There was an investigation.

John Callaghan, the surveyor, and another staff member representing the manager trooped down into the basement. In no time at all, the hidden bodies were discovered and I was reported to the general manager, Craig-Martin. I went into his office, quaking. He was sitting behind a mammoth desk, miles from me across the intervening carpet and, walking towards him, I realized how impressive he was. Impressive and remote. He didn't speak, just looked at me with cold eyes. After an awful pounding silence, which seemed to last an hour, he said: 'I've been trying to decide, Andrews, whether you are lazy or dishonest. After a lot of thought, I've decided you are lazy, and I will not dismiss you this time. But if I'd decided you were dishonest, you would have been out the door. Understand?'

I nodded and tried to say: 'Yes, sir.'

'All right. You don't lose your job, provided we can settle this mess.'

We settled the mess. For weeks, I stayed behind until nearly midnight, sorting out those files. I was delighted not to lose my job.

The frustrations of being a junior clerk were heightened by the fact that I knew nothing about the business. I had to greet the customers at the front counter and find out what they wanted. But they invariably launched into a spate of insurance technicalities I didn't understand. Nearly always, I was left madly straining to catch at least one coherent sentence which I could ultimately repeat into a knowledgeable ear. It was a guessing game, the stuff of sheer desperation, and I would be kicked, metaphorically, from one desk to another trying to find out whose job the enquiry might be. All the time, I would try to keep my eyes from those of the customer. Egg on the face is never pleasant. In time, I grasped a few details, passed an exam or two and slowly lost some of my embarrassment. But I still never saw myself staying in that job until my old age. I still had dreams of becoming a broadcaster.

Radio Éireann had been sufficiently impressed with my first live broadcast to give me another chance, and over the next couple of years I was called on to commentate roughly once every two months. My performances *inside* the ring, however, had to be cut down, thanks to a waspy chief clerk at work who took a dim view of me sporting (why on earth do people say sporting?) a bruised eyelid or hanging lip when I greeted potential customers. But, then, the National Junior Championships came around, and the St Andrew's Club found itself without an entry for the middleweight class.

By now I was a sort of twenty-year-old elder statesman to the committee – and a middleweight. The other members looked at me hard, wondering if my new-found committee responsibilities would combine with my ego to enter myself as the best middleweight we had at the time, even though I had not been training as assiduously as a would-be champion should. In committee, and playing the role of hero, I agreed to have my name go forward and start serious training at once. But I had a real puzzler a week or so later when Radio Éireann invited me to provide a running commentary on the semi-finals and finals of the Championships. Needless to say, I signed the contract and salved my conscience with the belief that I would be eliminated long before the semi-finals, which took place the last night of three. In the event, I did get through and had to confess to my trainer and seconds that I had a problem. They agreed to do their best to have me box my semi-final long before I was due on air. I was always a bag of nerves in the dressing-room. Before every fight, I inevitably found myself with legs shaking and my brain asking: 'What the hell are you doing this for? Why don't you get up, get dressed, and go home?' On this night, the nerves were added to my concern for the broadcast –more important to my future than any boxing title. My pal, Paddy Nolan, calmed me by showing me the time on his watch: there was a good hour to go before the broadcast and my fight was on next.

I won my bout and was through to the final much later that same night. But as I stood triumphant in the ring, my joy turned to despair when Paddy confessed he had put his watch back forty-five minutes to make me more relaxed. There was, in fact, only five minutes to go before I was due on air. I ripped my gloves off and dashed for the stairs leading to the broadcasting box to hear the sound engineer on the phone to the studio saying the commentator had not shown up.

Apparently he had watched me fight in the semi-final but, since he hadn't *expected* to see me inside the ring, he *hadn't seen* me inside the ring. This time, I really had been invisible.

Somehow, Paddy got my trousers on me and I got my breath back enough to do the commentary. There was not much time for rest or more nerves afterwards because I had to get undressed again to fight in the final – which, fortunately for me, was *not* being broadcast.

It was worth all the panic next morning when I read the headline: 'BROADCASTING BOXER WINS TITLE.'

It was unlikely anyone else was going to achieve that unusual, if not remarkable, combination.

The Hibernian promoted me to assistant surveyor, but the new job did nothing to fire my interest and I became more and more restless. The broadcasting bug had bitten and I wanted to be on air more often, no matter in what capacity. I had an overwhelming desire simply to be known, and as my ambition grew, so my insurance work decreased to the minimum I could get away with.

Outside the office, I was up to my head, neck and ears in our amateur dramatic company, Blue White Productions, with my friend Paddy Nolan. And when we weren't putting on plays, I was visiting the Radio Éireann station in Henry Street, trying to get in to see John McDonagh, who was Head of Production. The drama group, particularly, took up a lot of time, and the Hibernian's fire department must have been surprised when I bounded in enthusiastically and volunteered to take a late lunch-hour every day, and act as a sort of sentry while their office was empty. There was method in my apparent madness: a lot of arrangements for Blue White Productions needed to be made by phone and it would be invaluable to have an uninterrupted hour to get them done. A young lady named Maire Gannon stood in as switchboard operator during the lunch-break and I found her a willing conspirator in my telephone round-up. Paddy was my most frequent caller and because he worked in his father's business, where there were no managers or chief clerks guarding the company's time and finances, we were able to take our time sorting out what needed to be done for our dramatic company. Not that I was the only one he spoke to; his pleasantries with Maire grew into long conversations and often he forgot he was ringing me in the first place. Inevitably, they decided to meet, so they could see what each other looked like. The blind date grew into love and, eventually, they got married.

At first, Paddy and I put on little plays at the Bernadette Hall, but, as we got more ambitious, we hired the town hall, and staged bigger ones. Every time we put on a play, we had to pay royalties, so one day I decided to write a play myself. More correctly, I suppose, it was assembling a play. We had the drama group. We had actresses who could type, and a Hibernian insurance employee named Jack MacGowran, who was making quite a name for himself as a very talented actor, notably with Brendan Smith and his acting academy. And, as a bonus, my father, convalescing from one of his many bouts of illness, agreed to draw on his amateur theatrical experience to produce the play for us.

I had a title: *The Moon is Black*. We even booked the one-hundred-seater Peacock Theatre for two weeks at £10 a week – about four times my salary. What we did not have was one line of dialogue. That didn't worry me unduly, however, and I eagerly started on a tragi-comedy about a man ridden with guilt because he thinks he has murdered his wife when, in fact, she was dead already from natural causes.

Writing a play was harder than I had expected and the first rehearsal was due before I'd completed the first act. It was bizarre watching the cast say their lines when I hadn't a clue what the second act would be about. But worse was to follow: when the finished product was typed it was so short, I had no option but to keep writing new scenes to pad it out a bit.

And then, before the Moon could become even a dark shade of grey, disaster struck. Two weeks before opening night, Noel de Chenu, a university student due to play the juvenile lead, walked into the Hibernian's offices. Quickly, I grabbed a file and tried to make out he was a customer. He looked worried and came straight to the point: 'I'm sorry, Eamonn, but the Dean has told me, it's either study or plays – not both. I'm afraid I'll have to pull out of *The Moon is Black*.'

My world fell in on me. I couldn't think. I called an emergency meeting of the drama group for that night and we all agreed that the nerves of the cast, already stretched to twanging, could not cope with rehearsing with a new actor at such short notice. There was only one way out, we agreed: I'd written the thing; at least I knew the words. I would have to play the part. There was a big problem, however: I'd written the role for a frail tubercular lad – very popular in Irish dramas of the day – and I was tall, solid and in fine physical shape through my boxing training.

Trying to look small and thin and sickly was both madness and an impossibility – and most of the press notices tore the play, and me, to shreds. One critic pointed out that putting the junior middleweight champion in the part of the weak boy 'was not exactly typecasting'. But the notice that hit home was by Gabriel Fallon. He said something like this: 'Most of us get the measles at some time or another. Andrews has now had his literary measles. Let's hope he's got it out of his system and maybe next time he will write a *good* play.'

Despite such reviews, the play ran the full two weeks. And with that pathetic optimism essential to all actors we persuaded ourselves that, if only we had been able to book the theatre longer, the public would have been knocking down the doors to get in.

If the play was something of a disaster at least it can claim some credit for helping along the career of the talented Jack MacGowran. He joined Dublin's Abbey Theatre and started taking acting very seriously. Sadly, drink took a tight hold on him and when I met him occasionally in London I hardly knew him. I tried to get him into television, but he couldn't keep appointments. How he managed to become teetotal I never knew, except that he had good fortune in meeting Gloria, whom he married.

His film début was in *The Quiet Man*, with John Wayne, and his screen credits included *Doctor Zhivago*, *King Lear* and *The Exorcist*. But he was renowned more for his interpretation of the works of his great friend and fellow Irishman, Samuel Beckett.

Jack died in New York's Algonquin Hotel on 31 January 1973, after a bout of influenza. He was just 54. What a tragic waste.

I have one somewhat bizarre, but sweet, memory of him. I was just leaving the Ideal Home Exhibition at Olympia when I was stopped by the broadcaster, George Elrich, who pressed me to have a look at a collection of paintings by people in showbusiness in aid of the Water Rats Society. I was in a rush to get back for a *Today* interview and told George I had no time. Being a persistent Scot, he said I would at least have to buy a catalogue. I did so, with poor grace, I fear, and dashed off.

Waiting to go on air, I flicked through the catalogue and was amazed to find that so many of my show business colleagues had sketching and painting talent. Suddenly my finger stopped at the name Jack MacGowran. And the painter: actor James Mason. The price was £50. I rushed out to the hospitality room and asked someone to get in touch with George and let him know I wanted to buy the painting.

The next day, George phoned me, apologizing that the painting had not, in fact, arrived; James Mason was filming abroad and would be sending it direct from his home in Switzerland. Was I still interested? Yes, I was, but I now felt strangely doubtful about the whole project for some reason. To my surprise, George phoned again a few days later. He had spoken to Mason and had to confess that the painting was not yet done. But the actor had said that if I donated the £50 to the charity he would go ahead with it.

'Done,' I said. 'Even if he never delivers the picture, at least I can go around saying I commissioned James Mason to do a painting for me.'

Happily, James was as good as his word. The next time he was in London he brought the painting – a cartoon-style evocation of Jack – which I hung proudly in my study to give me an excuse to talk about my insurance clerk pal who became an actor of world acclaim.

Even though I was doing only half a dozen boxing commentaries a year, I did think I'd cracked it at Radio Éireann. I rolled the title, commentator and journalist, around my tongue with great joy and had the words printed, with my name, on some Woolworth's business cards. I also needed to put a phone number, but we didn't have one at home. To blazes with it, I thought, and wrote: Dublin 23027 – the Hibernian Insurance number. I prayed it would not prove too embarrassing if anyone did ring me there.

The cards helped boost my confidence and I handed them out freely to anyone I thought might be able to help me. Fortunately, I had a few left when it was announced that His Fistic Eminence, Jack Doyle, was to fight Chris Cole, a Mullingar heavyweight, in one of Dublin's rare boxing tournaments. Since I would not be able to afford a ticket, those cards – and the compelling, if misleading, words printed on them – were my only hope of seeing the fight. I found out the promoter was a gentleman called Gerald Egan and, with card at the ready, I began a series of assaults on his office in Commercial Buildings, not far from where I was working with the Hibernian.

'I'm Radio Éireann,' I told him over and over again, sweeping the whole complex organization under my wing. 'Boxing commentator, you know? Now what about a ticket?'

I might have been from Radio Iran, so far as Mr Egan cared. I wrote, phoned and went along umpteen times and hung around him. He drew down on himself protective mantles of deafness, annoyance and indifference – and I still did not get a ticket. I was furious, but not entirely dismayed. I still had one card to play – literally.

On the night of the fight, I marched up to Dalymount Park, the cleanest of my visiting cards in my pocket, ready to be drawn with the speed of Wyatt Earp. I was going to see the fight – and that was that. A big fellow barred the way through the press entrance. I flashed my card. 'Radio Éireann,' I said as nonchantly as I could. For a second, he was undecided and I had a sudden vision of Gerald Egan coming round a corner, recognizing me and having me kicked down the length of the approach.

The world stood still. Then the big fellow gave me a slack-jawed 'Awright' and motioned me in. People were passing me on the way to their seats and I got caught up with them and drifted towards the ring. But then I spotted a steward examining tickets so I slipped into a row of seats beside me and pushed on towards the far end. But another official with a huge steward's ticket in his lapel was waiting there, so I did the only thing I could – I sat down.

As soon as the official's back was turned, I slipped away to another, less congested, part of the arena and sat down again. I looked around me, fascinated. So this was the world of Damon Runyon. Dalymount Park was no Madison Square Garden, but what I was seeing of it was exciting. If only I could sit still . . .

Suddenly, I heard shouts and scuffling behind me and a great surging forward as hundreds of fans in the cheaper seats brushed stewards aside and heaved in closer to the ringside. It solved my problem nicely. I chose a section where the usurpers were at their thickest and squeezed in among them, safe.

My recollection of the fight is that Doyle, the humble lad from Cork who was fêted in Hollywood and married to a film star, lashed out with a first-round haymaker and put the Mullingar man on the canvas. Thinking it was all over, he went to a corner, winked to the ringside customers and patted his hair to make sure not one strand of his dark curls was out of place. He was still smiling his film-star smile to the ladies in the expensive seats when Cole got up and pole-axed him with a right. That was the end of the fight, and the beginning of pandemonium.

I had the big idea then that I'd like to interview Doyle. I don't know why because I wasn't working for any paper, but I started making my way to the tunnel under the stand, the crumpled bit of cardboard that was my visiting card clutched in my fist.

When I came to the first batch of gorillas barring my progress, I got frightened. 'Radio Éireann,' I said, in a voice I would be embarrassed to admit was mine. They leered or sneered or smiled, according to their lights, and let me pass into the long corridor behind them. With every step I took, the more convinced I became that I was making a ghastly mistake. As I approached more toughs at the end of the passage, fear set in again.

'Radio Éireann,' I said again. A thumb flicked in the direction of a dressing-room door.

I was at the end of the journey now: only one more centurion to pass, and this one had heard me say I was from Radio Éireann. He stuck his head round the door and bawled: 'Hey, Jack, fella here, reporter or som'p'n, to see yis.'

By this time I was terrified. I didn't want to see Jack at all. All I wanted was to stand in the background of this new world and soak up some of it. But how could I explain that?

I went into the room, and there was Jack, looking very sorry for himself, being fed a drink by his dark-skinned, beautiful actress wife, Movita. 'Hello, there,' he said.

For some reason, I handed him my grimy card, my fraudulent passport. I was convinced he would say something like: 'Ah, Radio Éireann is it? Well, where's your microphone and stuff? Or do you want me to go on to a studio, or what?' But after what seemed a long time, he just said: 'Ah, yes. Well now, you can tell your readers . . .'

I slipped the card into my pocket with more sleight of hand than any magician. Jack thought I was a newspaper reporter so I acted out the part. The relief flooding through me, however, played havoc with my concentration and the dialogue must have sounded like a wartime message before the code-breakers got to work.

Walking back down the now-crowded corridor, the tension was worse. The nape of my neck tingled. I couldn't bear to be caught now. I resisted the temptation to run and nodded knowingly at the lounging sentries. Once outside the stadium, I didn't look back till I reached O'Connell Street two miles away.

It was several days before I was brave enough to start boasting (in whispers) of the night I interviewed the legendary Jack Doyle.

Whenever I had time after work, I tackled Radio Éireann's head-quarters with greater zeal. But I still had the greatest difficulty getting past even the doorman. I decided then and there to make him my first friend in the station. What a happy and useful decision that turned out to be. But, having got past him, I really had nowhere to go: people weren't interested, even when I succeeded in meeting them.

'Eamonn who? Oh yes, boxing, yes, yes, yes. Could I get a part in a play? No, I hadn't really acted outside of school but – yes, I'll write to you about that. How about what? Well, that's not really my department, you should see . . .' And so it went on. Gradually, however, I wore them down and, with the help of my friendly doorman, who even allowed me to use the telephone without charge, I began to identify some of the key people.

There was the nutty, but key, man called John McDonagh, who was in charge of the lighter end of broadcasting. I set my aim at him for a start. He was easy enough to identify: he had very little hair, horn-rimmed spectacles almost the size of his face, he dribbled slightly when he talked, never seemed to sit still for a moment and all over his jacket, as well as cigarette ash, were pinned pieces of paper with reminders of things to be done – although I had a feeling that, once there, they were meant to be forgotten. He was a grotesque sight. I often had the feeling that if a strong breeze were to blow through his office, he would fly out the window, probably away altogether, if only to escape my never-ending visits.

Once I had the entry, he was doomed. I was convinced I could do any of his programmes better. At long last – a week is a lifetime on the way in or up – he gave me some minor parts in radio dramas and documentaries. But I never quite lost the feeling of being resented by those who had known each other for years, and who talked over my head during rehearsals about things I knew nothing of. It was an uncomfortable feeling, but I was determined to get on with it and try to get something of my own out of McDonagh – or someone else – that wouldn't depend on nervous servility to people whose power I had no way of getting at or even measuring. My doorman couldn't advise me, so I played it safe, for a while.

In the long run, I decided on a very dangerous course: to say yes to every offer of a job, and to answer yes to any query beginning: 'Do you know anything about?' The first part of the resolution was based on the belief that if I was heard on *any* subject often enough, at least people would get to know my name, and I would have a better chance of presenting my ideas to the mystery men I hadn't yet met. The second, even more dangerous, part of the resolution was based on the naïve belief that I could bone up on anything in a hurry, and learn enough to talk about or describe the subject, whatever it might be. I gave this a faint moral justification on the grounds that if I was *not* expert on the subject, I had a better chance of serving the public, the vast majority of whom would not be experts either. My own ignorance would help illuminate theirs.

I quickly came a cropper. When I was asked if I wanted to have a trial as a horse-racing commentator, I gave my standard yes reply, and proceeded to bone up in the ten days before the tests were due to start. I read all about the horses, the numbers, the colours, the trainers, the jockeys, but it was an impossible task for someone who had not been to a race-meeting before. I ended up at Baldoyle racecourse on the Saturday with a head full of knowledge that I thought would help me deliver a breath-taking commentary.

The station was using an open broadcasting box on top of the grandstand, and an old-fashioned ribbon microphone which picked up sound from all directions. With my borrowed binoculars, I began to realize that colours were not as easy to identify as flags of nations as

I had thought; and that the hoops and caps were bewildering to the novice. So I decided to concentrate on the numbers on the sides of the horses. I managed to get my race going well down the straight, past the commentary position, but I lost sight of them almost entirely on the far side of the course: the odd bobbing head meant nothing to me.

I kept the commentary going for the benefit of my critical judges in the studios, naming horses in any old position in the optimistic belief that when they reached the straight again I would sort them out properly by numbers. Alas, a few feet from my open window a knowledgeable, but irate, punter could stand it no longer.

'Rubbish,' he shouted, adding precisely what kind of rubbish he meant.

He also added, in clear, colourful terms, the information that the horse I had in front had fallen long ago. The horse I had second was, in fact, sixth. And the horse I placed third was last.

All this went clearly down the line to the executives judging my racing-commentary skills. No doubt they had little trouble crossing my name off the list of contenders for the job, for I never heard about it again. As it turned out, I was on a hiding to nothing, anyway. One of the other men on trial that day was a youngster named Michael O'Hehir, who went on to become one of the world's greatest racing commentators.

The experience taught me a lesson: if you take a job well within your powers, you're likely to be a happy man. Take one outside your powers and you'll probably spend the rest of your life in misery, fearing you'll be found out.

Soccer was not outside my powers so much as horse-racing. But I did get found out in a different way; and it resulted in the Hibernian and the budding broadcaster parting company.

I'd picked up the finer points of the game by watching Sunday afternoon matches, and was asked to commentate on a match involving the English Football League in Dublin one Wednesday afternoon. With my horse-racing nightmare still fresh in my mind, I felt it would be beneficial to watch the English stars play in Belfast the preceding Saturday, so that I would know who was who. The Hibernian worked on Saturdays, however, and when I pleaded to be given the day off, I was refused. Frankly, it didn't take me long to decide what to do: on the Saturday morning, my sister Kathleen rang the office to say I was too ill to come in, and I made my way up north to Belfast to join Brian Durnin, a full-time member of Radio Éireann's staff, who was also doing research for the forthcoming Dublin match.

At Dalymount Park, on the following Wednesday, my afternoon off, I described the first-half, then brought in Brian with the time-honoured cliché: 'What do *you* think, Brian?'

And my heart beat a little faster as I heard him tell all Dublin: 'Well, Eamonn, I think you'll agree, this English side isn't playing as well as when *we* watched them in Belfast last Saturday.'

I was sunk.

Joe Gallagher, the Hibernian's new general manager, sent for me the next day, and told me he had heard the broadcast. It was too late to bluff and I confessed I'd lied about being ill. A frown on his face, but a twinkle in his eye, Mr Gallagher suggested that it was probably time for a parting. He did give me a choice, but something inside told me I needed to quit if I was to do anything in the broadcasting world. Joe comforted me by saying I was doing the right, if risky, thing and I went home that night to tell my parents I'd decided to quit.

My poor mother was not sure what fit of lunacy had smitten her first-born, and disregarded my bombshell. But my father grasped my seriousness immediately.

'Why?' he asked.

I just said: 'Because I'm going to be a full-time broadcaster.'

He nodded, thought about it for a while, then said quietly: 'It's a big decision, Eamonn, but one you can only make yourself. You're throwing up a good job with security and prospects. But don't let that be the only consideration. If you really want the other thing, and it would make you happy, then you must do it. But there are a lot of broadcasters and actors without tuppence to rattle on a tombstone.'

My father was not at all well at that stage and hearing him talk like that affected me. There were hardly any full-time freelance broadcasters in Ireland and he must have felt it was presumptuous and foolhardy of me to think I could break through. But he did not try to influence my decision, and I was more than grateful to him.

The idea of going it alone had seemed attractive. The reality was frightening. I went back and forth to Henry Street, armed with ideas and scripts, but the jobs were few and far between, and I began to think I was the idiot of the century to give up a steady job for the unfettered world of the freelance.

5 PLAYBOY OF THE SOUTH-WESTERN WORLD

Gradually work began to trickle in and over the next few months I did everything, it seemed, except sweep the corridors of Radio Éireann. I wrote short stories. And quite a few documentaries. I even sold a keep-fit series for children to a delightful olde-world character named Miss Roddy. In some ways it was the best assignment I ever had. She insisted on me speaking slowly – the sage advice I had culled from personal boxing experience and dozens of library books – with the result that very few words went very far. I don't know if anyone ever did the exercises. I know I did, because I had to be sure they worked.

In those early Radio Éireann days, I became friendly with Seamus Ennis, an eccentric who had gone for the same job as I. He became a recording officer and gave the station's civil servants many a headache with his astonishing 'travelling expenses'. He was brought to heel many a time, but, since he could charm a bird off any bush, he nearly always got away with it.

The classic story concerns the occasion he travelled to Valencia Island, off the coast of Kerry. The only guest-house on the island was run by a Norman Ross, another eccentric, who refused to have his guest-house upgraded to a hotel, so that he could retain the right to refuse customers he didn't want.

Seamus was staying there when Norman told him that a Spanish trawler had come in for shelter from the Atlantic storms, and that several of the crew were in the public lounge next door. It was a heaven-sent opportunity for Seamus to collect some off-beat material – perhaps the Spanish version of 'What shall we do with the drunken sailor?' – and he assembled his equipment and went into the lounge to meet them.

The Spaniards wouldn't sing. Seamus's charm worked only in English or Irish, and the Spanish beat him. Norman had a suggestion: why not try a few pints of Guinness? It worked, and the next day Seamus set off with several new tunes in the boot of his car.

A few weeks later, an astonished civil servant reckoned Seamus

Ennis had done it again as he surveyed his expenses: 'To making Spaniards sing – 100 pints.'

I was then asked to do a Saturday-night interview programme called *Microphone Parade* and had to haunt hotels in search of visiting celebrities. Finding stars was the easy part; somewhat harder was getting them up to our little studio at the top of the GPO building for the interview, for Radio Éireann was too budget-conscious to pay any fee or expenses. My long hours hanging around hotel lobbies were often rewarded, however, when popular personalities of the day did agree to climb that tiny staircase.

By now John McDonagh had been succeeded as Head of Production by an astonishing, mercurial character named Larry Morrow. I was not familiar with his literary world, but he was obviously very much a character in it, although more journalist than literary man, more wit than wicker. He thrived on gossip and had a wicked tongue. He gave you the feeling he was conspiring with you against his pompous masters, but one had the uneasy feeling that, in the presence of those masters, he was decimating you through pursed lips. Once, he poked his head out of his office door, looked up and down the tiled corridor and hissed in my ear: 'The largest public lavatory in the world.'

He told me most executives seldom listened to the programmes they had commissioned, or shared the dreams and passions of the makers. On this basis, he taught me a trick, which I practised repeatedly. Although I did not have an office, I was keeping office hours at Henry Street. And as soon as I arrived, I would announce to the doorman, lift-man, or, indeed, a charlady, if I happened to meet one, that my programme the previous night had been sensational.

The idea was that the information would be passed on to someone who mattered. 'Good morning, sir. I hear Eamonn Andrews's show was sensational last night!'

Even if the ruse worked only once in ten, it could prove worthwhile.

Whether it was the result of such cheeky self-promotion, I never found out, but, out of the blue, I got an offer to be question-master in a new quiz show called *Double or Nothing* – not on radio, but at a theatre in Limerick.

It was the age of a new entertainment phenomenon in Ireland called Cine Variety; which meant cinema managers could avoid entertainment tax if they provided a certain amount of live entertainment as well as a film. This 'live' entertainment varied enormously across the country: it was pretty basic – and pretty awful – in some tiny hard-seat halls in tucked-away villages; but in big cinemas in large towns and cities, Cine Variety was the signal for some very fine stage shows. Dublin's mammoth Theatre Royal, as usual, topped the lot, employing enterprising home-grown talent, as well as first-class vaudeville acts from England.

The theatre also introduced a new quiz called *Double or Nothing*: members of the audience were invited on to the stage and asked a series of four questions each. If they got the first one right, they were given half a crown (12½p) and asked: Double or nothing? They could accept the money and leave the stage or try a second question for double the amount – five shillings (25p). If they got that question right, they could try a third one for ten shillings, and then a fourth for one pound. The quiz caught the public's imagination – and catapulted into the limelight a fast-talking, personable young actor named Eddie Byrne.

And an ambitious, young, fast-talking broadcaster named Eamonn Andrews.

The quiz was so successful in Dublin, the owners of the Savoy Theatre in Limerick were introducing it there and wanted me as question-master. I jumped at the chance and borrowed £170 to buy a Morris 10. Sadly, the car was suffering from severe senile decay and collapsed many times during the whole day and most of the night it took a friend and me to drive the hundred-odd miles. But we got there eventually, frozen and cramped and weary, fit only for bed. It was a hectic and inauspicious start to a hectic, but memorable, period that would shape my life.

And that lovable, ancient Morris, affectionately called 'Moggy', was to share it all.

If I'd ever seemed quiet and retiring in Dublin, I now erupted as a playboy of the south-western world. I learned that fellows drank various liquids which liberated the inhibitions, loosened the tonsils and engendered a liveliness of behaviour. In due course a certain former assistant insurance surveyor abolished his inhibitions, became possessed of the loosest tonsils within the sound of a donkey's screech, and had (on occasions) behaviour-patterns which would have left Pavlov's dogs nowhere. All this was during off-duty hours, of course. The show, meanwhile, had to go on.

I had done a little compèring at concerts in Dublin, but I'd never been asked to hold an audience on my own. But the southerners were fun-loving, receptive people who liked *Double or Nothing* and it became a nightly favourite. The show gave me invaluable experience in keeping my wits about me, to be ready for unexpected answers and quips, or help the tongue-tied or give someone a clue.

I was doing sponsored lunch-time spots on Radio Éireann and would set off for Dublin immediately after my last performance at the Savoy. It was nearly always a terrifying ordeal, driving through the night: I hated being blinded by the headlights of cars coming the opposite way and would pull into the side of the road, frightened and furious. But it would happen further along the road and I'd pull in again. The continual stopping and starting and being frightened and angry would leave me exhausted by the time I reached Dublin in the early hours. I never got over that hatred of driving at night.

I would grab a few hours' sleep before going to the studios, then dashing back to Limerick for the evening show. The prodigal son was seldom seen at home. My family were aware a nomad (*a*) arrived and (*b*) left while they were (*a*) asleep or (*b*) either at work or at school.

Once, I persuaded Alec, the Savoy's stage-manager, to drive to Dublin with me; he'd never been there and I welcomed the company. I picked him up on the bridge over the Shannon at five o'clock in the morning. He had been up fishing most of the night and for most of the journey sat beside me like a sack of cabbages, sunk in vegetable silence. We got to Dublin later than usual and I had to rush straight to the studios.

'Grab yourself a cup of coffee or something, Alec,' I said. 'And I'll pick you up around here at two o'clock.'

I rushed off, leaving him sitting there. When I got back a couple of hours later, he looked as if he hadn't moved.

'Did you see the city?' I asked.

'Ah, sure, no, Eamonn,' he replied. 'I didn't like to get off the car.'

That was all: no further explanations. I couldn't understand him. I thought he was daft to sit in a car on his first trip to Dublin. Anyway, he didn't seem bothered and we happily set off for the return journey.

We were going well until we reached Monasterevan. Now, those responsible for designing this little town were either cunning or else had a weird sense of humour. For suddenly, without warning, a twelve-foot stone wall appeared on the main approach road. A driver had two options: to turn right and end up with a flat face; or try to negotiate the ninety-degree *left* turn and enter the town's main street.

Addled by tiredness, I saw the wall rather late. I jerked the wheel left with all my might and waited for the crash. Moggy's back wheels lost their grip and slid round in a tasteful arc. The rear slammed against the kerb, but Moggy kept going forward. Then my door fell off and I found myself sitting in the road, watching, in a detached, dreamlike way, as Alec, erect as a stick in the passenger seat, headed for a pub. The bonnet missed a plate-glass window, but the left bumper knocked a chunk of drainpipe and the right one opened, somewhat abruptly, the front door of a house next to it.

Alec was shaken, or shaking, or both. The pub's owner came out, and so did his neighbour, who turned out to be a local police sergeant. Then a man from a nearby garage came and stared and shrugged, a look of hopelessness wandering across his features. We pulled Moggy away and part of the pub's drainpipe came away in sympathy.

'You'll have to pay for the damage,' the publican said.

I was more concerned about getting to Limerick for the show. 'Will she go?' I asked the garage man.

'Look at that,' he said, a car-door in one hand and the radiator-grille in the other.

'The damage,' the publican was saying. 'What about paying me for it?'

And all the time the sergeant was telling me not to worry about anything as far as he was concerned.

Finally, the garage man put Moggy together again, informed me cautiously that I *might* make it to Limerick, and refused to accept anything more than half a crown for his trouble.

But there was no getting away from the publican and I had to pay him thirty shillings for his broken drainpipe.

Alec and I clattered out of town, the bumpers, radiator-grille and door piled in the back of Moggy, and reached the Savoy Theatre at precisely the time I should have been introducing the show. I ran out from the wings, dust on my suit, face and hair.

For years afterwards, the broken drainpipe on the pub wall stared back at me every time I passed through Monasterevan. And I kept wondering about my thirty shillings.

I did try the journey by alternative transport twice. But the experiences were so nerve-wracking that I couldn't wait to get back to Moggy. Two American friends at Shannon Airport owned a Flying Flea aircraft and I persuaded one of them to give me a lift to Dublin in return for some radio publicity. I had never flown before, and certainly had never seen such a small plane: it was like a king-size kite and I closed my eyes as we bumped down the runway. After we'd been airborne for a while, I shouted to the pilot: 'Hey! Can I smoke?' He looked at me and suddenly we started to plummet. We landed in a field and the pilot got out. 'Now you can smoke,' he said. I was so confused, I didn't think to explain that I hadn't been that desperate for a smoke. But it was the second flight in the Flying Flea that convinced me that old unreliable Moggy was the safest form of internal travel. High above central Ireland, we started to run out of petrol. Frantically, the pilot took us down, closer and closer to the roads . . . looking for a petrol station!

I had a wild time in Limerick, most of it in the company of a marvellous, crazy Galwayman, named Des Staunton. He had those very light-blue eyes that nearly always – in an Irishman at least – betray an uninhibited zest for life, and he swept me along with him at an intensely furious pace that left me gasping afterwards. In the week, he was a dedicated aircraft maintenance engineer. At weekends, he was a carefree lover of life, game for anything that promised a good time.

He'd arrive and say: 'Right, Eamonn, Galway – are you on?' I always was and we'd point Moggy in a westerly direction and take off for several hours of non-stop action. I soon discovered that the various liquids for which fellows had a friendly toleration were potent, as well as invigorating. This was illustrated clearly in a Galway hotel at nine o'clock one Monday morning. I came down, ready to head back to Limerick, and found Des sitting, zombie-like, at the breakfast table. Two other statue-like apparitions were at the next table, but I barely noticed them because I was anxious to get going and did not intend having breakfast.

'We'd better be off, Des,' I said.

'Right you are, Eamonn,' Des said. 'But first I want you to meet two friends of mine here.'

He gestured to the men at the next table. 'Fellas, this is a pal of mine, Eamonn Andrews.'

The men got to their feet and offered their hands to shake mine when – bang! – they folded, jack-knife-like, across the table. It was like a rehearsed double act – but it was no act. They were paying the penalty for a night that had stretched too long – even for Galway. I never did get their names. But I left that hotel, convinced I would recognize their snores if I ever heard them again.

For all I knew, Des had been up all night with them. But his blue eyes never wavered and his step was firm as we headed for the car. As usual, he was ready for anything the day might offer.

That sojourn in Limerick lasted only a few months, but I crammed so much in that it seemed like years. In a sense, it was just as well Cine Variety came to an end because, physically, I could not have gone on much longer. I returned to Dublin and, later, Des went to Canada. One summer we spoke about getting together, but sadly, we never did. And by the autumn he was dead. I never forgot that wonderful, wild, blue-eyed man from Galway. Nor did I ever forget how hard it was saying goodbye to all the friends I'd made in Limerick. Ma Sadlier's hotel had been my home from home all the time I was there, and while my farewell party went on, I sat on the stairs and cried.

I had never felt so sad about anything before.

6 DOUBLE OR NOTHING

The offer that was to change my life came when Eddie Byrne temporarily left *Double or Nothing* at the Theatre Royal, to go into acting. Impresario Louis Elliman, who also owned the Savoy in Limerick, decided I was worth a spell at headquarters, so to speak. I would have to do two shows a day for seven days a week for £30 a week. Naturally, I grabbed the chance.

The publicity that surrounded my take-over made my debut a huge ordeal, however. While the Savoy had been small and intimate and cosy, the Royal was one of the largest cinemas in Europe, and I was gripped by excitement and a tingling fear in the moments before I went on. And the fear got worse when I spoke into the microphone and couldn't hear my voice come back to me over the amplification system. I wasn't afraid of words, though, and went through the usual introductory patter before asking for four volunteers from the audience. The fear was tingling inside me as I introduced the first contestant; I was far more nervous than he and, in my nervousness, I made a tentative wisecrack. From the darkness beyond the footlights a fantastic sound rolled down to me: the sound of an audience laughing. My tenseness eased. My fear vanished. I knew it was going to be all right.

Whenever I stopped to think of my shyness, I was astonished at what I was doing for a living. I still did radio work, but usually there was just an inanimate microphone and me – perfect for someone so withdrawn. And yet here I was, running on to a huge stage, painfully aware of all my deficiencies, and performing before huge audiences. The show made me more well-known in Dublin and people would come up to me in the street as though they knew me. I found it very exciting and flattering, and the more people I met, the more the main burden of shyness wore off. It never left me at parties, however: I was still petrified of everyone hushing and shushing, waiting for me to sing my party solo. People never seemed to understand the huge difference between talking to three thousand unknown – and unseen – people from a stage and standing up in a living room under close scrutiny from, perhaps, a small gathering of friends whom you can see very well.

For me, the Theatre Royal was a cross between an Aladdin's Cave and a naughty nightclub. Cool, detached front-of-house management and backstage hilarity-cum-hysteria were linked by two extraordinary managers – Charlie Wade and Jimmy Sheil. Charlie veered from pursed-lip, narrow-eyed discipline to bottom-pinching schoolboy innuendoes about as subtle as a seaman's parrot. Jimmy seldom raised his voice, seemed permanently at an angle of thirty degrees forward, his feet moving as if wound from a spring between the ankles and kneecaps. His nose wrinkled constantly, as if there were a nasty smell from everything going on around him, and his eyebrows took off into his hair at the unbelievable chicanery constantly being reported to him.

Jimmy was always on the brink of discovering some world-shattering talent, or of launching an enterprise that would make not only his fortune, but mine. He drank prodigious quantities of large whiskies and his face at times reminded me of the head of a matchstick just before it burst into flames.

He was a gentle, loyal, infinitely funny character. He hated the system, whatever it was, and defied the laws of medicine and science to live longer than any of us thought he would. Seriously ill, he so hated the hospital routine of the happy, smiling doctor bustling into the room day after day with the same question that he channelled what little strength he had to prop himself and snarl: 'Well, how are *we* today, Doctor?' It almost destroyed the unfortunate man's professional confidence.

When Jimmy died, he had the last laugh on us. We could say what prayers we liked at the funeral mass, but there was no funeral and no body. Jimmy had arranged to have his mortal remains given to the College of Surgeons for research and study.

I never felt an insider at the Royal; Eddie Byrne had become very much a fixture in Dublin theatrical life and I was, after all, only replacing him temporarily. But Jimmy did his best to make me feel at home.

After the second stage show, the feature film would bring the day's entertainment to an end. While it was on, I would meet Jimmy in the Circle bar. Favoured figures were discreetly allowed in there without buying a ticket for the show and it was developing into an unofficial showbiz nightclub. When it closed, Jimmy would invite me up to his office, with either the current star of the show or a less well-known, but equally colourful, performer. Few of these after-hours guests stuck it out as long as Jimmy and I. Sometimes when they had gone and a sobering influence was needed, Jimmy would telephone Olivelli, the Irish-Italian restaurateur next door, and order two flowing bowls of well-oiled, cheesed-up spaghetti to be brought round. I would usually have to be up relatively early the next day for a radio broadcast before the matinée at the theatre. Sometimes, I envied those languorous Thespians who rose languidly at noon, but I never did learn to lie-in. Work was always on my mind: I felt too insecure to place all my eggs in the Theatre Royal basket. Or the radio one, for that matter.

Luck plays a part in everyone's career and a huge slice came my way with the appointment of a new executive at Radio Éireann: Frank McManus, the teacher-cum-novelist who had read my poetry a few years before. When he had settled into his new job, I went to him with an idea. A kindly police superintendent at Kilmainham Castle agreed to make certain files available to me and I wanted to adapt them for a true-life radio crime series. Mr McManus loved the idea and I got cracking. Researching and writing the series, however, turned out to be much harder than I'd expected and, with all the other radio and theatre work I was doing, it was not long before I started running behind on script deliveries.

Mr McManus was normally kind and understanding, but did rage at me from time to time when I was particularly late delivering. One of these times came when I was doing a sponsored programme in an upstairs studio.

Where was the latest crime spot script? he angrily wanted to know.

My usual panic set in. For not only was there no script, there was not even an idea for a script. With everything else I'd been doing, I hadn't got around to getting the material for it. But I could hardly admit this to an executive of the station, who needed programme information for advance publicity.

I bluffed and stalled and hedged, and finally Mr McManus said: 'Well, have you a title? Just let me have the title.'

'Er, no, I, er, I haven't decided on one yet.'

'Well, what's the story about then?' Mr McManus's voice rose in irritation.

Of course, I hadn't the faintest idea. Somehow I heard myself babbling on about a burglary. But it wasn't very helpful; Mr McManus pursued me down the phone for more detail. Panic led to inspiration and then to invention: I found myself talking about a car escaping across the Curragh and killing a sheep, and this being the vital clue in the mystery.

Bingo!

It immediately gave Mr McManus an idea. What about 'Pulling the Wool over Crime' for a title? I grabbed it with relief. I had a sponsored programme to get on with; any title would have suited. But no sooner had Mr McManus slammed down the phone, than my relief turned to dismay and then, again, to panic. I was now committed to writing a fictitious story about a supposedly real crime involving a burglary, an escaping car and a dead sheep.

That afternoon I headed for my kindly superintendent and begged him to find a case to fit the title. To my relief, and his eternal credit, he did. And somehow I managed to come up with enough scripts to get to the end of the series. But Mr McManus was never aware how much of a sweat it was.

By now, sadly, I was so busy I had almost lost touch completely with my boyhood pals, although Paddy Nolan did drop into the Royal now and then for a chat. His blind date with Maire Gannon, from the Hibernian, had worked out wonderfully and they were now married. Paddy took his new responsibilities very seriously.

Double or Nothing continued to draw the crowds. Even for run-of-the-mill prizes, we were in great demand and had hefty commission-aires standing by to stop would-be contestants battling each other to get on stage. The show was a great target for impecunious university students and I often suspected we were supporting half the higher education facilities of the city. One such student, I learned later, was the actor Peter O'Toole. It wasn't hard to imagine him producing that little-altar-boy-lost look to win the audience's sympathy and prompt me to give him a few clues so that he could pick up the prize money.

O'Toole became something of an eccentric. But then, in the late forties, the Theatre Royal had a handful of characters who, at times, would have made Peter, at his most unpredictable, seem like an usher at a funeral. The theatre was like a miniature, self-contained town; a secret garish society visited sometimes by the outside world.

One larger-than-life character who never ceased to amaze me was the organist, Gordon Spicer, a Yorkshireman who told me he had studied music at Oxford. He was a drunk of the highest degree – a musician of infinite delicacy and a hoarse, croaking companion of delicious wit. He had a dreadful piggy face, a Chaplin moustache, with a smile under it that saved the rest of the face, a greasy felt hat, a badly fitting threadbare overcoat, but well polished boots. His face was almost permanently bruised and seldom without sticking plaster or stitch, mainly because of the stone steps leading to the flat where he lived with a dog, Danny, and housekeeper, Dottie.

Apparently, Gordon was rarely able to keep his balance on those steps by the time he had reeled home from whatever hostelry still tolerated his sardonic presence. But no matter how drunk, no matter how steep the fall, Gordon would instinctively clasp his little hands behind his back and let his head and body take the brunt. The theory was obvious: so long as someone could prop him up at the organ next day, the hands would still be able to perform their fairylight task.

Pauline Forbes was practically custom-built for the role of a 'real trouper'. Her father, Dick Forbes, wrote most of the sketches for the post-war shows and Pauline appeared in many of them either as an 'orphan Annie', a craggy stepmother or sexy siren. She also sang. To try to get her away from the knockabout sketch image, she was dolled up for one show, in a long dress, soaring blonde hair-do, earrings – you name it. Behind her, solemn concert-style drapes, a piano centre stage and seated at it, levered into a boiled shirt and tails, Gordon

Spicer. Jimmy, the manager, noticed signs of wear in Gordon during the first house and lost track of him almost immediately afterwards. He searched nearby pubs, but the 'concert pianist' was nowhere to be seen. The second house started. Pauline came on to warm applause. But there was no sign of Gordon. Jimmy's heart stopped. The orchestra crashed out the opening chord and then, suddenly, like two snakes coming out of two baskets, two hands appeared from beneath the piano and started to play . . . perfectly. Gordon had been lying prostrate beside the piano stool, in a world of his own, until that chord reached into that mysterious corner of the brain that says: the show must go on.

Gordon kept his job. And his general contempt for his audiences. Christmas Eve rolled up and Christmas Eve, special as it is, was even more special in the Theatre Royal, due entirely to the licensing laws. Once inside the theatre, you could drink to your heart's content; you didn't even have to watch the show or film. No matter how long the show ran, the bars could serve for a further thirty minutes after curtain down. It was bonanza time for the management and a heaven-sent stocking-up opportunity for those who put thirst before turkeys and other family commitments. Jimmy and Charlie must have sold the house over many times on the basis that only a small proportion of their clientele actually wanted to sit in the seats. The place was jammed: bars, aisles, foyers.

All was well until organ recital time and Gordon rose up out of the depths, perched on top of the gleaming, flashing monster. The song sheet on the cinema screen might as well have been projected on the Dublin mountain tops for all the notice the audience took. That didn't seem to offend Gordon; but when he switched to a selection of his favourite classical pieces and the noise from the trough below grew louder, he got angry. He pressed a button and sent the organ soaring as high as it would go. He pulled out all the stops, playing as loud as electricity and human endeavour could achieve, in an attempt to drown the ghastly, shouting customers below him.

He played on and on and on. Jimmy ran down to the orchestra pit and shouted at Gordon to come down. If Gordon heard him, he didn't show it. His little piggy eyes were glassy with hatred and his moustache bunched up under his nose with the effort of pumping as much volume as possible into the huge theatre. Jimmy searched desperately for a trip-switch. No success. Suddenly he had an inspiration. George Rothwell, who was playing in the Savoy, just the length of O'Connell Street away, knew the secret of the trip-switch. Jimmy dashed to a phone, spoke to the manager, and George was soon in a taxi hurtling to the rescue. Jimmy mopped his brow with relief when George arrived and disappeared into the orchestra pit. Seconds later, the organ started descending slowly, with Gordon still playing angrily. Jimmy, his relief now turning to fury, strode towards the pit, no doubt thinking about what piece of his mind he was going to give Gordon. Suddenly he stopped in his tracks, a horrified look on his face. The monstrous machine was beginning to rise up again. Only this time Gordon had a companion . . . George!

During one season of *Double or Nothing*, Gordon was otherwise engaged and Norman Metcalfe became resident organist. One of his duties was to play tricks with popular tunes, which contestants would try to recognize.

Norman was a staid, respectable and talented musician. But also moody. We had fallen out over something and he started to bug me in all sorts of ways. One of his tricks was to barge into my dressing-room, create some minor havoc and barge out again. He knew this irritated me, because I liked to spend time before the quiz quietly studying the questions and preparing whatever new ones were needed.

I warned Norman I would take drastic action – and one day I did. I locked him in the dressing-room, and went off to the tea-lounge to have a leisurely meal before drifting backstage in good time for my part of the show. Suddenly I heard my music cue; I ran on to the centre of the huge stage as the orchestra finished the chord and scrambled out for their fifteen-minute break. I went through the usual patter, invited contestants from the audience and started off with the first few simple questions.

And then it was time for the musical knowledge spot. But below me, the organ seat was empty. No musical tricks. No Norman Metcalfe. I was the only one who knew where he was. The key to my dressing-room was in my pocket. I raced to the side of the stage, threw the key at the stage manager and hissed a request to unlock Norman from my dressing-room two floors above.

He took forever to arrive, and heaven only knows what the audience were thinking. But, finally, a sheepish, understandably hostile Norman slid on to the organ seat and we completed the quiz.

It took the rest of the night to restore order to the chaos Norman had created in my dressing-room – and the rest of the month before he and I were speaking again.

Another Theatre Royal story that caused much merriment down the years concerned the legendary Billy Cotton and his band; they were annual visitors to the theatre and took over the whole second half of the programme. Billy was a motor-racing fanatic, and on one of his trips he learned that the Irish Motor Racing Championships were on in Cork. He entered himself as a competitor and told his son, Bill, to front the orchestra for the two Saturday shows – something Bill Junior often did in Britain.

Of course, a band show at the Theatre Royal meant that the pit orchestra was free to leave; and leave they did. The final show that Saturday night was also the final show of the week and while young Bill was jigging around in front of the band, he suddenly realized there was no pit orchestra and that, presumably, it was down to him to end with the national anthem. Thinking quickly on his feet, he jigged closer to his piano-player and hissed: 'Pass the word. After the last number, the Queen.'

Fortunately, the piano-player was more aware of history than Bill. He knew that the Republican national anthem is 'The Soldier's Song' – and gladly passed that on to the band, not the British one.

Bill reckoned he would not have made it to the firing squad.

As if I was not doing enough, I now decided to extend my range of activities. Deep down inside me, a little voice was telling me I should be a film star, and when I got a suitable break in my working schedule, I enrolled at the Gaiety School of Acting, run by Ria Mooney, one of Ireland's most distinguished stage directors. I tried hard and enjoyed the schooling, doing plays, rehearsing speech and learning movement. But I was not totally dedicated, nor single-minded enough, to be an actor; and anyway, there was little or no money in stage acting.

Far more attractive was the publicity and fame and money attached to films – and the studios where I could realize my dreams of stardom were in England, not Ireland. I'd never been there, but an American pal, Greg May, studying at Trinity College under the GI Bill of Rights, seemed sure a mail-boat trip to London could lead to fortune. I didn't need much persuading: through *Double or Nothing* at the Savoy and Theatre Royal, I'd met many English performers, and I honestly thought that some of them would be assembled, by magic, in the capital to open all sorts of doors for me.

Two such people were the Tanner Sisters, who harmonized in fishnet and feathers, and had all the saucy glamour of show business and seemed to know everything and everybody.

How was I going to impress those two beautiful birds? Aha! Stockings were impossible to get in England – they would be ideal. Just before Greg and I left, I commissioned one of my sisters to go to Cassidy's in George Street and buy not two, but three, pairs. The influential sisters, I reasoned, might have a friend.

My obliging sister rushed home with change of a fiver and the stockings in a brown paper bag. I stuffed them haphazardly into my cardboard suitcase and promptly forgot about them as we headed for Dun Laoghaire to get the mail boat.

We were met for a farewell drink by one Jimmy Fitzsimmons, brother of Maureen O'Hara, the actress, who was now world-famous in Hollywood. The excitement was tremendous. Jimmy, much younger than me, affected a worldly-wise approach to the whole adventure, gave advice about this and that and then presented us with a bottle of whiskey. The Lord knows how he came by it. He surely could not have bought it.

The boat was bleak and cold. We could not afford berths. We found a corner and sat there sipping the whiskey, miserable as hell. By the time Holyhead clanked in front of us, at a dark, inhospitable two o'clock in the morning, we were feeling little pain. Somewhat unsteady on our feet, we headed for the customs.

'Anything to declare?'

'Nothing.' I said, hearing the slur in my over-enunciated reply.

In addition to my cardboard case, I had a canvas-zipped holdall. I tried to open it on demand, but failed. The zip had jammed. So too, presumably, had I. The customs man ordered me to open the case. The little brown paper bag was on top.

'What's that?'

'A pair of shilk shtockings.'

'One pair?'

'Yess.'

By now, the little bag was in his hands and he was opening it. Between finger and thumb he slowly drew out a pair of silk stockings.

'One pair?'

'No . . . two pairs.'

He lifted this first pair high in the air and then let the stockings sink, coiled and lifeless, on the bench beside the case. He began the finger and thumb pinching bit again. Out came another pair of stockings.

'Two pairs?'

'No, three pairs.'

'Three pairs?' The eyebrows climbed towards his hairline and his head was cocked superciliously in disbelief.

'Yess. Yesss. Three pairs . . .' I grasped him by the lapel and stuck my face into his. 'Wanna bet?'

My freedom must have hung by a silk thread. He stared at me for what seemed like forever. Then he waved his hand and told me to go.

I just wasn't worth his powder.

The trip was an anti-climax. I sat for hours in casting directors' waiting rooms, spent hours and hours travelling in buses and trains and tubes across bewildering, massive, impersonal London and to the film studios in the countryside. But there was a colossal indifference to my hopes of becoming a screen idol; apparently I looked too much like Keiron Moore, another Irishman hitting it big at the box-office. I saw the light very quickly, and abandoned all hopes of breaking into movies.

Instead, I used my time to try my luck at the BBC. But the corporation, like the film industry, was in no rush to snap up my talent and, with money running out, I decided to abandon The Great England Adventure. I returned home disappointed, slightly disillusioned, but far from downhearted. They may not want me today, but they will tomorrow. I was sure of that.

There was no brass band waiting to welcome me back to Dublin, but somehow I felt life would never be the same again: it must be possible to break into the outside world somehow. Dreams of movie stardom quickly vanished, but hopes of a job at the BBC were as high as ever. And, at least, I now knew where Broadcasting House and Upper Regent Street were. Being back in Dublin was like those big yellow criss-cross lines at busy road junctions with the order: DO NOT ENTER THE BOX UNLESS YOUR EXIT IS CLEAR. I was very conscious of needing an exit, very keenly aware of the frailty of the freelance career and the jealousies and hindrances of people not prepared to take the same kind of risk themselves.

I badly wanted a job in England, but I did not plan to leave Dublin permanently; I wanted to come back with enough capital not to be at the mercy of every small wind, and enough experience to force the respect of those little people in places of power who thought home-grown must be second best.

Meanwhile, I needed as many strings to my bow as possible. I had to continue to earn a living; and although no one at home ever asked me for a penny, I knew that my contribution would hardly go amiss.

I persuaded the *Irish Independent* to pay me for a weekly column and got more involved in the magic, if suspect, world of sponsored radio. With maiden-like reluctance, Radio Éireann decided to lease fifteen-minute afternoon segments to firms anxious to advertise. Anything that smacked of commerce, smacked of sinfulness, however, and the station's civil service mandarins would police the contents of the programmes, words and music, with a barely disguised distaste that had to be experienced to be believed. Producers of sponsored programmes in Dublin tore their hair out in metaphorical handfuls when the Director of Music banned records on the ground of morals, musical taste or even worse, that it was a souped-up classic.

Can you imagine an authority banning, on moral grounds, such numbers as 'Who Were You With Last Night?', 'What Do You Tell The Missus When You Get Home?', 'Gigi' (with its innuendos about little girls), and the 'highly suggestive' 'I Want To Get You On A Slow Boat To China All By Myself Alone'!

At one stage, Dr Arthur Duff, a kind, cultured gentleman, was given the sole job of arbitrating with the producers of sponsored programmes. He was a lover of music and somebody must have hated him to give him the job of listening to rock and roll, jazz and all the awful in-betweens the public hungered for, but official RTE loathed.

Arthur would sit, hunched on a chair, long, tapering fingers on his forehead, eyes closed, groaning quietly and, more often than not, saying in a broken little voice: 'Well . . . I suppose . . . it's all right . . . but . . . it's dreadful, isn't it?'

And then he would stumble off, no doubt to be abused by his superiors for being weak yet again.

I signed a contract to introduce these spots at four guineas a time. But my début under this arrangement was disastrous and nearly finished my sponsored-radio career before it began.

The sponsor of my first show was Kavanagh, whose selling line was 'Pure Food Products'. I waited for the signature tune, 'You Are My Sunshine', to fade down, then came in with my first line of script: 'Good afternoon, welcome to a programme of music brought to you by Kavanagh's, makers of *poor* food products.'

I nearly had a fit when I realized what I'd said. I was convinced that the gaffe would mean my sponsored programme days were over. But, to his eternal credit, the firm's owner, Paddy Kavanagh, never mentioned my blunder to me – even though he got a lot of good-natured stick about it every time he went to his golf club.

Next, I did a two-handed programme with Louis Spiro, an ex-singer who owned a cleaning firm called Imco. Louis still had a great yen for show business and he had created two dreadful characters, Spotless and Stainless, for his radio spot. I was one, Louis the other, and we kept up a stream of patter which could only be beaten for corn by the world's largest wheat prairie. Louis had to fight hard to get these masterpieces accepted by the station, which considered any sponsored programme a form of radio pollution and Louis's as even worse than that. I enjoyed the experience the show gave me, however. And, besides, Louis was a nice fellow, who knew ears of corn when he saw them, but viewed them as orchids if they sold his product, which they did.

He got away with breaking most of the copyright rules. Set to well-known tunes, we had such tasteful gems as: 'A cleaning and a dyeing and a pressing for you' and 'Women get weary wearing that same shabby dress, and when she's weary try an *Imco* clean . . . and . . . press.'

Useful as these shows were, I needed another string to my bow, and the chance came when I struck up a friendship with Dermod Cafferky, the Arrow Advertising Agency junior who brought round the discs and scripts after they had been cleared by Radio Éireann's all-holy censors. Dermod was as bright as the button on his shirt and, between us, we hit on the idea of packaging the advertising segments ourselves and then selling them to the station. We didn't have enough money to buy our own recording studio, so we approached a charming, brilliant, but unbusinesslike, recording engineer named Peter Hunt, who was running a little studio more as a hobby than a commercial enterprise. He was delighted to join the proposed venture.

I was keen on the business because I was convinced I would not survive very long as a broadcaster in Ireland. The system was a monopoly, largely controlled by civil servants, most of whom knew nothing, and cared less, about show business. Also, there were so many cliques to which I didn't want to belong, or couldn't join, so many part-timers picking up pin-money, and so many bosses confusing ambition with greed, that I felt I would be squeezed out sooner than later.

We were joined by Lorcan Bourke, whose connection with the theatre and the old Strand Electric Company was so involved that you could have dropped him in any major town or city in Great Britain and somebody from the theatre world would have known him. Lorcan wrote his own rules and had an extraordinary canny judgement.

We completed the company when we discovered a young man,

Fred O'Donovan, who had, as they say, his office under his hat. Fred had had some experience as a stage manager in theatre, and was very keen to break into the radio world. We invited him to join us as the only salaried full-time member of the company apart from my sister, who was secretary and general factotum, and he accepted, provided I agreed to call the new company: 'Eamonn Andrews Studios'.

I was reluctant to have my name up there, but finally agreed. I was also sad to part with one of our more ingenious strokes in having called our original company Broadcasting Company, which must have driven Radio Éireann bonkers, since anyone looking up the word 'broadcasting' in the phone-book would find us first. Considerable pressure was exerted to stop us using the name.

Soon after I began another season of *Double or Nothing*, Lorcan brought his wife, Kathleen, and young daughter to my dressing-room after the show. Lorcan also ran Bourke's theatrical costumiers in Dame Street and I'd met his wife before. But I had never met the stunning dark-haired beauty now standing before me in the crowded dressing-room. Lorcan must have sensed my interest. With the hint of a twinkle in his eyes, he gestured towards her and said: 'Eamonn, I'd like you to meet my daughter, Grace.'

I held out my hand. 'Hello, Grace.'

It was just after the show. The dressing-room was packed. I had to move fast or the chance would be lost.

'Can I see you home, Grace?' I asked.

If she was surprised that I was trying to make a date so soon after meeting her, she did not show it. Her eyes laughing, she said: 'Yes, all right.'

From then on, I didn't have much to say; I was mesmerized by Grace's beauty and not too interested in whatever else was going on. Eventually, Lorcan finished his drink and shepherded Kathleen to the door, leaving Grace with me. At the door, he turned round.

'Remember,' he said. 'She's *my* daughter.'

Moggy had been replaced with an apple-green Ford Prefect, which I'd parked nearby. After charming her in true Sir Galahad fashion, I led Grace to it and got in with (I thought) an attractive manly flourish.

I put in the key and switched on, my mind racing with ideas on where to go so that we could get to know each other.

But all that came out from under the bonnet was a dry, hopeless rattle. The car was out of petrol.

Fumbling around in embarrassment, I remembered there was a petrol station a matter of yards away. Grasping desperately at sang-froid, I said: 'Ah, well, she's a thirsty so-and-so. We'll get a can of juice and be away like the wind.' But standing in the roadway, going through my pockets, it dawned on me that I had no cash. Not a bean. Even more embarrassed now, I asked Grace to lend me some money and she gave me ten bob, which was enough to get us to our homes.

We had regular dates after that inauspicious beginning. Grace – who, I quickly learned, preferred the Irish equivalent name, Grainne – worked in the family business and she would pop out during her lunch-hour for a drink or bite to eat. Time was always a problem, because the Royal was a seven-day-a-week job – and I was involved in other business ventures, too. The more I saw of her, the more I liked her. But that was as far as it went. She seemed the sort of girl I'd like to marry, but I didn't think my financial status sound enough to propose.

With boxing commentaries, sponsored radio programmes and *Double or Nothing* at the Royal, I was well-known in Dublin. But something in me kept telling me that England was where I should be, and the chance to go back there came when a dynamic man from another branch of show business quickstepped into my life with an offer I could not resist. He was Joe Loss, and when he brought his band to Dublin for a two-week engagement at the Royal, my *Double or Nothing* spot caught his eye. After a few days, he asked me to go to his dressing-room. He had a proposition to put to me.

I popped in after the show. Joe came straight to the point: how would I like to do the quiz on tour with his band in England? I couldn't believe it; I thought he was joking. When it sank in that he wasn't, my heart started racing: the offer, of course, was too good to even think of turning down, but again, I could try my luck at the BBC. I'd sent countless letters, tapes and discs and got nowhere. Maybe the personal approach might do the trick.

I jumped at Joe's offer and he said his agent, Leslie McDonald, would be in touch with me to talk money. When he was, I almost blew it, helped by Charlie Wade who appointed himself my financial adviser. The lordly Leslie offered me £40 a week. It seemed reasonable enough to me, but Charlie persuaded me to hold out for more. This didn't cut any ice with Leslie, who told me, disdainfully, that he thought the whole idea was silly and that he was confident of talking Joe out of it.

At home in Ireland, I trembled with terror. The biggest chance of my life was about to disappear. I told Charlie I was going to accept £40, but he told me to be brave and stand up because they desperately needed me. He was quite clearly prepared to spill the last drop of my blood. I said I couldn't take the chance, but Charlie argued and argued and, finally, cajoled me into sending a final face-saving telegram in which I said everything was OK, but I was not going to pay Leslie any commission. Amazingly, it worked – and I received a letter confirming that I would be part of the twenty-week tour throughout England, Scotland and Wales at £40 a week (no commission). I broke the news to the family, saying the tour was simply a short-term holiday trip and invested £8 in a return flight to England. The fact that I booked a return did not mean any loss of faith; dozens of impresarios would be clamouring for my services, of course, but I would have to go back to Ireland at some point to see the folks and clear up a few outstanding commitments. Flying was something of an extravagance, but even if it had taken my last penny I would have needed it as a morale booster. For, deep down, I had great twinges and twitterings of uncertainty.

They were unfounded. I felt like a poverty-stricken student being invited to join the university and that tour with all the different digs and landladies and theatres in different towns and cities, was the most enlightening and exciting experience of my life. Joe's musicians were different from any people I'd met before and I was fascinated by them. They seemed hard and tough, and yet very likeable. They had been everywhere, seen and heard it all. In their company there was no mercy, no place for the over-sensitive character. From them, I learned about camaraderie. But I also learned something else: that no matter how warm the friendship, you were on your own when you stepped into the spotlight. The boxing ring or the stage, there is not much to choose between them.

Standing in the wings, about to appear in front of my first English audience, I trembled with nervousness. And when I heard Joe's tremendous build-up, I was half-paralysed. A build-up is fine, but it has to be justified. My début went well, however, and launched me on a hectic, breathless tour of one-week dates up and down the country and over the borders into Scotland and Wales.

In the couple of weeks before the tour began I went to the BBC's headquarters at Portland Place a few times. I sauntered through the high, bronze, stiff swing-doors, seemingly brimming with confidence, but I was always baulked at the reception desk. The personal approach was terrific in theory. In practice, it was useless.

The pubs around Broadcasting House were almost as much a part of the building as the studios and the canteens and the never-ending offices. The George – nicknamed the Glue Pot – was patronized mainly by executive types, features producers, Light Entertainment, music and the occasional journalist. The Stag seemed to house the drama department, with a touch of outside broadcasts, while the Cock Tavern was solidly sport. The price of a half-pint of bitter was enough to get one in and all three pubs were patronized by aspiring employees like myself. In Ireland, it was customary to buy drinks for anyone you chatted to, which created a 'school'. But in these three packed pubs there wasn't this deadly round system; people didn't expect me to buy drinks for maybe six people. I was able to mix with all those influential BBC staff for the price of my own drinks. It was bad insofar as it made the pubs synonymous with work; but I don't know how many a radio idea that flowered would have been pollinated without it. Certainly the BBC building itself was quite impenetrable without a formal appointment.

I had two options: I could go back to writing letters and hope my persistence would persuade someone to see me; or I could start using the BBC pubs to try to make some contacts over a pint or two. I did both.

I chose the George and, happily, renewed a friendship with a rugby-playing giant of a man from Donegal, whom I had met in Dublin a few months before. He stood out like a mountain top: square jaw, tufts of hair on his face, honest blue eyes, shoulders that stretched for ever and an ambling gait. He was the most unlikely man one ever saw in BBC administration. He was also one of the kindest, most patient, unselfish men I'd ever met. His name was Brian George and he seemed to know just about anybody who was anybody at the BBC.

Brian never had a bad word to say about anyone. He collected out-of-work actors, writers, musicians – lame dogs of any kind. And his lovely English wife, Anne, was always ready to turn on a smile, turn down a bed and stretch the supper to whoever Brian brought home to his clattering, child-brightened house by the Thames at Sonning, near Reading.

That 'whoever' was frequently me. The ritual was always the same: I would meet him in the 'Glue Pot' and we'd have a couple of pints before taking a taxi to Paddington to catch the 6.55 P.M. to Reading, where Brian had parked his battered banger.

Brian loved his pint and if we got to the station a shade early, we'd always squeeze in a very quick one; one way or another, it was always a wild, coat-flying race for the train. Brian was so well known the ticket collector let him sail through even after the whistle had gone, and there would be a flurry of leaping and banging and gasping, and we'd be off heading for what I knew would be a happy, homely visit that might include yet another quick half-pint in the French Horn next to Sonning station, unless Anne was ready to serve dinner at once.

Alas, Brian made one leap too many at Paddington. After his farewell party at Broadcasting House, he made yet another mad dash to beat the guard's whistle, but missed his footing and, three days later, was dead. He was a kind, kind man and I owed him a lot.

It was through Brian's help that I got to see Tom Chalmers, Head of Light Programmes. He said he would come and see me perform with the Joe Loss band, but never got around to it. Then I got to S. J. de Lotbinière, the seven-foot-tall Head of Outside Broadcasts, and persuaded him to listen to a recording of my latest boxing commentary.

'Well . . . yes,' he said. 'It's good . . . but, listen to this.'

Then, to my well-concealed rage, he played me a recording of the most successful voice on radio – that of Stewart MacPherson, a slick and voluble Canadian, who had first made his mark commentating on ice hockey. On boxing, he was way ahead of anything I'd heard, and certainly could not have been more of a contrast to the Empire tenor of the BBC's own Raymond Glendenning.

MacPherson was clearly a favourite of the Outside Broadcasting bosses, but he was moved into Light Entertainment and suddenly seemed to be into everything: *Ignorance is Bliss*, *Twenty Questions* and Heaven knows what else. He wrote a national newspaper column and his name and voice seemed to be popping up every day of the week.

After making me listen to MacPherson's much-loved style, Lotbinière then brought out one of Glendenning's boxing commentaries and played that. Clearly, he was saying: 'Now, my boy, this is how it should be done.' I gritted my teeth and listened. How could I tell such an influential executive that I thought I was better than both of them?

Lobby then played my tape again. 'It *is* good enough for broadcasting,' he conceded. 'But, you see, we pay only ten or fifteen pounds for a commentary. And we'd never consider paying your expenses to come over from Ireland.'

I grabbed this tiny chink of light. 'Oh, I would certainly pay my own fare just to be given the chance,' I said enthusiastically.

It clearly wasn't as easy as that, however, and Mr Lotbinière ended our brief conversation by telling me, as gently as he could, to be patient.

I started wearing down the famous Anna Instone, who was in charge of the most desirable morning record-request programme, *Housewives' Choice*. The fact that I was 'Southern Irish' was something of a problem, she said, but she promised to do her best, although the most one could hope for was a run of two, perhaps four, weeks. To me, that would have been the acme of recognition, so I decided to give Anna no peace.

I'd also succeeded in meeting Jack Solomons, the boxing promoter, in his Windmill Street gymnasium, and was not at all modest in describing my commentating prowess. Jack gave me something of a glassy eye, and it was to take me another year or two before I could get him, or anyone else in Britain, to focus on me in that capacity.

On the outside looking in is an agonizing business: the stronger your belief that you can do the job on the inside, the sharper the pain. But with the Loss tour about to begin, I didn't have time to brood. I thought positively: at least, in the George pub, I had some important people nodding in my direction – even if they couldn't quite remember, or pronounce, my name!

I was something of a curiosity to the band boys. I didn't talk like them, dress like them or play like them. I knew nothing of their mysterious world: the digs, the dames, the barbers and the betting shops, the clubs and the characters who are hungry to peer into the seemingly romantic world of backstage show business. I learned later that Joe's musicians were paragons compared to many other men of music, but to me they had a whiff of danger, a heady air of freedom. I became an admiring friend of most of them. They taught me, as they say, more than my prayers.

We travelled around the country mainly by train, whiling away the miles playing poker. Most of the time I just sat and listened. When I did play, I lost.

Living in theatrical digs was a new experience for me and I enjoyed it; we stayed at some weird and wonderful places that offered the most amazing value for money. In one big Midland town, a pub called The Grapes offered bed and breakfast, lunch, afternoon tea, if we were around for it, and a meal at eleven o'clock at night for just £3 a week each. *And* there were special facilities at the bar after hours.

Back in Ireland, my mother had no idea just how well I was eating, so she decided to help out. At each new stage door, I would find a bundle of Irish newspapers individually wrapped and separately addressed to me. Back in the digs I learned to open them very carefully so that I didn't damage wafers of streaky bacon or razor-sliced back rashers folded neatly inside the pages. I was very popular on Mondays and Tuesdays with the lads who happened to be sharing my digs. Once or twice, my mother got carried away and sent me above-board packages of Irish black and white pudding and sausages which she knew were a breakfast favourite of mine. However, by the time the security department of the post office had identified the strange contents they could have walked to the stage door unaided, so I sent my mother a grateful but cautionary note.

One of the larger-than-life characters in the orchestra was a young Scottish saxophone player named Harry Bentz. Discipline was the last word in Harry's dictionary, but I found his brash, bouncing, show-off style quite attractive, if sometimes nerve-wracking. When we were playing the Glasgow Empire, I discovered the crazy licensing hours – or rather lack of them – that meant the pubs were closed before the show was over. Harry had a solution: a few of us would buy crates of beer and he would have them stacked in a jeweller's shop down the road owned by one of his uncles. There was no problem with drinking vessels, since the shop had plenty of tankards. It had something else, I hadn't bargained for – a stop-watch. The crates were well on their way to being empty when Harry remembered Dublin and its famous Guinness, and bet me a pound he could drink a pint faster than me. With all the experience I'd gained at the Theatre Royal's stage-door pub, Mulligans, I felt very confident. Two pint-tankards were set up on the counter and a Jewish bass player from the East End named Sid Burke was put in charge of the stop-watch. Ready, get set, go. The beer flowed down smoothly, but Harry seemed to have given up almost before he had begun. I had no time to feel smug. Before my tankard was half-empty, he was picking the money off the table. I couldn't believe it. His drink was gone! It was probably what made him such a powerful saxophone player. Apparently he didn't even have to swallow, he just dropped the pint down like a stone.

That wasn't my last drinking encounter with Harry. At the very end of the tour, in Bradford, the boys and the instruments were taking a coach to Liverpool, then a boat to the Isle of Man. I was catching the train to London on my way home to Dublin. There would be no time for farewells. I asked Joe if I could buy the boys a drink in a nearby hotel between the first and second houses. There wouldn't be much time, but this suited me quite well since I was depending upon my last week's wages to see me through. Joe agreed and murmured a cautionary word of moderation.

What I didn't know was that Harry had either fallen in love with the blonde, bouncing vocalist, Elizabeth Batey, or that she had fallen out of love with him. Whatever it was, there was a romantic problem, and Harry had been secretly drinking to drown it during the afternoon. When he arrived for my farewell noggin, he was already well gone. And when the orchestra assembled on stage for the second house, he was promptly sick into his saxophone. Joe seethed with rage but hid it from the punters. He discreetly moved over towards Harry – conducting and smiling all the while – and hissed at him to get off the stage. Harry stumbled into the wings and bumped his way upstairs to the band room, where he fell down unconscious. Apparently, Elizabeth discovered him and ministered to him in some way not revealed to me. Whatever she did worked and, sometime after she'd gone to sing her numbers, Harry stumbled back downstairs for the second half of the show. The orchestra was playing 'Twelfth Street

Rag', which entailed three of the band stepping up to the front microphone for solo contributions. Harry was meant to be one of them. Standing in the wings, he saw two of his colleagues go forward, and to Joe's astonishment and rage, staggered over to join them. Joe could do nothing. Harry kept aggressively elbowing his way closer to the microphone, almost losing his balance in the process. It was like one of the old Bud Abbot–Lou Costello routines. Somehow the number finished and somehow Harry got back to his place on stage. After the last number, I tried to explain my innocence to Joe, but he brushed me aside angrily and rushed on to his dressing-room, slamming the door behind him. Harry arrived, saxophone in hand, hitting the walls as he walked. Dan Treacy, the road manager, tried to stop him getting into Joe's dressing-room, but Harry swept him aside and burst in. Joe, who works at the pace of a professional boxer, had just taken off his soaked shirt.

'I resign,' Harry slurred.

Standing at the other end of the corridor, I heard Joe yell: 'You'll bloody well resign when I tell you and not before. Get out! Get out!'

Had he waited in the corridor, Harry would undoubtedly have been fired that night. As it was, he lasted a few months longer. It's a funny old world.

The band went on to the Isle of Man and I went back to Dublin, hoping to pick up enough of the threads to stitch together a living. I had left with £10 and returned with ten, but not a penny banked. I didn't mind. The experience would have been worth a million if I'd had it to spend.

One of the programmes I went back to was *Microphone Parade*. I shared it with Terry O'Sullivan, an ex-Irish Army officer who became one of the best daily-newspaper columnists I have ever read. Terry worked for the Irish Tourist Board which put him in an ideal position for spotting good candidates for interviews.

Our cruel and canny producer paid us £2 (rising to £4) for each interview in a total of five. Although I was in theory the producer, he had the final say on which ones were acceptable, so there was pretty tough rivalry between Terry and myself as to who got the odd one in five interviews – even though I had a slight headstart with my additional three or four quid for putting the show together and linking it live on the Saturday night.

By now, I had a growing connection with the show business and sporting worlds, which helped me pick up some notable inter-viewees, most of whom went to considerable trouble to climb to our little studio at the top of the GPO, sans fee, sans expenses. Gene Tunney climbed up there. So did Sir John Barbirolli at one end of the musical scale, and that gentle pianist, Charlie Kunz, at the other. Charlie was being paid £500 a week, plus a percentage at the Olympia Theatre. But when, from the depths of my innocence, ignorance or arrogance, I asked him if he would play something on the air, he said charmingly: 'Of course.'

Sir John Barbirolli didn't play, but he left me with a memory I never forgot. He explained in his husky voice how he had been brought up in Bloomsbury; and how so many of the buildings he loved and treasured had been razed in the wartime blitz.

'I love to come to Dublin and walk amid your Georgian architecture and be reborn again,' he said.

I was thrilled when the American actor, Burgess Meredith, and actress Paulette Goddard agreed to do an interview and asked for a preliminary meeting at the Hibernian Hotel. Pay cheques were slow in coming, and I was broke at the time, with just about enough to buy a tin of cigarettes to steady my nerves and help me in the role of bland host. As we chatted in the hotel foyer, I eased the tin towards Burgess, who took one of my precious cigarettes and blew a great cloud of smoke just over my head.

All was well. All was agreed. And we arranged to meet a couple of hours later at the studio. Burgess stood up and oh-so-casually closed my tin and slipped it gently into his pocket. I was horrified but, of course, in no position to protest. Twenty years later a certain friend of the actor told me he was unlikely to have lifted the tin by accident! Indeed, Burgess didn't even offer me a cigarette later at the studio. But it was worth it, even though he turned out to be much more of a theatrical egghead than I had bargained for.

Eithne Dunne, the beautiful and talented Irish actress, who appeared on the New York stage with Burgess told me a delightful tale about him.

At the height of his Hollywood fame, Burgess decided to act in the *Playboy of the Western World*, that haunting, and, in its day, controversial play by J. M. Synge. To her joy, the little-known Eithne was invited to play opposite him in the part of Pegeen. She had to make personal appearances with Burgess and a public relations man as part of the pre-play publicity, which was totally new to her.

One appearance was at a women's club luncheon – a fearsome experience, as far as I was concerned. Eithne was nervous to begin with, but positively terrified when the chairwoman stood up after the lunch and started savaging the play and all that it stood for – and, in particular, its sexual connotations. She thumped the lectern to shaking point in her determination that no child of hers would be allowed near a theatre showing such filth.

Eithne trembled. Burgess whispered: 'Say nothing. Just leave when I do.'

The moment the speech finished, he was on his feet. 'Ladies,' he said, with steely charm. 'Remember, when you look at the *Mona Lisa*, it is not the Mona Lisa that is on trial. Good afternoon.'

And out the three of them swept.

Microphone Parade was a great grounding for keeping cool while brushing with celebrities. I was never a head-hunter, but, nevertheless, believed that famous people were not famous by accident (given the obvious historical exceptions equivalent to standing on a land-mine) and have always felt curious to explore and admire their achievements.

Name-dropping does, of course, have a simple pleasure all its own, heightened when it becomes a game of name-dropping to infuriate name-droppers. In searching for a really good name-drop in relation to *Microphone Parade*, I remember that Ronald Reagan was one of my guests.

As President of the US Actors' Guild, he came to Dublin and, with others, hosted a benefit show for the Catholic Stage Guild at the behest of that show-business phenomenon the Franciscan priest, Cormac O'Daly, who happened to be chaplain. I always felt a Catholic Stage Guild in Dublin was like forming a league of decency in a convent. But Cormac was such a lover of theatre and theatre-folk the world over, it was worth it for that alone. What Mr Reagan said vanished from my mind ages ago, but whatever it was he said it charmingly and succinctly.

When I interviewed him for *Today*, he was Governor of California and no doubt we talked weightier things. Way at the back of his eyes, behind all the charm, was an uneasy hint of a shadow when I reminded him of our first meeting in Dublin. At least *I* had remembered *him*!

All this time, however, the BBC was still on my mind and in my rare quiet moments, I would think about another bombardment of letters. I always held off; something in the back of my mind told me to take S. J. Lotbinière's advice to be patient and bide my time.

And then I read that Stewart MacPherson was leaving England to go home to Canada, and my patience was replaced with a tingling excitement. I was confident I could replace him either as a commentator or quiz show host and I contacted Brian George immediately, asking him if he would mind putting my name forward.

A week or so later a letter arrived from the BBC, inviting me to present myself at the Aeolian Hall in Bond Street. I was, it appeared, on a short list of six for the job of quiz-master of the comedy show, *Ignorance is Bliss*.

A couple of days later, another letter arrived concerning the audition. It was from a gentleman I'd never heard of and he wanted to meet me in London. His name was Maurice Winnick.

He looked like something out of one of those Hollywood musical extravaganzas. He wore a Homburg and overcoat with astrakhan collar, smoked a huge Havana cigar and, after the audition for *Ignorance is Bliss*, introduced himself to me as 'the guy who owns this goddamn show'. That was not quite accurate: the show was owned by an American TV company, but Winnick had the British rights, and after every broadcast the announcer said: 'By arrangement with Maurice Winnick'. Certainly he seemed very influential, and when he invited me to his flat in Park Lane to discuss what might happen if I got the job, I accepted readily.

Waiting there was another gentleman, less flamboyant, shorter, much quieter. His name was Teddy Sommerfield. He sat in the background most of the time, listening as Winnick and I talked about what I had been doing in Ireland. Winnick seemed to be amused at everything I told him and when I revealed the fees I was getting, he would turn to Teddy, so they could chortle at the quaintness of it. Things would be different for me in England, he said, drawing deeply on his Havana; not because of the goddamned BBC, but because of everything else that would go with it and what he could do for me.

Did I have any idea what MacPherson had been earning? No, I didn't. He told me some astronomical figure I was in no position to dispute. All this could be mine, he said, and poured another generous whisky as if to underline the point. I was in a daze. I felt I was clinging to the spire, with the devil beside me.

So what did I have to do to acquire these riches? I asked.

It soon became clear that Winnick was more interested in a stage tour of *Ignorance is Bliss* and wanted to be my sole agent for twenty per cent of my gross income. Teddy, he said, would handle the management side for fifteen per cent. I was very chary of signing anything at that time and anyway, I didn't even know if I had the job. I thanked Winnick for his offer and said I'd think it over. He was not too pleased with that. The BBC would be making their decision very soon, he said, and he could bring a lot of influence to bear on who they chose.

I went home to Dublin, confused. When the family asked me how things had gone, I played it down. I was used to rejections and I wasn't going to get too excited in case another one was on its way. A week or so later, however, I received a telegram from Winnick saying he needed to speak to me urgently about the show. Would I fly over to London again? Naturally, I was excited. But with the excitement came caution. I was not going back into that jungle alone.

I called in my old pal, Louis Spiro, from the IMCO sponsored show. Louis reckoned he knew a lot about London (which I didn't) and a lot about showbusiness (which I didn't). He was also a Jew and would understand the workings of Winnick's Jewish mind.

We flew to London together and checked into the expensive Athenaeum Hotel, more for appearances than anything else. Winnick produced a contract which we went through carefully. Louis was against me signing it, but Winnick started putting the pressure on: if I didn't sign a seven-year contract with him he could make sure the BBC did not appoint me, he warned. Totally confused, I sought the advice of my friend, Brian George, and other BBC employees in 'The Glue Pot'. They too, warned me not to sign anything with Winnick.

More meetings were arranged with the hawk-faced, cigar-puffing Winnick. He made certain improvements to the contract, but they were all pretty peripheral. Quite honestly, the thought of a seven-year contract with anybody gave me the shivers; I knew nothing about the world he was describing. Certainly it never occurred to me that, perhaps, the BBC had made up its mind to offer *Ignorance is Bliss* to me and Winnick was desperate to sign me up before I found out.

A final meeting was arranged in Winnick's Park Lane flat. More sandwiches. More booze. More pressure. He now stated categorically that I would not get the job if I didn't sign his contract. And even if I had passed my audition he could stop me getting the job. He had, he implied, someone inside the BBC on his payroll who was in a position to influence the decision. I felt Winnick might be bluffing, but there was no way of knowing for sure.

As the night wore on, that flat above Park Lane became unreal, menacing. My dream of getting on to BBC Radio was so close to being realized that I was literally trembling. My nerves must have been obvious to these two men: Winnick, the loud wheeler-dealer, the traditional tough-guy cop, and Teddy Sommerfield, tiny, with large limpid eyes, jet-black, swept-back hair and night-time pallor, the sympathetic smiler.

Eventually, in the early hours, Teddy left. Winnick occasionally put his arm around my shoulder, treating me as the equal I clearly was not. He dangled before me stories of the untold riches he had put before so many, including the fabulously wealthy Stewart MacPherson, omitting to tell me the number of times he had sued, or threatened to sue, the shrewd Canadian. Winnick sneered at the pittance I was earning from Radio Éireann and made it clear I'd never have this kind of chance again. He poured drinks. He blew smoke. He made me feel a provincial hick. He wanted to do me a favour, he said, then get on with some more important things in his life. My nerves closed in on me. The smoke got thicker and the talking tougher and I began to feel claustrophobic.

To go to London, to join the BBC, was what I'd wanted all along. I wanted the job, the chance to prove myself. But now that it was close, now I was at the very point of pulling up the stake, I was paralysed with fear.

Eventually, dawn broke – and with it my resistance. I agreed to sign both contracts: one with Winnick for stage options; the other with Sommerfield for management. I tried to salvage some pride by insisting on a pathetic condition: that I would not be obliged to perform any material that would offend against my faith or nationality. The cynical Winnick must have had a sly smile behind his cigar at that one.

Documents were produced – huge, crackling pieces of parchment – and Margot magically glided back into the room to witness my signature. The agonizing was over. I'd done it. I had signed away the next seven years of my life. We all smiled at each other and shook hands and talked of the glorious future ahead, and then I found myself on my way out of that stuffy, smoke-filled room and going down in the equally stuffy lift, Winnick's promises that the world was my oyster ringing in my ears.

It was five o'clock. Park Lane was deserted. I walked across to Hyde Park, my head pounding. I grabbed some railings. I leaned over them.

And was violently sick.

I was worried about going back to the Athenaeum to confess my weakness to Louis. But I had nowhere else to go. I crept in and flung myself on the bed. I couldn't sleep. I just lay there, the rotten taste of whisky filling my mouth, listening to my heart beat fast and thinking of a future I couldn't even dimly begin to understand.

In the morning, my head ached with a dreadful hangover from the drink, the tobacco, the tension – and the fear of what I was letting myself in for. Louis was philosophical about what I'd done. But all the way home to Dublin I was tortured by the thought that I had ignored everyone's advice and done the wrong thing.

It was this fear of the unknown that forced me not to give up my sponsored radio programmes and newspaper column in Ireland. I had thirteen weeks on a national radio show to prove myself. I was confident I could do it . . . but not that confident to leave myself with nothing to fall back on if things didn't work out. I just was not that much of a gambler.

The fees were not big on either side of the Irish Sea, but air-fares were fairly reasonable and I was able to fly over for the *Ignorance is Bliss* broadcasts and back for my Radio Éireann spots. I fell on my feet by meeting a charming young man, named Ken Riddington, who lived in the basement flat of a boarding house his mother ran just off the Bayswater Road in West London. At that time Ken was an out-of-work stage manager and he offered to let me share the flat if I went fifty-fifty on food and phone calls. For me, it was a marvellous arrangement and I snapped it up. In all the time we shared the flat, we had only one serious row. That was when Ken asked me to take care of his cactus plants while he was away working, and I did . . . by foolishly watering them faithfully every day I was there.

With my appointment as the new *Ignorance is Bliss* question-master, the publicity machine swung into action. My three colleagues and I made personal appearances, and gave interviews. A photograph of the four of us even appeared on the front page of the *Radio Times* – a prime spot coveted by performers as much as oilwells are by Texans! For me, it was heady stuff after the Radio Éireann technique of: 'What did you say your name was?'

The Irish papers were full of it, too. The 'local lad', it seemed, was on his way to making good. It was an exciting time for me, but a very sad one, too. For in March 1950 my father died.

I'd never been as close to him as I would have wished; but we were almost beginning to talk to each other as adults when the heavy smoking and those long treks to work finally took their toll.

It is a lament of too many sons that they never really knew their fathers. Certainly I wish I'd known at the time that he was proud of me; that he used to boast a little to his workmates about my prowess in the ring and my modest success with the pen. He must, at the very least, have been pleasantly astonished that his son actually broadcast on the BBC, that strange and impregnable world millions of miles away from Fairbrothers Fields, and his amateur acting days in St Teresa's Hall, a physical jewel in the Temperance Society's spiritual crown.

I knew my father was anxious about the huge step I had taken in my career and I would have loved him to be around to see it proved to be the right one. But I'd hardly begun the thirteen-week series that was to change my life when he slipped away in his sleep.

9 AN ELEGANT DÉBUT

Ignorance is Bliss was a success and after its final broadcast Maurice Winnick exercised his contract for it to go on tour at theatres around the country, with a stage version of another radio show, *Twenty Questions*, the rights of which he also owned.

If I had expected the tour to be like the wonderful times I had with Joe Loss and the boys, I got a shock. The show was quite dreadful and, not surprisingly, business was bad. This was always blamed on one thing or another – poor management, not enough advance publicity or whatever – but the end product was rumblings of discontent among the three stars – Harold Behrens, Gladys Hay and Michael Moore.

Having had just that thirteen-week exposure on radio, I was the least known. But I enjoyed myself, even though I dreaded that dragged-down feeling, stepping on to a matinée stage and being able to count the audience without moving my head.

I got on reasonably well with Gladys, Michael and Harold, but jealousy started creeping in when the show went to Ireland and the papers concentrated on that 'local lad makes good' angle again. I didn't help matters with a little ruse while we were playing Bournemouth. The sun was shining and the touring manager arranged for a picture of my three colleagues and me in a rowing boat to appear in the local press. Sadly, the stunt did little to stimulate business, but it gave me an idea. Since we were due to play the Olympia Theatre in Dublin the following week, I arranged for the picture to be sent to my old friend, John Finnegan, who was the Dublin *Evening Herald*'s theatre critic. I was somewhat taken with the photograph because it showed me as a fine manly figure, stripped to the waist, rowing my colleagues over the waves.

And I was delighted that the *Herald* decided to run it – even if some artist in the photographic department did emasculate 'Tarzan' Andrews by painting a white singlet over my hairy chest. The picture, helped by previous publicity about my BBC contract, worked wonders at the box office: people were curious to see what had happened to one of their local boys, thrown into waters infested by all those foreign sharks that had gobbled up so many Celtic morsels before. But the more business we did, the lower my popularity with my colleagues sank; every line written about me widened the gulf between me and them.

When another journalist friend, Arthur Gahan, of the *Irish Press*, came to my dressing-room for an interview, I had another idea. And I had enough bottles of stout with Arthur to ask him for a favour.

'Please, Arthur,' I implored, 'write something about one of the others.' And I explained why.

Ignorance is Bliss was not his country by a long chalk, but I quickly filled him in on what the show was about. He plumped for Gladys, the 'Fat Lady' of the show, and the butt of Michael's merciless poems and Harold's vaudevillean wisecracks, and I took him along to her dressing-room. After introducing Arthur to Gladys and her husband, I left. But less than a minute later, there was a shout, a crash, then a door slamming. I rushed out. Arthur was slumped against the corridor wall, blood trickling from his mouth.

'What happened?' I asked.

'Dunno,' said Arthur, wiping away the blood with the back of his hand. 'I just took out my notebook and asked her measurements when her husband hit me and threw me out.'

Poor Arthur had failed to understand that Fat Ladies on stage are not fat ladies off it.

There was little I could do but apologize . . . and offer him a compensatory bottle of stout.

There was not a vacant seat during that week at the Olympia, but, back in Britain, business dropped again and a worried Winnick called a crisis meeting. Things were so bad, he said, that the cast might have to take a cut to keep the show on the road. I was worried, too. I asked Teddy Sommerfield's advice. He told me to keep my mouth shut; he would deal with the matter. No one agreed to take a cut and the show did fold in Cardiff a few weeks later.

I travelled back to London, grateful, more than ever, for Ken

Riddington's hospitality in Lancaster Terrace, and worried about what I was going to do next. The enforced hiatus in my determined bid to achieve fame outside Ireland gave me a chance to return home, not only to see the family, but also to see Grainne.

In that autumn of 1950 money was tight, but my hopes were high. I had no work lined up, but I was not exactly unknown after thirteen weeks on the radio and a couple of months appearing in theatres around the country. With Teddy Sommerfield or by myself, I went anywhere where there was a chance of work; I saw all manner of people, trying to persuade them to give me a re-start in radio. But it seemed hopeless. No one wanted to know – and, as winter drew nearer, I began to get desperate. Had it not been for Ken's warm friendship, it would have been a miserable time. As it was, he was a good friend, always there, it seemed, with a comforting smile and encouraging word when I returned after yet another hapless day. At least, in that flat, there was always the prospect of a warm, if very basic, meal. Ken and I shared the shopping, usually for celery, radishes and lettuce to supplement the cheese suppers; or, on better days, when we had a tin of Irish stew, carrots, onions and potatoes that hid the scarcity of meat. By judicious injections of fresh vegetables, we would make those stews last a week, or even longer.

I spent a lot of time in Maurice Winnick's tiny office in Hanover Square, looking into all the possibilities of work, but they remained just that – possibilities.

The relationship between Winnick and Sommerfield was never clear to me; nor was the way I was split between them. The only thing they seemed to have in common was the fact that they had both been bandleaders: Winnick most successfully, Sommerfield somewhat anonymously.

Winnick was a gambler down to his socks and loved to play the big, American-style packager. He smoked expensive cigars, tipped with fivers and poured champagne as if there was more in the tap. Sommerfield, on the other hand, was a penny-pincher, using envelopes at least twice, making notepads from half-used notebooks and filling his guests' glasses with ice before pouring them drinks.

Titles and tycoons meant a lot to Winnick. He seldom missed an opportunity to use them to impress business contacts or even clients, and once he put on the performance of a lifetime for my benefit. He was sitting behind his big desk, trying to interest me in one of his schemes, when a godsend of a phone call made him feel ten feet tall: it was from someone in the Royal Household. Winnick chewed his Havana with relish and boyishly repeated enough of the conversation for me to get the drift of what it was all about. He was, it appeared, being invited to take his orchestra to a function at Windsor Castle.

'Yeah, yeah,' he drawled, 'that's fine by me. How much?'

Long pause.

'You gotta be joking.'

Another silence at the Winnick end.

Then he yelled: 'Prestige! Lissen. I just been round to my tailor for a new tuxedo for functions like that and do ya know what? He charged me 250 fucking prestiges!'

He skipped that particular royal assignment.

The Light entertainment bosses recognized that Winnick's show-business instincts were often right, but most of his bold, brash ideas were resisted by that frustratingly prim BBC line: 'We don't do things like that . . . It's not policy . . . That sort of thing is all right for Radio Luxembourg . . . The Governors wouldn't like it . . .' I had grown to like Winnick and often felt sorry for him when he found himself up against this brick wall.

It was inevitable he and Sommerfield would split up and when they did, it was bitter: when Sommerfield left, taking me with him, Winnick snarled at me about anonymous phone calls and threats about the Inland Revenue and said he knew who was behind it.

Meanwhile, Teddy was taking care of the prestiges. He took me aside and solemnly assured me, those sad, sad eyes staring at me, that he just couldn't manage on his commission; if I wanted him to continue, it would have to go up. It did. And so did I. I ended up grossing more in a year than I would have dreamed possible in a lifetime.

It was thanks to Winnick, however, that I landed a plum reading job with the BBC, just when my pounds were beginning to turn into shillings. A few months before the Sommerfield split, Winnick had made contact with Patrick Harvey and Michael Bell, two charming, debonair university types, who were producing *A Book at Bedtime* for the BBC. It had an up-market flavour to it and I wanted the spot badly. Winnick got hold of an old tape machine and I recorded passages from John Steinbeck's classic *Of Mice and Men* and Frank O'Connor's lovely little story, 'First Confession'. Winnick handed the recordings to Messrs Harvey and Bell, along with the most appallingly obvious charm that embarrassed me no end.

The gentlemen must have liked what they heard, crude though the tapes were, because, just when I was thinking I'd never crack it, I was offered – joy of joys – the most prestigious contract I had had. The book Patrick had chosen for me to read was George A. Birmingham's *Spanish Gold*.

Reading *A Book at Bedtime* meant something more than just delivering the narrative. One also had to simulate the dialogue, trying to indicate and separate the various characters by nuance, accent or audible impediment. I worked hard trying to 'create' the characters, paying particular attention to the key person in the story, a Church of Ireland curate, who was an affable practical joker. I felt that the lilt and bounce of a Northern Ireland accent would suit him admirably: happy, tricky, likeable, clearly definable from the rest, including a colonel to whom I tried to impart a broad stage English accent. The magic date came round and we went on air. Patrick was pleased. That most doubtful barometer of all, one's personal friends and family, showed only Fair, however. Then came the bombshell. Patrick had something to discuss. Would I meet him at the BBC Club across the way from Broadcasting House? There had been a letter to the Director-General, Sir Ian Jacob, from a Professor Wagner of (to the best of my recollection) Manchester University.

He abused my performance in no uncertain terms and I could see my career toppling from the top of Broadcasting House into the gutters of Regent Street. Professor Wagner said he was familiar with Canon Birmingham's works and that the curate in the story had clearly been educated at Trinity College, Dublin. Why, therefore, had

I given him the accent of a Belfast slum? It was an insult to the Church of Ireland, he protested. My career had now washed past Oxford Circus and was well on its way to the sleazier side of Soho. Patrick was reasonable about it, but I could detect a distinct tremor of alarm behind that urbane, pipe-smoking front. I explained that Trinity College was awash with Northern Irish, and to assume that a divinity student must have anything but a Northern Ireland accent was a very tenuous assumption indeed. I ignored the bit about the Belfast slum because I had no idea of the nuances of Northern Irish accents any more than many would have of the Cork or Kerry or Galway regional tone.

I had an inspiration. Brian George was not only Northern Irish but also Church of Ireland. I rang his office. Fingers crossed, I asked him if he had heard my broadcast. Yes. And enjoyed it.

Had he found anything offensive towards the Church of Ireland? What the blazes was I going on about?

'Brian, would you join me for a pint? I'll explain to you.'

Brian's reassurances were all that Patrick Harvey needed to stiffen his resistance to Professor Wagner. The next day he wrote to him – with a copy for the Director-General – explaining our defence and maintaining that being a Trinity student did not preclude a Northern accent.

Patrick wound up his letter with: 'Anyhow, I suspect you just don't like the North of Ireland accent.'

Professor Wagner replied with a charming letter, conceding the point made, and inviting Patrick to tea any time he was passing. And he confessed: 'You were quite right. I don't like the Northern accent. I'm from Cork!'

Can you believe that! Can you believe that a career could have been in jeopardy over such a trivial incident?

That *Book at Bedtime* reading set the wolf back a few paces and then I landed what was to prove a wonderful shop window for the wares I had to offer – *Housewives' Choice*. I could not believe my luck. It was only for a fortnight, but in terms of getting known, those two weeks were more valuable than all the thirteen I'd spent on *Ignorance is Bliss* – even though the restrictions on the disc jockey hampered my style. I had nothing like the free hand I'd had on record shows in Ireland. The housewives' requests were selected by one person, the balance of the records decided by someone else and the various do's and don't's explained by kindly, but cautious, producers. It was amazing that anyone's personality ever came through on *Housewives' Choice*. The show did mean that potential employers knew where they could hear my voice, however, and I was asked to read short stories and do film commentaries, such as Pathé Pictorial.

Towards the end of 1950, a dark Scotsman named Angus McKay offered me the job of presenter for BBC's *Sports Report* – and, again, I'm indebted to my pal, Brian George, for paving the way. Angus had heard me on *Ignorance is Bliss* and thought: 'There's a voice we might think about for *Sports Report* some time.' Later, he saw me in the pub with Brian. I had to leave suddenly and Angus asked if I was 'that fellow Andrews' from *Ignorance is Bliss*. When Brian said I was, Angus said: 'I'd like to see him some time. When he's around again will do.'

Angus promptly forgot about it. But Brian didn't. And a couple of weeks later he introduced Teddy Sommerfield and me to him over a pre-arranged lunchtime drink. I was invited to visit the *Sports Report* studio 'just to see it going on'.

After the programme, Angus asked me if I would like a try-out on an overseas sports broadcast. I jumped at the chance. Angus seemed pleased with the result and in November I broadcast my first *Sports Report* – a programme that was to thrill, excite and worry me for twelve exhilarating years.

Later, I also presented a programme called *Sports Review* for the BBC overseas service. Letters came from all over the world and one, in particular, put me in a quandary.

It was from a youngster called Asaf in West Pakistan and he wrote:

My Dear Eamonns,
How are you? I am very fond of football and will be very glad if you will send me a picture of yourself and write how you became a player. Please write S. Matthews address to me as well. I am

fourteen years old and play as outside right, but I am not so good, but I practise very hard.

Some exercise which I do include running, skipping, running fast and stopping at a certain point, etc. I will be very happy if you will write some dodging tricks to me also . . .

I had a problem. Asaf was the only person in the world who linked me with Stanley Matthews, the legendary England outside right. Should I write back and tell him the awful truth? Or put on a football jersey and shorts and send him a picture together with a letterful of dreamed-up dodging tricks? Or perhaps I should just send him Stan Matthews's address and hope that when the correspondence started, Stan would keep my terrible secret.

Television was developing fast, but I was hardly interested. It fell into the category of being a possible source of income if one could wangle a few interviewing jobs. That was the way I thought about it on those rare occasions when I did think about it. As for *appearing* on the screen, it never entered my head.

Then came an opportunity to do a boxing commentary for BBC Television from the Empress Hall. Just before the fight, the producer, Peter Dimmock, suddenly turned to me and said: 'Eamonn, I'm going to try something. At the end of the fight I want you to hop into the ring and do an on-the-spot interview with the winner. Nice and short, and it doesn't matter if he's puffing and blowing and surrounded by yelling fans.'

'Should I wear a dinner jacket?' I asked.

'Yes, yes, you'd better whip away and get it,' Peter replied – and I dashed off to the flat by taxi.

By the time the preliminaries were over, I was ringside, suitably attired in the required black and white, bow-tie clipped snappily on to my fresh white collar. When the fight ended, I leaped up and ducked under the ropes as I had done many times as an amateur boxer.

But this time there was a warning click and something went loose on my neck. The bow-tie was hanging by one clip from one side of my collar just as I was about to be seen by the watching millions. I did the only thing I could. Just before I straightened up, I snatched the loose-hanging bow right off, and slipped it into my pocket. I would not have scored many points for sartorial elegance on my TV début. But then, I'd always been an 'invisible' man on radio and the idea of actually being seen on a small screen by millions of people still did not thrill me.

Part II

In the summer of 1951 I was still unmoved by the prospects of television when the BBC decided to try out a weekly panel game from America called *What's My Line?* A panel of four celebrities had to try to guess the occupations of members of the public by asking questions based on one piece of unhelpful information, given by the chairman. The BBC decided to have two resident chairmen, who would appear on alternate weeks – a gruff, seemingly irascible intellectual named Gilbert Harding and me. Although radio was still my favourite medium, I accepted the offer.

Imagine my surprise when I was introduced to the producer, Leslie Jackson, at the BBC studios in Lime Grove, Shepherd's Bush. As we shook hands, he said: 'You were a boxer at St Andrew's Club in Dublin, weren't you? So was I.' I was so taken aback, very little else registered about that evening; however, I did meet the four celebrities who were to make up the début panel: Ted Kavanagh, a witty scriptwriter, Barbara Kelly, a bubbly Canadian actress, Jerry Desmonde, a comic's stooge, and the writer Marghanita Laski.

I did the first show and, thankfully, got through without any embarrassing mishaps. But Gilbert Harding had a nightmare début, which caused quite a stir. The cards giving challengers' occupations got mixed up and Gilbert started one game off, thinking a panel-beater was a male nurse. The more the challenger answered the panel's questions truthfully and accurately, the more impatient and irritable Gilbert became.

'Can your job be done equally well by a woman?' asked one panellist.

'Yes,' replied the panel-beater.

'No,' roared Gilbert, thinking of the male nurse.

Eventually, with time running out, an exasperated Gilbert announced that the challenger had won. And that he was a male nurse.

'But I'm not,' said the confused challenger. 'I'm a panel-beater.'

That was it. Gilbert let fly with one of those magnificent bursts of rage that was to become his television trademark. 'This,' he thundered, 'is the last time I appear on television.'

It was not the last time; later, he became one of the panel. But he did not want the chairman's job at any price: someone else could hold the sword of Damocles. That person was me. I was invited to be resident chairman. The show, which went out live every Sunday night, became a hit with the public.

Suddenly that summer, all those tiring days trying to sell my voice to BBC bosses, all those impoverished weeks of making the stew last, seemed far away. I had, it seemed, broken through.

That simple little programme was to change my life. From being a reasonably well-known radio broadcaster, I became, almost overnight, a face. I acquired that new, meaningless description for people who can neither sing nor dance nor juggle nor play the harp – a Personality. Television Personality. Very soon I took it for granted that I was recognized wherever I went and had to learn to live with it.

Mind you, the names my new-found 'friends' – or sometimes enemies! – gave me would make me smile. Overnight, I was addressed as Raymond or Aaomon or Eemon and, once, even as Amen Andrews!

But the best by far was the beauty bestowed by Barbara Kelly's husband, Bernard Braden. I appeared on his breakfast radio show and was introduced as – wait for it – Hymen Andrews! No doubt it gave Britain's listening millions a giggle that morning. It certainly appealed to Grainne. From that day, I was always Hymie to her.

The 'Personality' has to decide whether to be a prima donna, an actor in the grand manner, a *star*, or just assume that one is making new and equal friends at a rate rather faster than normal. I – more or less – tried to aim for the latter.

It wasn't just me, of course. Gilbert Harding was the classic example: from a minority-audience, slightly egghead radio voice, he suddenly had the nation hopping up and down waiting for his next outburst or pronouncement on some piece of pomposity that might catch his eye.

David Nixon was an unknown, or almost unknown, cabaret conjuror until his droll style and pre-*Kojak* charm brought him fame and fortune. Isobel Barnett was probably known only as the decorous doctor wife of her charming solicitor husband, Sir Geoffrey Barnett, until *What's My Line?* struck.

Gilbert was a great panellist. If I'd been more experienced I'd have enjoyed the game – and him – more. As it was, I was often terrified out of my life when I met Gilbert glowering along the corridor of Lime Grove, clearly having had a gin or two too many and ready to argue with his own toenail.

At one stage, Leslie Jackson and I had an idea that, if Gilbert became too incoherent, abusive, or whatever, I would stop short of him and question the other three while Jacko kept the cameras away from him. But it was a silly idea and totally unworkable.

I enjoyed that early heady success of *What's My Line?*. But I realized the time was right for something else – something that had nothing to do with my career. Being part of a hit show gave me a luxury I'd never enjoyed before – stability. The future looked bright. And I knew now who I wanted to share it with.

One weekend in August I went back to Dublin, marriage on my mind.

In the two years since my ten-bob loan for petrol started our relationship, marriage was never mentioned; not that Eamonn seemed ever in Dublin long enough to bring up the subject. We spoke a lot on the phone , though, and he wrote hundreds of romantic letters that left me in little doubt that I was the only girl in his life. I used to love receiving these beautifully written letters and came to look forward to them, expect them. Once, when I felt Eamonn was neglecting me, perhaps thinking more of work, I decided to remind him of my existence with a cheeky telegram. It rebounded on me with amusing results. For when I dictated it over the phone, my strangely spelt Christian name – obviously a new one to the operator – appeared on the telegram not as Grainne, but as Granny! Eamonn fell about and for months afterwards called me nothing else!

I certainly wanted to marry him and had, in fact, told my mother so the day after Eamonn had driven me home from the Theatre Royal. She was talking about Peg Monaghan to whom Eamonn was apparently engaged, and I said: 'He's the sort of man I'd like to marry.' I meant it, too. He seemed somewhat bumptious and a little too sure of himself for my liking and I hated the white socks he wore with his sports jacket and flannels. But I'd always liked big, strong men, and there was a strength and a dominance about Eamonn that attracted me.

Since marriage was never mentioned, it came as a shock when Eamonn proposed. But it was done so lovingly, if formally, that I found myself saying 'Yes' almost immediately. The location he chose was the Bull Wall, a romantic spot on the edge of the sea at Dollymount. I remembered the Bull Wall very well, Eamonn had stopped there on the way home from the Royal two years before. He was very sure of himself then but came on too strong for my liking and I resisted his advances that night. One balmy August night two years later, however, I had no need: Eamonn was the perfect gentleman, going down on one knee by the wall overlooking the sea, and asking, ever so formally: 'Will you marry me?' Suddenly, a strange feeling I'd had since the previous night became clear. Eamonn had returned to Dublin from London and I'd taken him home for supper. Throughout the evening, there had been an odd tension between us, as though he had something on his mind, but didn't know how to bring it up. Now, beneath the moonlight at Dollymount, Eamonn revealed that he'd wanted to propose the night before, but couldn't because he hadn't told his mother. He had done so first thing the next morning.

Having said 'Yes', I now had to tell my own parents. But when we got home, at around midnight, only Mummy was there. She was delighted at the prospect of having Eamonn as a son-in-law, but I still needed Daddy's blessing. We were all so excited, there was no question of leaving it until the next day, so we settled down to wait for Daddy to come home. He finally rolled in about 3 A.M., very happy indeed with the world. When he heard our news, though, he didn't show Mummy's enthusiasm. He liked Eamonn, of course, but he was the sort of man who didn't relish the thought of losing a daughter. In the old tradition, they went into another room for a man-to-man talk, presumably about what sort of future Eamonn's career prospects could offer me. They talked and talked for ages, it seemed, and all the time Mummy and I were at the keyhole, trying to hear what was being said.

Finally, they came out, all smiles; Daddy kissed me and said I had his blessing to become Mrs Eamonn Andrews.

The next day Eamonn brought me an engagement ring I'd always dreamed of – a five-stone diamond, which was the most beautiful thing I'd seen in my life. It was far too big for me, but I didn't care and tied it to my finger with a big piece of string so it wouldn't slip off, rather than send it away for alteration and be without it, even for a single day.

The night before our wedding three months later is a blur for me. There was a huge gathering of people in my parents' home, but I spent the whole evening in bed with a blinding headache, brought on by nerves. A doctor gave me an injection, which eased the pain, but I was not well enough to go downstairs to meet all the guests, many of whom had come from London. During the evening Eamonn came up to chat about the next day, and when he left to go downstairs, I shouted: 'Don't forget to wear black socks!'

His mother had kept up a steady supply of the white ones she knitted for him, and I was determined to get rid of them. Eamonn must have told everyone what I'd said because I heard a big laugh from the living room.

The 9 A.M. wedding at Dublin's Corpus Christi church got off to a disappointing start, not only because it was raining, but because there wasn't a soul about: not one single neighbour, it seemed, was bothered at watching the bride leave for the church. My wedding-day nerves quickly replaced my disappointment, however, and before I knew it I was being led up the aisle by my father and standing beside Eamonn, immaculate in tails, at the steps to the altar. After the ceremony, I realized why no one had been outside my house – they, and thousands of others, it seemed, were thronging the street outside the church.

Somehow our car got through the crowds and we were on our way to The Four Provinces for the reception. On the way, Eamonn said he was dying for a smoke and asked the driver to stop for some cigarettes. Our man pulled up at a pub, went in for the cigarettes – and came out with two whiskies as well! Eamonn downed both whiskies, lit a cigarette and, as he later joked, we both felt much better.

At five o'clock in the afternoon, Eamonn was behind the wheel of Daddy's car and we were heading south-west for our honeymoon in the coastal resort of Parknasilla. It was not the most memorable of honeymoons: frankly, I think I was too tensed-up and immature to enjoy it. Honeymoons should be taken later in life. And we did . . . frequently.

The wedding, though, had been a magical affair and Eamonn wrote to my father, telling him, in his own eloquent manner, what it had meant to us and how much we appreciated what he had done. That letter, one of my most treasured possessions, was the beginning of the type of relationship Eamonn wished he could have had with his own father.

This is what he wrote:

> Dear Lorcan and Kathleen,
>
> Things are so lackadaisical and lazy in this part of the world that it's almost impossible to summon up the determination to write a letter . . .
>
> I need hardly tell you that we're both very happy indeed, and very keenly aware of how much of that happiness we owe to both of you. It was wonderful what you did for both of us; and as I said and meant on Wednesday, I could never hope to thank you enough.
>
> You can certainly be proud of everything you did and the way in which you took the whole place by storm. But the people and the papers have already told you that.
>
> What they haven't told you is that if I was proud at even being accepted by Grace and yourselves, I was prouder than a million peacocks at the princely way you set us off in this new life. I don't have to speak for your daughter, but for myself I can only promise you I will try to live up to in every way the trust and generosity you have shown.
>
> On the more personal side I was sorry I was too full to say more to you on Wednesday. But words do not come to me easily on an occasion like that. All I can tell you is that I was deeply aware of the sacrifice you had made and the loss you were feeling. Even in this letter I don't like being quite so serious, but I will try with all my heart to make Grace as happy as you have – which is something I can do with your help and advice, which I know I will always have for the future.
>
> Now, an end to the seriousness, but not to the thought. We're

having a whale of a time but looking forward like mad to seeing you at the end of the week.
Love,
Eamonn

A week after we returned to Dublin, we were on the move again – to a flat Eamonn had rented. Whether it was the sadness at leaving my family and friends and my homeland, or sheer married bliss, or a combination of both, I don't know, but I never stopped crying from the time we left Dublin till we arrived in England.

After our honeymoon at Parknasilla, we returned to Dublin then set sail for England, where I'd rented a first-floor flat in Priory Road, West Hampstead. It was a bitterly cold time and the task of trying to entice heat into the main room was enough to corrupt a saint. Not that it affected me as much as Grainne. No sooner had we arrived than I was off around the country interviewing people for the BBC's *Welcome Stranger* – another programme my old pal Brian George helped me get.

Grainne was marvellous. Here was a newly married young girl who had left her family, her home, her country to be left alone in a strange city for three or four days every week – yet she never complained. I was quickly aware that my nomadic existence would not be good for the marriage, however, and made a mental note that the touring business was not for me.

To help ease Grainne's loneliness, I bought her a gorgeous black poodle pup. We saw it in a pet shop in Baker Street and I suggested buying it for her birthday. I changed my mind when I heard the price: fifteen guineas seemed astronomical to me. But as we walked out into the street, I saw the look in Grainne's eyes and gave in; clearly, it was love at first sight. I was glad I capitulated; that puppy quickly became part of our lives. We called him Quiz.

That lovable, faithful dog, and our love for each other, helped Grainne and me cope with being apart so much and as my career as a broadcaster strengthened, so did our relationship. Outside the marriage, I was hard-working and disciplined; inside it I was happy and carefree. Grainne and I didn't have a care in the world.

And then a shock revelation kicked our happiness right in our faces.

The flat had been converted from a large Victorian house and I hated it. From the moment we moved in, I set about changing everything, but it was a waste of time; it was one of those places that was never going to look right. And it was freezing, too. The rent of £12 a week was outrageous in 1951 and when I wasn't reorganizing things, I was out hunting for a house we could buy. I couldn't wait to move.

It was the year of the exciting Festival of Britain, but, quite honestly, it was a lonely time for me. Eamonn was away working three days every week and, although his family and mine came over to stay every so often, I spent most of the time on my own. Once, a cousin called Dominic Behan, brother of the famous Brendan, turned up and promptly asked Eamonn to lend him £5. I was embarrassed, because in those days £5 was more than many people earned in a week. But Eamonn handed it over, as he always did, if asked. He was always a soft touch.

We were in that flat only six months, but our stay was not without its dramas – and in one of them, I was scarred for life. Gilbert Harding had given Eamonn a pressure cooker as a present for me. They were fashionable in the early fifties, but I wouldn't use one now if you paid me. This one refused to open because of a blocked vent. I loosened the lid – and the whole thing blew up, sending the lid and boiling water into my face and on to the ceiling; the blast was so violent, it took the plaster off. Eamonn's mother was staying at the time and she went into such shock I had to call the doctor myself. He dealt with her, then covered the burns on my face with Vaseline and gauze and ordered me to bed. When Eamonn came home later that day, he was horrified; but, fortunately, he couldn't see how bad my burns were. Later, he had to host What's My Line? *and made a point of telling the panellists what had happened. All of them were sympathetic – except Gilbert; he was only bothered about the cooker he had bought for me. 'Oh God,' he said. 'Not* my *pressure cooker.' I think his lack of concern bothered Eamonn.*

With Eamonn now a television celebrity, we received many invitations to film premières and theatre first nights. Having been on my own for more than half the week, I was always keen to go and relished the task of making myself a different evening gown for each occasion. Out of all the faces I saw at those glittering galas, one has stayed sharply in focus for more than thirty years – Joan Collins's. I forget the function we were attending, but I've never forgotten how stunning she looked that night. There were many gorgeous young women there, but Joan, in a slinky black dress and white fox stole, was the most beautiful. People talk of how good she looks for her age now, but they seem to forget she was always beautiful. Another person I remember liking on sight was Kay Kendall the actress, whom I met when Eamonn and I spent a weekend in Jersey where he presented the stars appearing in the world première of The Importance of Being Earnest.

Kay, it seemed, was short of cash and tried to sell Eamonn her mink stole for £150. Eamonn liked the idea of me having a mink, but didn't like the price and politely declined. Kay was a zany character with a bubbly personality and a lovely sense of humour, and it was a sad loss when she died tragically of leukaemia in 1959 at the age of thirty-two.

Although Eamonn was famous, we were just like other young newly-weds. We liked the idea of 'doing the town', but we enjoyed being on our own just as much, and some of our most pleasant moments were spent just strolling arm in arm on Hampstead Heath. When Eamonn was away working, he would write beautiful letters or notes on cards, always in the green ink that was to become his trademark. Or, if he was too busy to write, he'd send a cheeky, but still romantic, message by telegram.

Despite my loneliness, they were happy times. We often talked about it: we would say, well, we haven't got everything, but at least we're happy. Sometimes though, even in the middle of a romantic moment, a crushing wave of pessimism would engulf me, and I would say it was all too good to be true, and something was going to happen to spoil our happiness. Sadly, I was proved right. We'd been married eighteen months when I got pains in my right knee and started limping badly. I was always moving furniture around in the flat, and was convinced the pain was merely a strain. Eamonn knew all sorts of cures from his boxing days, but no matter what he suggested, the pain didn't go away and the limp got worse. Finally, my doctor sent me to a specialist at Great Portland Street Hospital, who told me I had either arthritis or tuberculosis.

I was horrified and, naturally, upset; it was the biggest fright of my life. The specialist said he hoped it was TB, because he could cure it, but he would not know for sure until he had done a biopsy.

'That will have to wait,' I said. 'I'm going on holiday to Italy this weekend.'

The specialist shook his head. 'You'll have to miss the holiday. The biopsy needs to be done at once.'

Eamonn was out of the country at the time, so when I got home, I rang Teddy Sommerfield, and asked him to contact Eamonn and break the news. Teddy, bless him, did just that, then jumped in a taxi and came round to comfort me. I was grateful for the company, for he was one of the few people I knew in London.

Eamonn flew home the next day and said we should seek a second Harley Street opinion. The first specialist said he did not mind us doing that, but he would wash his hands of the case if I didn't go in for the biopsy immediately.

The fear of the unknown terrified us. Nobody knew much about TB or arthritis in those days and we had no idea what they were going to do to me. But I had little choice: I had to cancel our holiday and have the biopsy.

They found I had TB, which was making the gland in the right hip the size of an egg and two days later I was on the operating table having it removed. When I came round from the anaesthetic, I saw Eamonn standing beside the bed holding a bunch of tulips and just looking at me. When he saw my eyes opening, he quickly turned his back and started talking to a doctor. A minute or so later, he turned back to me, but his eyes were still glistening and I knew he had been crying. I was still woozy from the anaesthetic and cannot remember much about that July evening except that it was the first time I'd seen Eamonn cry, and that I was lucky to have someone who loved me so much.

They told me I was going to be confined to bed for three months; and that it was best to be in a ward with other patients. They had a hard job convincing me. I didn't want to be in a ward. I was bitter and resentful at being bedridden, thinking all the time, Why Me? Why Us? and I wanted to be bitter and resentful in a private room, not a public ward. Finally, I was persuaded that a ward with other people would be better for my morale, and early in August I was taken by ambulance from the imposing grandeur of Great Portland Street Hospital to the wooden, makeshift Royal Orthopaedic Hospital in Stanmore, Middlesex.

My stay there was to open my eyes. If Eamonn's initiation into what life was all about had been touring with the Joe Loss Band, mine was living in that ward with nineteen other women. As a lesson in life, it was unbeatable. In some ways, I'd led a sheltered life, protected from certain aspects of human nature, and those months in that ward were a revelation to me.

The twenty of us were a mixed bag: different classes, different religions, different personalities; some brave and stoical; others cowardly and whingeing; many kind and obliging; a few cruel and difficult.

One woman must have had a sexual problem because every so often, she would shout: 'I want a navvy.' We were horrified.

It took time, but, eventually, I became accepted as one of the gang. We were all stuck in bed, but we were determined not to let it get us down. We had parties for the nurses: they brought the sandwiches, we provided the wine. The camaraderie was great and we had lots of laughs. I made many friends.

Eamonn was wonderful, making the long trek from town to see me every day after work, then going back again, often to work again. All I had to talk to him about was what was going on at the hospital or to moan about my lot. It must have been boring for him, but he was always patient and never uninterested.

I had a great deal of curiosity value because Eamonn was on television. People who knew he was visiting would come up to the window behind my bed and stare at him while we talked. Eamonn didn't mind and I'm sure would have signed autographs, if asked, on his way out. The woman in the next bed, however, didn't watch much TV and was astonished that Eamonn should attract so much attention. One day, she said to me: 'It's not as though he's George Formby, is it?' I told Eamonn on the next visit. He found it hilarious.

I find it hard to understand now, but his star status even embarrassed me for a while. Sometimes he couldn't make it to the hospital during official visiting times because he was working, so the hospital allowed him to come at all sorts of times when, of course, there were no other visitors around. I felt a bit self-conscious that we were given this special privilege, which is a bit silly because everyone who watched TV would have known why he couldn't be at the hospital at visiting time.

Eamonn was charming to everyone he met and his popularity soared on our anniversary when he arranged for some show-business friends to put on a show for us. For some reason, he also brought a Catholic priest, Father O'Toole, who sang a cheeky song called 'Courting in the Kitchen'. No one in the ward could believe a priest would sing such a song; they felt it must be one of Eamonn's singing pals dressed up in theatrical gear borrowed from the

BBC. *But a genuine priest he was. And the next day he – and Eamonn – were the talk of the ward.*

Christmas came and went and then, in January, I was told the traction was coming off my leg. I was euphoric; in my innocence, I assumed that meant I was going home, but I was wrong: I would have to stay in hospital for at least another four months having physiotherapy to build up wasted muscles in my leg. That was disappointing enough, but what was worse was having to wear a built-up shoe. I was tormented by the thought that I would never walk properly again, but the shoe was merely to ensure that I didn't put any weight on my bad hip.

I was finally discharged in April and left the hospital the same way I'd gone there – on crutches. Eamonn had bought a ground-floor flat and decorated it ready for my arrival. Waiting there with him was Bianca Fury, who had been a ward orderly at the hospital; she had secretly accepted my offer to work as our daily help and cook and resigned a month before I was discharged.

Eamonn had been advised to take me on holiday as soon as possible and, although it was not convenient with his bosses, he insisted on having a four-week break from What's My Line? We went to Cap Ferrat and had the most blissful time, lazing around in the sun. Getting in and out of the sea isn't the easiest job in the world when you're on crutches, but I managed it: with the help of Eamonn's muscles.

All that delicious French food over four self-indulgent weeks did not help my weight problem, however, Having been inactive for virtually ten months, I'd ballooned up by around two stones, and when I returned to London, Bianca's splendid cooking did not help matters.

She would cook breakfast, elevenses, lunch, tea, dinner and supper, and because I was taking Vitamin B I was always hungry enough to eat all she served up. In no time, I'd put on another stone. Eamonn was too polite to say anything, but I could tell he wasn't happy about it. I wasn't over the moon, either: I'd always been figure-conscious and hated the sight of myself. But there was little I could do about it: I was still on crutches and unable to do any exercise to take the weight off. And what made it worse was that every time I went for a check-up, I was told to carry on as I was – with strictly no dieting.

Eventually, however, I was told my hip was cured. I could lose my crutches – and the excess weight. I can't describe the relief. I cut out more or *less everything and set out to get back to what I was the year before. I had a fixation about it, but it still took six months.*

11 MY OWN GUEST

The shattering news of Grainne's hip problem made my mind whirl. I was worried, but I knew that worry was the most unproductive thing in the world; not only for myself, but for Grainne, too. I turned to prayer and to another great healer for a worrier: work. I worked and worked and worked, and when I wasn't working, I was at the hospital, trying to cheer Grainne up.

At first, I feared that even if she was cured, she would be left with a limp. It played on my mind: she was so young, so vibrant; it would be awful for her. But then I began to take notice of other people in her ward. I saw people with polio who couldn't use their limbs. I saw people with frightening diseases, who were not only taking it, but matching up and being cheerful.

Suddenly a limp didn't seem so bad. If that's the worst that Grainne will have, that's OK by me, I told myself. The important thing is that she must get up and get out.

After that, my mind was easier, although Professor Seddon would never commit himself when I asked him how it was going. 'It's going according to plan,' was all he would say.

Grainne was always asking after Quiz, our poodle, and one night she said she would like to see him. The ward sister was kind enough to grant permission and the next evening the little fellow put in a bedside appearance, much to Grainne's delight. Later, I drove with him to Holborn where I was having dinner with a friend, Bunny France, and his mother, Eileen.

It was pouring when I left and I got lost behind Euston Station. I saw a policeman sheltering in a doorway and got out to ask him where I was. Then I got in and started crawling in the downpour towards West Hampstead. It took me an hour.

I opened the car door and looked in the back. No Quiz. I rang Bunny, assuming I'd left him at their flat, but I hadn't. It dawned on me that the dog had got out while I was speaking to the policeman. I had no choice but to go back to the Euston area to look for him.

Somehow I found the same policeman. 'I thought you'd be back,' he said. 'Your dog jumped out when you opened the door.'

'He's at the police station then?' I asked hopefully.

' 'Fraid not, sir. He was too fast for me.'

My heart sank. It was well past midnight and I had a busy Saturday, with three sports programmes, ahead of me.

But Quiz *had* to be found. I started driving slowly through the dark, wet streets looking for him. It wasn't long before some policemen in a patrol car flagged me down and wanted to know what I was doing coasting around the back streets. They were a bit sceptical about my explanation at first, but then sent me on my way, promising to look out for Quiz themselves.

At three o'clock, and almost out of petrol, I gave up the search. I was worried out of my mind, but I had to get some sleep. I did two broadcasts, then rushed to the hospital to see Grainne before I went on air again.

'How's the little fellow?' she asked, almost as soon as I sat down.

I hadn't the heart to tell her the truth. 'He's fine,' I said. And changed the subject.

Later that day I had a phone call from the police who told me the dog had been spotted in the Euston area. After my third broadcast, I dashed off and started scouring the streets again.

I searched most of the night with no success. Then, at nearly midnight, I saw some taxi-drivers sitting around chatting in a shelter at King's Cross. Desperate now, I told them about Quiz and said: 'If you'll go out and look for him, I'll pay whatever is on your clocks, plus tips. And a fiver to the man who finds him.'

But by three o'clock Quiz still had not been found, and, reluctantly, I went home. At the hospital later that day, the inevitable question: 'How's Quiz?' Again, I lied. I didn't know how to break it to her.

That night Teddy Sommerfield offered to join the search and we spent several hours combing the streets. But again, no luck. Now fearing I'd never see the lovable puppy again, we called at the police station. I was far from hopeful, but, amazingly, was told that a man had indeed reported finding a poodle. Teddy and I went to an address in Grays Inn Road. The man and his wife were out at a pub. We waited and waited. Finally they returned. Yes, they *had* found a poodle. My heart was thumping. I couldn't bear it now if the dog wasn't Quiz.

But the couple were reluctant to part with him. 'How do we know he's yours?' they asked.

'Just let me see him,' I pleaded. 'If it *is* Quiz, he'll know me straight away. Then *you'll* know.'

Grudgingly they allowed us in. Quiz was there – thin and worn by his travels. He gave me a tired licking welcome, but the couple still seemed unsure. I suggested going to the police who had a description of Quiz. Reluctantly, they agreed. And although the couple freely admitted they wanted to keep the dog, they said I could have him back. Suitable compensation was arranged and we all left.

'By the way,' said the wife, 'what do you call the dog?'

'Quiz.'

'Blimey,' she said. 'We've been calling him Charlie.'

I went home to West Hampstead, tired but happy. And relieved that I wouldn't have to lie again on my next hospital visit.

I had not been given a release date for Grainne, but one thing I knew she would need when she left hospital was a ground-floor flat. I found a perfect one at Lancaster Gate and took photographs of each room so that Grainne could design a colour scheme. She changed her mind half a hundred times, but what did it matter? She was beginning to show an interest in getting out and about again, and that was a marvellous sign.

At long, long last Professor Seddon said Grainne could leave and suggested I took her on holiday. I was in the middle of *What's My Line?*, but that was nothing compared to Grainne's health. She was my most important consideration and I told my bosses that I was taking her away – even if it meant I would lose the show. Everyone was kind and understanding, however, and said a replacement would take over as chairman while I was away. I booked four weeks at a quiet, little pension in the South of France resort of Cap Ferrat and bought a new car with an opening hood so that Grainne could get plenty of fresh air whenever we drove.

For me, the day she came out of hospital was as exciting as any of my broadcasts: I was on an emotional peak, my heart full. Seddon was still not committing himself on whether Grainne would ever fully recover, but I didn't mind: at least she was out of that hospital and heading for the tranquillity of one of the most beautiful spots on the Riviera.

Days were spent sitting or sprawling on warm sandy beaches. Nights were spent sipping coffee and cognac, watching lizards immobilizing themselves on the walls and ceilings, then scampering to gobble a fly or moth. Sometimes we would go for a drive into Nice or Monte Carlo. For a woman, however, wind doesn't do much for the hair, so the car-hood was always up, shutting out all that fresh air I wanted Grainne to have.

Shortly after arriving in Cap Ferrat, I bought a paper to see if there was anything about Ron Randell, an Australian actor who was standing in for me on *What's My Line?* There was – a lot! He had, it seemed, made quite an impact by blowing kisses to the women in the audience and the paper carried a big photograph beneath a banner headline. Ah, well, I thought: good luck to him. But then I had nagging doubts and fears. Maybe I would not have the show when I got back.

My fears proved unfounded: when we returned a month later, I learned the BBC still wanted me. It was with some relief I threw myself back into work . . . and I even won a diploma myself for beating the *What's My Line* panel.

It happened the night Jack Solomons, the boxing promoter, was due to be the mystery guest, but didn't turn up because of fog. Producer Leslie Jackson said it was too late to get someone else and suggested I play a dual role – chairman *and* mystery guest. The idea for this spot in the programme was for the panel to try to guess the celebrity's identity while blindfolded. After they had put on their masks, someone signed in for me, then walked heavily to the seat beside me. A second or two later, he sneaked quietly away, leaving me to adopt a dual personality.

I had to ask myself questions, then hop to the other chair to answer them in a high falsetto voice that almost choked me. I argued and whispered and laughed with myself for five or six minutes of hilarity that had the studio audience in fits. I was delighted to beat the panel, and got them all to sign my diploma before, in all solemnity, I presented it to myself.

The show was dropped in 1955, but given a reprieve a year later and quickly bounced back into the top viewing figures. Around the same time, it had its first royal visitor – Princess Margaret. When the announcement was made, I expected the BBC's organization in general, and the show in particular, to go into a flat spin; but the only signs of agitation came from behind the scenes where dozens of smartly dressed BBC dignitaries appeared, as if they had been poised in the wings waiting for the royal visit to happen.

The moment of greatest interest and excitement that night was meeting the Princess after the show. She had a fine gift for putting people at ease, and it was good to hear her say she enjoyed the programme.

A few years later, Princess Anne paid an unofficial, unpublicized visit to the studios. It was all very informal and quite charming, and everyone connected with the show played the game of knowing she was there, but pretending she wasn't. The last challenger was a breeder of Welsh mountain ponies and the programme ended with one of them being led on stage. After I closed the show, panel, celebrity guest, various nabobs and myself went into the wings, eager to continue chatting to Princess Anne. But when Her Royal Highness came through a side door and saw the beautiful Welsh pony, she went up to it without a glance at the glittering front and backroom talent assembled for her. She seemed to spend the rest of that visit petting and talking to him.

As chairman of *What's My Line?* I had to think quickly – especially if I dropped a clanger. One famous occasion when I did just that concerned a young challenger who was a waiter.

It was the custom to provide a piece of information, such as the way the challenger earned his or her money – self-employed, salaried or wage-earning. But this particular night, I threw the panel into hilarious confusion by giving the game away immediately. After the young man had signed in, I turned to Barbara Kelly and said solemnly: 'Your free piece of information is that he is a waiter.'

The silence baffled me. I couldn't remember what I'd said. I felt sure it was: 'Your free piece of information is that he is wage-earning.'

Suddenly it dawned on me that I'd blundered. Something had to be done – quickly. I turned to the bewildered young man and whispered to him that, for a few minutes, he would have to pretend he was something other than a waiter. We decided on a steeplejack. A case of instant elevation, if not promotion.

Another time the audience fell about laughing was when a ship's captain told how his good intentions had rebounded embarrassingly on a voyage to South Africa. He had been asked to give VIP treatment to a certain young lady, and gave her a seat at his table. The girl was so shy, however, that she hardly said a word, apart from 'Good morning'. The captain was at his wits end; no matter how hard he tried, he could not draw her out.

One meal-time in heavy weather, the girl watched, intrigued, as the waiters hurried around, sprinkling tablecloths with water.

'Captain, why are they doing that?' she asked.

Delighted she had said something, the captain explained: 'It's an old trick. When the ship begins to roll in heavy seas, knives and forks slip and slide all over the place. Putting water on the cloth gives them a grip, you see.'

The girl's eyes brightened. 'Oh,' she said, cheerily. 'I must remember to wet my bed tonight.'

It was, the captain told the *What's My Line?* audience, the last thing the poor girl said on that trip.

Before that momentous Festival of Britain year drew to a close, I was to apply the yes-to-everything technique again – and barely got away with it.

'Do you know anything about chess?' was the question from the distinguished producer, Derek Burrell Davis. I had already done a few things for him and he was happy enough to give me an extraordinary booking to commentate on a 'living' chess match in which schoolboys were the 'pieces' on a huge board. As soon as I got the offer, I bought every instructional chess book I could lay hands on. On the day, my ignorance was not too obvious because, fortunately, the boys got a little confused and I was able to cover for them in what, no doubt, was a grand and patronizing manner.

I never tried the 'yes' technique again.

Millions today will not even have heard of Gilbert Harding. But in the early fifties he was an explosive personality whose TV outbursts frequently made headlines. His temper was genuine, although many cynics said his clashes with me were planned to make viewers switch on the show. Nothing was further from the truth.

He never believed he was as great as the public thought he was and had a sense of guilt about the money he was paid. But he worried that *What's My Line?* was trivial and he should be attempting greater things. During our last lunch, I tried to put his mind at rest, telling him he was in a unique position of having one foot in the intellectual camp and one in the lowbrow camp.

He was the great interpreter who could speak for the common man and the professor; he could translate both their points of view into something they could both understand. My rationalization seemed to console him. He looked genuinely relieved and thanked me.

Behind the bellow and the bluster, Gilbert was a kind and religious man whose annoyance and temper never lasted very long. He suffered instant repentance whenever he realized he was in the wrong and was always sending flowers to ladies he'd offended, or to the wives of men who had felt the lash of his tongue.

He was very attached to his mother and would tell me how she scolded him whenever he was rude to me on screen. One time when my own mother was over from Ireland to see the show, I took her to meet Gilbert in his dressing-room. His mother had recently died and when he started talking about her, he started to cry. The public, who saw only the short-temper and irascibility, would have found it hard to believe.

I was in Dublin when I heard Gilbert was dead. It was a terrible shock. Suddenly I felt very, very lonely.

Professor Seddon still would not commit himself. I would look at Grainne closely and think to myself: 'I *know* she's cured.' But all he would say was 'I must have more tests, more X-rays.' It went on and frustratingly on.

And then one day, one most wonderful day out of the blue, he asked to see her and said the words we had been longing to hear: 'Now I'm sure. You are cured. Completely cured.'

And she was. Without even a limp.

While Grainne had been recovering, work poured in for me and I had accepted offers to work on two children's TV programmes – *Crackerjack* and *Playbox*. I liked working with children; in fact, I never understood anyone who did *not* like it. I agreed with the man who said there is no such thing as a bad child: if one has the time and patience, one can unlock the loudest or the slyest and find the wide-eyed wonder that is a child. Mind you, when a bright seven-year-old bopped me in the eye, it took me all my time not to bop him back.

All the major stars came along to twinkle for the children. Until Cliff Richard appeared, I thought that screaming girls were specially provided by producers as a sort of accepted sound effect of twentieth-century claque. I couldn't have been more wrong. The moment he came on stage and started singing, girls in the gallery started jumping and shrieking as though someone had let loose half a dozen mice. I stared at them, petrified that one of them might jump too high and too far forward.

We had several letters of complaint and one particularly interesting one in defence. A mother said she had been concerned that her teenage daughter was mixing with older girls who drank more than was good for them. The girl had then returned from a party in the north of England where Cliff had been guest of honour and told her mother: 'I'm never going to drink. Cliff wouldn't take anything except orange juice.' It proved, perhaps, that there are two sides to every song.

The highlight of my *Crackerjack* career was when the Queen paid a visit to watch the show, then greeted the crew and cast on camera.

On that occasion, a strange atmosphere of paralysis and panic prevailed. It almost took over in the big studio at Children's Television Centre in Shepherd's Bush. I noticed shadowy figures moving around, pacing out how many steps it would take from here to there, mumbling gallant replies in mimed rehearsal, lest the Queen should ask them a question. One executive traversed and re-traversed six yards of space round a camera, vainly trying to work out how he could do it without turning his back on Her Majesty and getting tangled up. The more he tried to work it out, the more he looked like someone not all there, rehearsing – with an invisible partner – an impossible dance. I pretended not to notice.

In the end, it all went well, although I never understood how our guest star that day, Harry Secombe, managed to stand still and refrain from his customary giggling when the Queen was speaking to him! They were happy days, those *Crackerjack* days.

I wanted to try a new style programme, interviewing people as well as playing records and I went to my BBC radio bosses and suggested The Pied Piper. I could sense a slight reluctance immediately. 'What kind of people?' they asked.

'Oh, well, Noel Coward's in town,' I said. 'People like that.'

'You won't get him for a start,' they said.

'If I get him, can I carry on with the idea?'

Oh, yes, that would be grand, I was told. So off I went in search of the Master. He was appearing at the Café de Paris and I haunted it until I got to see him. He listened patiently as I told him my idea. Anxiously, I asked: 'Will you do it?'

'Certainly, dear boy,' he replied. 'When?'

I told him the date and the time, and said I'd send a cab for him.

'Not at all, dear boy, not at all,' he said. 'I'll be there.'

And he was. And the BBC let me carry on interviewing surprise guests on the show, which went out live every Saturday night.

I found Coward's brilliant, almost hypnotic, personality dazzling. But not so dazzling that I shied away from asking him about something a Chicago theatrical agent named Joe Glaser had told me. Joe, who dropped such names as Louis Armstrong, Duke Ellington and Rosemary Clooney at the slightest opportunity, said he was going to offer Mr Coward a record fee to appear in Las Vegas.

One could not pierce the suave polish of Noel Coward, however. When I put Glaser's promise to him, he replied coolly: 'Surely you realize by now that *everyone* who appears at Las Vegas does so for a record fee.'

At the end of our chat, I played 'Mad Dogs and Englishmen' and it was amusing to hear Noel Coward the person interrupt Noel Coward the recorded voice to bid me goodnight with the customary Cowardian courtesy.

After that *The Pied Piper* took off and stars of the day – including Gracie Fields, George Formby, Bob Hope, Eddie Fisher, Lena Horne and Rudy Vallee – would drop into the studio to tell Britain's listening millions what they were up to. Bob was about to entertain American forces in Iceland and when I asked him if the cold would bother him he shook his head and said: 'No, I'm half man, half blubber.'

Norman Wisdom failed to arrive on time for one show. I'd already told listeners that a mystery guest was on his way and I had to cover up somehow. Then we learned Norman was about to walk in and one of the technicians heralded his arrival with sounds of a jet-plane whistle, honking of cars and a screech of brakes.

The tiny comedian sat down, breathless and bewildered. 'How did you get here, Norman?' I asked.

'On a bicycle,' he replied.

During *The Pied Piper*'s run, I would play records at home to try to get a balanced programme. Grainne would go round the bend because, every time she came in, she had to walk around on tiptoe, picking her way among more than a hundred discs scattered over the floor. I nearly went round the bend, too. For after listening to records for three solid hours, I would lose all idea of what was good and what wasn't.

One record I wasn't allowed to forget was by Don Charles and his

Singing Dogs. Tommy Lawton, the England footballer, told me one day: 'My little daughter, Carol, has a poodle named Cognac. When he heard all the howling on the record, he leapt at the radio and practically scratched it to pieces before we hauled him off. The next time you play a record like that, Eamonn, make sure you issue muzzles and chains.'

I still loved to write, however, and I got the chance to read one of my monologues on *Henry Hall's Guest Night*, one of the top radio shows at the time. Ironically, it was so successful that it led, a few weeks later, to a cabaret performance that was the worst professional moment of my life.

The monologue was as hammy as the corner-store delicatessen, but Henry, or his producer, liked it and I was on.

The story concerned a young boxer and an old boxer, along the classic teacher-student line, with the teacher retaining one trick to himself – a mixture of Hazlitt and Aesop, maybe. But in this bout the old boxer went blind. How's that for a punchline?

Shortly after the broadcast, I was invited to appear in a cabaret in aid of the newspaper organization's charity, Old Ben, and preened myself at being asked to include my boxing monologue. Subsequently, I was invited to appear on BBC's *Picture Page* – one of the first 'popular television' programmes – at Alexandra Palace, but, happily, the timing was such that I could do the appearance and get to the Connaught Rooms for the charity cabaret.

One of the items on *Picture Page* was a test to check the effect of alcohol on driving ability. TV's first chef, Philip Harben, and a young film actress called Diana Dors were among the contestants. And after sipping various degrees of alcohol, they had to sit behind a driving wheel, with a simulated road ahead of them, to be tested for speed of reaction to danger and general driving accuracy.

Afterwards, all the performers and guests gathered in the hospitality room for drinks. I asked for a gin and tonic, but one of the charming dispensers of BBC hospitality – much more lavish and lethal in those days – must have added the contents of one of the alcohol-laden test tubes, because, on the way to the Connaught Rooms, I began to feel decidedly queasy. A great fuss was made of me at the hotel, however, and I finally found myself launched on to a tiny platform that passed as a stage.

The place was packed. The cigar smoke was rising. But they were an attentive audience and my jokes seemed to be going down quite well. Then I reached the finale: my Boxing Monologue. No problem here, since I'd written every word.

I launched into it. The audience gave me their rapt attention. But as I approached the climax, I couldn't, for love nor money, remember what it was. I skated around, adding words, hoping for my own inspiration to come back and re-inspire me. It must have become quite meaningless and I could hear conversation rising like water in a stuffed sink. Somehow, I finished the piece and got off the stage.

I never appeared for Old Ben again.

If I'd read half about science as I had done about boxing, I would have been able to split an atom at the drop of a microscope. Yet, even in my most altitudinous flights of fancy, I never dreamed I would commentate on a world heavyweight title fight – the great crown of boxing. So it surprised me when, in the spring of 1955, the BBC quickly agreed to my idea of covering the fight between the US champion, Rocky Marciano, and Britain's Don Cockell in San Francisco. There were certain economic advantages for the BBC, since I'd decided to invest in a trip to America anyway to see what I could learn from a country that was producing more television than anywhere else in the world. Negotiations started for getting broadcasting rights, facilities and air time – and yet another dream was about to be realized.

Before I left, the BBC's Light Entertainment Chief, Ronnie Waldman, told me he had heard a lot about a programme in the States. 'Take a look at it while you're there,' he said. 'I'd be interested to know what you think.'

The show was called: *This Is Your Life*.

13   THE BIG FIGHT

I flew to New York with Sir Winston Churchill. Well, that's a slight exaggeration: we travelled on the same Comet! I, like all the other passengers in Economy, was surprised and not a little thrilled that he was on the flight, but there was very little fuss and, seemingly, no preferential treatment for the great man. He and a few aides sat up in First Class, apparently oblivious of the excitement his presence was causing behind.

Churchill was an old man then, but he seemed to have more stamina than most of his party. He spent nearly all the time playing cards, and wore out three or four partners. When the jet touched down in New York he looked as alert as though the journey was just beginning.

I deliberately hung back as we all got off because I wanted to take a photograph of the famous statesman. But President Eisenhower's plane was waiting on the tarmac to take Sir Winston on his way and security guards were all over the place, saying: 'Immigration, this way.' As I hung back, waiting my chance to snap Sir Winston, a big fellow in a stetson walked over and stood in front of me. 'Immigration – *in!*' he barked.

'I just want to take a photograph of Churchill,' I explained.

The man didn't move. 'Get in!' he said.

'Who are you?' I asked.

'Security.'

'What do you mean – Security,' I said. 'I've just travelled across the Atlantic with this man. If I'd wanted to do anything to him, I'd have done it before now. I'm staying right where I am.'

'Get *in!*'

'No.'

The man was standing practically against me, but he took a short step forward and breathed in a great gush of air, which expanded his chest with such ferocity that it sent me and my camera hurtling backwards through the Immigration door. The door slammed, and I stood on the inside, fuming helplessly. I fumed for a week afterwards.

I found New York the sort of city where I'd hate to be out of work. It has a toughness that leaves you thinking that unless you do your job well and are a success, nobody wants to know. Nobody has time to know.

Unlike London, however, it is easier to get in to see a top man, although you will be told within ten seconds if your idea is no good. 'We've heard it all before, bud, sorry, thank you, come and see me again, goodbye . . .'

On that trip, I had an experience of this no-nonsense approach that I never forgot. At the time, Ed Murrow was a journalist running a very successful series of in-depth TV interviews, called *Person to Person*. He had captured some famous and intriguing people and I badly wanted to persuade him to do a *Person to Person* on *himself*. But he was not the easiest person to get to.

My BBC pal, Brian George, helped me out again. He had known Ed during the war when the American was a correspondent in London and gave me a letter of introduction, which I sent round to Murrow's Manhattan office. It worked. He agreed to see me the next afternoon. Now it was down to me to get weaving with some friendly persuasion.

The following day I found myself with time to kill, and dropped in to see Aubrey Singer, the BBC's New York representative, who worked on the thirty-third floor of Rockefeller Plaza, the same building where Murrow's office was. During our conversation I asked Aubrey precisely where the great interviewer's office was.

Aubrey pointed. 'Just across there. Why?'

'Oh, I'm seeing him this afternoon,' I replied.

Aubrey looked surprised. Then he said: 'I'll come over with you now and show you where it is.'

I was delighted; I felt I had reinforcement for my task. For Murrow was almost an institution in America and a meeting with him might have its problems, despite my letter of introduction. As we waited to be shown into Murrow's personal office, I asked Aubrey: 'Is he a nice fellow?'

Aubrey shook his head. 'I don't know,' he said. 'I've never met him. I thought I'd take this opportunity to come over with you and meet him.'

My heart sank. What a fine time to tell me. I didn't have time to dwell on it, however, because we then went in and were greeted by a smiling Murrow, who put us at ease right away.

The whole occasion was nice and chatty and informal, and had nothing to do with the reason for my visit. I sat there in a daze as Aubrey and Ed got themselves into a deep discussion about farming. Suddenly, after what seemed like a couple of hours, Ed looked at his watch and whistled through his teeth. 'I've got about ten seconds to an appointment. Was there anything particular you wanted to see me about, Eamonn?'

Ten seconds!

I was caught off-balance. Almost apologetically, I started to tell him. 'I was hoping you'd do a *Person To Person* with you in the middle and me doing the interviewing . . .'

Murrow stopped me in mid-sentence. He got up and waved his hand in a gesture of finality and dismissal. 'Aw, no, can't do it,' he said. 'And, anyway, if I ever do, I've promised a pal of mine here. Can't be done. Sorry.'

And then he leaned across his desk to shake my hand and said, 'Been very nice meeting you, thanks for calling,' and it was all over and Aubrey and I were walking out the door.

That sort of fast, unwrapped decision, I found, was typical of American business. There was no wavering, very little sentimentality and money was a great god. I was not sure it was a good thing.

I was lucky enough to be shown parts of Manhattan the tourist doesn't see. But my guide wasn't a native New Yorker – it was an Englishman named Eric Maschwitz, who had just been appointed BBC TV's Head of Light Entertainment. He knew New York from way back in the Prohibition days when he'd spent several years there as a writer, and took pleasure in showing me around for three or four days. He also told me how the city's gangsters in the twenties came to call him the Cat Doctor.

One night, it seemed, he was taken to a speakeasy on the night the house cat was about to give birth to kittens. Nobody knew what to do: men who wouldn't think twice about pulling a gun were standing around biting their nails, nervously. Eric, however, had had experience of the situation and immediately helped deliver the kittens. It won him the respect of the speakeasy's clients – and its owners – and he had only to come to the door after that to be given a warm welcome. 'Sure, sure, come in,' he'd be told. 'Hey, fellas, here's Massoowits –the cat doctor.'

In the few days as my New York guide, Eric showed me parts of the city that amazed me – and the most remarkable feat of recovery that amazed me just as much.

We had been on the town for several hours and had consumed liquid in proportions no one would call meagre. Just before midnight, Eric remembered a Swedish smorgasbord he wanted to take me to. We went there and partook of schnapps and Lord knows what else with some of his pals.

It was past 2 A.M. when someone ordered yet another drink. I groaned inwardly. I was making a guest appearance on the US version of *What's My Line?* the next day and wanted to get back to my hotel and sleep. When I looked at Eric, I knew that he had had one too many. I felt unusual relief; it meant we'd be leaving soon, surely.

Eric dropped his head to his chest and closed his eyes. He stayed like that for a full thirty seconds, as if in prayer or deep meditation, then suddenly looked up and shook his head, like a boxer, to clear his brain. He clapped his hands. 'Right boys,' he said brightly, 'let's go to The Round Table.' And we were off again.

Half an hour in The Round Table and then we were on our way to Eddie Condron's Club. By now I was past worrying about my TV appearance later that day and the only thing I clearly remember is hearing the band play the romantic classic, 'These Foolish Things', and introducing Eric as the co-composer. Once again, I was basking in someone else's limelight.

I couldn't match Eric's staying power, however, and reeled off into the night, in search of that welcome pillow. I slept like a baby, no doubt dreaming of those long ago days when I'd never heard of *What's My Line?* and New York was as remote as the Sioux Indians.

* * *

When I flew on to San Francisco for the big fight preparations, I quickly learned why no one gave Cockell much of a chance against Marciano. Outside the ring, the hard man from the Bronx was gentle and charming but when he started sparring, it was as if a red mist had come down over his eyes and driven him into a rage. What he did to those sparring partners was frightening and I didn't hold out much hope for Cockell's chances.

The Americans take care to protect their fighters, as I discovered, to my embarrassment, at the weigh-in in San Francisco's City Hall. I'd got to know the 'Rock' fairly well during his training and when he saw me, he grinned: 'Hello, Eamonn.' I held out my hand and said: 'Hello, Rocky.' Suddenly, someone behind me gripped my hand in what felt like a steel claw and forced it back. A thick voice rasped in my ear: 'The Champ don't shake hands on the day of a fight.' A shiver ran down my neck.

I was always nervous before a radio or TV broadcast, but that night I was screwed up more than ever: the awareness that my voice would be winging out across the Atlantic and into British homes at three o'clock in the morning suddenly hit me and gave a heightened sense of thrill. My nerves vanished, of course, the second the bell went for the first round and my commentary, I learned later, went down well in Britain where interest in the fight proved to be higher than anyone at the BBC had imagined. Marciano did, indeed, beat Cockell, but not before the Battersea boy put up a show of courage for nearly nine rounds that earned him glowing tributes from partisan American fight fans.

My experiences at the big fight convinced me that the American cop was in more danger of causing more riots than he stopped by bearing down, on working journalists and public alike, with drawn baton and warnings that sounded like war-whoops. And that conclusion passed before my mind's eye at a Buckingham Palace garden party the following month. The garden was packed and, when the Queen and Prince Philip appeared, what looked like a line of a thousand people surged forward, eager to see and touch them, no doubt. Just when it seemed the Royal couple might be engulfed, a gent in a bowler hat, walking in front, simply lifted his umbrella a few inches above the ground and waved it gently – not even admonishingly – at the oncoming crowd. They fell back, as if they had been struck by a magic wand and waited docilely.

That garden party was the time the Andrews scored a Royal 'first'. We didn't have a limousine, so our friend, Bunny France, kindly loaned us one. What's so unusual about that? Well, Bunny is an undertaker and the car he provided was, yes, a hearse. Surely no one had arrived for a Palace party in one before!

When I tuned into *This is Your Life* on American television, my first reaction was: this *is* television. I thought the creator and presenter, Ralph Edwards, had pulled out too many stops and coloured too many purples, but I felt we could pitch it right for British audiences. I cabled Ronnie Waldman, telling him I'd love to do it at home.

Later, Ronnie told me that the BBC governors (why they were consulted, I never knew) recoiled from the formula as being very un-British, too sentimental and 'all-that-tosh-you-know'. All they would agree to, under Ronnie's gentle pressure, was to give it a trial on a monthly basis. If it didn't work, it could be dropped from the schedules without too much trouble.

A number of suggestions were made for a possible opening subject and finally it was decided to surprise the great footballer, Stanley Matthews, who was riding high on one of his many crests of popularity. Most of the preliminary investigations and contacts had been made by the time Ralph Edwards and his mini-team arrived here. When I say mini-team, the outstanding member of it, in fact, was very maxi. He looked like a bear, in so far as any human being can. He was tall and soft and paunchy and spoke in a kind of European growl. I think he was Polish. He was Producer. He still looked like a bear, despite his tiny moustache and the bottle-top glasses. His name was Axel Grunberg. We talked with him a lot and found him a kind and gentle and helpful colleague, unlike the sharp-shooters we'd been warned to expect. He had one astonishing trait. He started to tell us about one programme in particular that Ralph had done. He recalled a touching confrontation and what it meant to the story, and as he talked I didn't know where to look. Tears were rolling down his face. A sob was chugging at his voice. He took out a handkerchief almost as big as himself, wiped away the flow and apologized. This was to happen several times. Ralph was not at all surprised when I told him about it.

'Yes,' he said. 'Quite a problem that at times. His production assistant has had to take over once or twice when Axel's glasses got so steamed up he couldn't see the action.'

What a lovely, lovely man. I went to see him in Hollywood many years later, after he'd retired, and it was the same old story: the eyes filled, the glasses steamed and the voice wobbled and we had a wonderful time.

Everything was going to plan. There was great pre-publicity about the new programme and Ralph called what was to be the final meeting on the Wednesday before the Monday transmission – live, of course. When we arrived at his apartment in ye olde worlde St James's all hell broke loose. Someone on the *Daily Sketch* tabloid newspaper had leaked the story that Matthews was to be the first subject for *This is Your Life*. Stanley was up in the Lake District fishing, unaware of the hullabaloo, and Ralph wondered if we could see to it that he didn't see the offending paper. We had to remind him that our main news-papers were national rather than local; and that, in any event, there would be no way of protecting Stanley from the casual comment of a fellow-fisherman, or a neighbour when he returned from his trip. The time left was shatteringly short and heads were put together immediately to think of a story that could be presented quickly.

At this point, I had a personal dilemma: I was writing an overnight column for the *Star*, a London evening paper, and had led my story with a piece about Ralph Edwards and *This is Your Life*'s début. By now, the first edition was already on the streets and, in view of the Matthews situation, I needed to update the story. I asked to be excused from the meeting to telephone the Features Editor and re-draft the column. I was some time and, when I rejoined the meeting, I sensed a coolness. It dawned on me that the Americans in the party had probably thought everybody working for Fleet Street must be tarred with the same brush; that I was no longer a good risk, so to speak. It seemed a bit wild, but all the more likely when they said they had decided to head up to Television Centre to see Tom Sloan, then boss of Light Entertainment, to see what new plans they could put into action. They said they would contact me later.

I really did feel hurt. What I didn't know was that, while I'd been on the telephone, someone had pointed in my direction and mouthed the possibility of doing me! There were two obvious reasons: one, I was available on the night: and, two, that most of the people I knew could probably be rounded up in a hurry. The big problem now was to get rid of me, which they did, of course. I went home to Maitland Court for lunch and was soon cheered up with a call from Television Centre to say they'd come up with a smashing subject for the programme: Freddie Mills, the former light-heavyweight champion of the world and a very good friend of mine.

What did I think? I said it was a great idea and they suggested that, as a sports broadcaster, I could persuade him to take part in a pilot programme the following Monday. If Freddie was free, this would be easy because I knew he was on the look-out for that sort of thing. I told them they should make a formal approach first. They did – and were back to me in a shot to say that Freddie had agreed. This meant I could occupy Freddie all afternoon at Lime Grove Studios while preparation for the programme proper went on in the Television Theatre, round the corner at Shepherd's Bush. The big snag, of course, was that I would miss seeing how it was all done. However, it was a case of that or no show. Of course, the team had told Freddie all about it and he knew the score . . . although he did admit later that he started wondering at one stage if he had fallen for a double-double bluff.

I rang Freddie to tell him that, after we'd completed the sports programme, I was going to watch the new *This is Your Life* programme; would he like to join me in the audience, where there were to be a number of celebrities, including Ben Lyon and Bebe Daniels and Boris Karloff? He agreed. Of course, he would! I told him we'd drop back between shows to Maitland Court, have a bite to eat and that we'd be collected there and taken straight to the theatre. Poor Grainne was petrified. She had to hide the dress she was going to wear, and pretend she was staying at home and not interested in seeing *This is Your Life* that night; she thought the car would never come to take us away. Another car was immediately behind to whisk her round to the stage entrance of the old Empire while we went in the front.

The crowd was moving in as we got there. Suddenly I thought everything had gone wrong. In a corner, I spotted Don Cockell,

Britain's former heavyweight champion. Convinced that he was part of the Mills story, I told Freddie to wait inside the door, then I rushed back and hissed in a bewildered Cockell's ear that he wasn't meant to be seen; and to go to the stage door – quick. Poor Don! He must have thought we were all liars on the programme. Here he was, appearing on my show, and he had, no doubt, been told that his appearance would be a big surprise for me. I rushed back to Freddie, hoping he hadn't seen Cockell. We were shown to our seats. The show started.

Ralph made his introductory remarks and came down into the audience, talking to various celebrities. Then he came to Freddie and me and introduced me to the audience. When he asked me who was sitting alongside me, I said, smugly, that it was, of course, the very popular Freddie Mills. More applause. Ralph gave me The Red Book, and asked me to read what was on the cover. When I saw it, all I could say – may my Irish ancestors forgive me – was 'Oh, blimey!' There it was under my nose – EAMONN ANDREWS – THIS IS YOUR LIFE!

After that, it was a blur. I couldn't imagine how they had persuaded my mother to fly, much less walk on a stage, but there she was, and my sisters, my brother, my old pals, the amateur drama group I used to help run, one bubbly member, Maureen Wright, being flown all the way from her emigrant home in San Francisco, my old insurance colleague and later international actor, Jack MacGowran, Joe Loss, Don Cockell, of course, and Jim Fitzgerald, the lad I'd beaten for the Irish middleweight junior title.

It took me days to recover. It was an experience that would have been worth it at any time. But with me about to do the programme myself, it was gold dust.

The month's trial of *This is Your Life* was successful. And the show was on its way to becoming one of the most popular programmes on British television. For the production team involved, it was always a nerve-wracking experience keeping the identity of the subject secret and never a week went by without one drama or another. But the Danny Blanchflower episode takes some beating. It taught me that if I was not to go through life a nervous wreck I should regard the unexpected as the expected.

When we decided to make the famous Irish International footballer a subject for the 'Life', I was convinced nothing would go wrong. Danny was a radio and TV performer as well as a soccer star and by no stretch of the imagination could I imagine him being averse to publicity. So, when I prepared to spring the surprise on him, I was quite relaxed.

Knowing we had no hope of getting the shrewd Irishman to the Television Theatre without him suspecting something, we arranged for him to go to a different venue, thinking he was doing yet another football broadcast. Without his knowledge, everything would be taped, to be played to the theatre audience and viewing millions half an hour later. A fast car would be waiting to take Danny to the theatre to watch the opening sequence and enjoy all that was to follow.

Danny turned up at the little news studio opposite Broadcasting House all right. And, as a secret camera whirred, I got as far as saying: 'Tonight, Danny Blanchflower, this is your . . .' But as I was about to present him with The Book, Danny fled like a greyhound from a trap. Angus McKay, the BBC's Sports Editor, lunged forward to try to stop him and caught hold of his coat. But Danny wriggled out of it and rushed through a door and down the stone steps, shouting: 'Let me out. Let me out.'

He was due to play in the Cup Final in a week or two and as I chased after him, I had this dreadful vision of him slipping and breaking a leg. He reached the main exit door safely, thankfully. It was locked. Danny was white and taut. I told him to relax; there were no cameras on him. He didn't want to know, just demanded his coat back. Outside, I tried to persuade him, but his mind was made up: he wasn't doing the programme and that was that. The theatre was full, I said; backstage, many of his friends were waiting to greet him. That was our concern, he said. He hadn't invited them.

I went upstairs and phoned Leslie Jackson to tell him he had no programme. It was a great, great disappointment; weeks of preparation had gone by the board; hundreds of pounds in fares had been wasted – and a theatre full of people now had to be told they could go home.

I couldn't let it go at that without a fight. With just fifteen minutes to go, I went to the BBC Club where Danny had gone with Angus McKay. Again, I pleaded. Again, Danny refused. Resigned now, I told Danny that a car had been standing by to take him to the theatre; he might as well use it to take him home. But, again, Danny turned down the offer. He was taking no chances, he said. He'd take the tube.

After that, I always expected the unexpected, and never relaxed until the guest of honour was sitting on stage and the programme rolling.

The next time I went to New York, I took Grainne with me. It was a trip I'll never forget, not just because of her experience with the dry Martinis, but also because I was treated like a VIP in the legendary 21 Club and told I could easily become a dollar millionaire. Let me take the second point first.

Mark Goodson, one of the game-show partnership that owned, among other properties, *What's My Line?*, seemed convinced I could repeat my British TV success in the States. And he took me to the 21 to try to persuade me to leave England and live in New York.

'If you stay here, Eamonn,' he said, as the 21 Club fussed around him, 'I can guarantee to make you a national figure. If you want to know what that could mean in terms of money, take your *What's My Line?* counterpart here, John Daly. For doing the show, he gets $250,000 a year. But that's only the start. He gets the same again for other TV work, plus thousands of dollars from personal appearances and sponsorships. That kind of money could be yours, Eamonn.'

It was very tempting. And, sitting there, reflecting in Goodson's glory, savouring at second-hand every moment of the sure, smooth sophistication of New York success, I took the offer seriously. Of course I wanted to be rich and famous and be treated like a king – who wouldn't? But did I want to live in America? Did I want to turn my back on everything I'd worked for in Britain? Could I bear to tear up all my roots, not only in England, but Ireland, too, and leave all my family and friends, simply to be richer and more famous in another country?

I decided to talk the whole thing over with Grainne that evening.

Deep down, I knew what her feelings would be, but it would be good to have a long chat about it and consider all the pros and cons. Well, the talk about our future and all the exciting possibilities it held didn't happen that night in New York. And that's where the dry Martinis come in.

On my previous trip I'd experienced Greenwich Village, the unique quarter on the west side of Manhattan, alive with jazz and art and poetry, and all sorts of fascinating characters. Grainne jumped at my suggestion to go there.

We popped into a particular bar I'd enjoyed before and invited Grainne to try a dry Martini. She wasn't a practised drinker, by any means, and looked doubtful. 'Go on,' I said, 'the American dry Martinis are very good.'

What I'd forgotten was that dry Martinis, American-style, are served in mountainous conical glasses. Grainne's eyes popped when the waiter put the drinks on our table.

I smiled at her shock. 'Go on, get that down you,' I said. 'Then we'll press on to the Village and I'll buy you a nice dinner.'

Grainne enjoyed the dry Martini. And a little later, when we popped into another bar, she had another one. Our thoughts turned to eating and we moved on to the edge of the Village looking for a restaurant I'd liked on my previous trip. Once I'd got my bearings, I suggested we had another drink before going on for dinner. Grainne, now clearly enjoying herself, agreed and promptly downed another dry Martini. Now ravenous, we stepped out into the Manhattan evening, looking forward to dinner and that chat about our future. I started walking in the direction of the restaurant. But Grainne gripped my elbow tightly. 'A taxi,' she whispered, in a voice that didn't sound like hers. 'Get a taxi. Take me to the hotel. You and your dry Martinis!'

The night was young. Greenwich Village was alive, vibrant, beckoning. We were to bask in its excitement and talk about being millionaires and living like kings . . .

Not that night we weren't. All Grainne wanted was her head on a pillow in our room at the Warwick Hotel, amid the relative tranquillity of Sixth Avenue, more than fifty blocks up town. She never made it to

Greenwich Village. Nor, to my knowledge, did she ever have another dry Martini, American-style.

We did get around to talking about moving to the States, however. And she, like me, felt a 3,000-mile move, and a transformation in lifestyle, was not what we needed or wanted at that stage.

One of Manhattan's most famous restaurants, frequented by everyone who is anyone, is Sardi's. Getting a table there at any time is difficult, but Grainne and I found ourselves there three times in two days – thanks to three marvellous hosts who wanted only the best for us.

Firstly, Piers Powell, who had worked in London as American correspondent for the *Star* evening newspaper, called our hotel and invited us out to lunch. Piers, a very gentle, correct Englishman, had connections at Sardi's and got a table for three. We had a glorious meal and immensely enjoyed our first look at the legendary show-business venue.

The next day, Larry Lipskin, then head of Columbia Pictures, called at the Warwick and said he had a marvellous surprise for us. He was taking us to lunch, but he was not telling where. All the way to Sardi's, he kept mum.

Once again, the meal was terrific. But we couldn't spoil it for Larry by telling him we'd eaten there the day before.

That evening, a good friend named Barry Gray, known all over New York as an ace radio man, called at the hotel to take us to dinner. He had booked a table at a place we would love. That's right – Sardi's. We feigned surprise and pleasure to spare Barry's feelings. But the evening was an ordeal. Instead of it being a relaxed, enjoyable occasion, Grainne and I spent the whole time tensed up, waiting for the embarrassing moment when a waiter came up and said: 'Nice to see you here again, sir.' Happily, no one gave us a second glance.

Before we returned home, Barry invited me on his radio show and I decided to surprise him by wearing an extraordinary pair of cuff-links given to me by a Californian friend the night before. One side of each was a watch which ticked away normally. There were no hands, however.

'What does it mean?' I had asked my friend.

'Nuttin',' he replied. 'But they'll sure drive your friends mad.'

That's why I wore them on Barry's show. He was bound to be fascinated, I thought; and they would make a conversation piece, should we run out of ideas. I could not have been more wrong: with Barry, you never run out of conversation; and, secondly, he didn't bat an eyelid when I showed off the cuff-links. To the New Yorker, nothing is unusual. There's nothing he hasn't seen before.

In those days, Barry's show came from a posh restaurant between 11 P.M. and 2 A.M. He would discuss any subject: politics, religion, the latest play he had seen – anything and everything, in fact, that came into his mind or was sparked off by his guests, which ranged from the President of the United States to the newest comedian on the scene.

On my first appearance I found Sammy Davis Jnr on one side and a comedian, Jack Carter, on the other side. Sammy jumped right in by asking me, in what he felt was an English accent, all kinds of questions on cricket: 'I say, old boy, what are the maximum and minimum dimensions of a crease.' I protested that cricket wasn't my strongest point, but this only encouraged him and he hammered away at it. Carter joined in and I just sat down, silent for the most part, or blushing or doubled up with laughter.

I went back on Barry's show several times after that, and always thought that the British Arts Council could do worse than sign him up. He was a gangling talker who was never lost for words and, for me, symbolized the best of what was left in real American radio – an oasis of conversation in an endless echoing desert of top twenties and top thirties.

I returned to the States in May the following year. On this trip, I realized a dream: I sailed to New York aboard the *Queen Mary*. For this unforgettable experience, I have to thank a tiny Liverpool Irishman named Alfie Cain. And for the pleasure of meeting Alfie Cain, I have to thank the imagination of Phyllis Robinson, the producer of *Welcome Stranger* back in 1952. One day, she had hit on the idea of me doing my interviews on one of the majestic Queen ships, and the Cunard Line agreed for a production team and myself to travel in the US-bound ships to Cherbourg and pick up the homecoming Queen for the return journey to Southampton.

We crossed the Channel in the *Queen Elizabeth* and I was in a state of perpetual amazement at the grandeur and size of everything. What a marvellous way to travel to America, I thought. And when we learned it was too rough to disembark at Cherbourg, my heart jumped: maybe we would have to stay on board all the way to New York! My hopes rose further, after several hours' delay, when a steward told us: 'No sign of the weather improving. You may as well go to your cabins and get some sleep.'

I dropped off, fingers crossed. But after what seemed only minutes, someone knocked on the door and said politely: 'Expect you'll be pleased to know it's calmed down a lot, sir. Better get dressed pretty sharpish. The tender will be leaving the ship soon and you wouldn't want to miss it, would you?'

The *Queen Elizabeth* came mighty close to having a stowaway that voyage!

We made our *Welcome Stranger* recordings on the return trip aboard the *Queen Mary* – and that's when I met Alfie Cain. He was chief bar steward and he had met all the greats who had travelled to and from New York on the ship; he had mounds of autographs and photographs of stage and screen stars, politicians, tycoons and sportsmen. And he also had a never-ending fund of stories about the New York waterfront which fascinated me. He knew a lot about boxing, too, and, all in all, made me eager to travel out on the *Queen Mary* as soon as I could afford it.

I didn't make it until four years later, in the May of 1956, when I went over to make a guest appearance on *What's My Line?* in New York and take a closer look at what was happening generally in American television. I was also flying on to Los Angeles to cover the Sugar Ray Robinson–Carl Bobo Olson world middleweight title fight for the *Sunday Dispatch*. A passenger on the voyage out was Lord Rothermere, who owned the paper, and one night he invited me to dinner. I presumed it was because I was working for him, but I was wrong. He wasn't aware of it and, in fact, asked: 'What are you going to do in America?'

I told him about *What's My Line?*, then said: 'I'm going on to LA for the Robinson–Olson fight.'

'Are you? Are you?' he mused. 'Mmm – very nice, too.'

'It certainly is,' I replied. 'And thank you. Because you're paying for it.'

Rothermere just smiled and asked me if I'd like some more cheese.

My agent, Teddy Sommerfield, was on the trip, but he felt seasick most of the time and I spent nearly all the five days listening to Alfie's stories or trying out the ship's facilities, courtesy of the master, Captain Sorrell.

I'd seen the celebrated Manhattan skyline before but never from the Hudson river. Sailing towards it that morning was a breathtaking experience, and I would never forget my sense of disbelief as I stared at the skyscrapers stretching for the dawn clouds.

We expected a long wait to get off, but, to our surprise, were sent to the front of the immigration queue and waved through with great speed. It was all down to a strange gentleman named Lou Indago, whom Freddie Mills's father-in-law, Ted Broadribb, had arranged for us to meet. Lou was a small man, with hooded eyes and he talked of 'toids' and 'voids' and 'boids' and 'coibs' in a Brooklyn accent. I knew nothing about him, but the picture began to emerge of a man deep in the boxing world, who would deliver mysterious messages, who would keep in the background until summoned by the boss, who knew all the secrets, but told none.

A couple of days after we arrived, Teddy and I were talking business in my hotel room when the phone rang. Teddy picked it up. 'This is Lou here,' the familiar Brooklyn accent drawled. 'I wanna talk ta Eamonn.'

Teddy did not approve of Lou; he was convinced he was linked to the underworld. He covered the mouthpiece and whispered: 'It's that Indago man. Do you want to speak to him?'

I wasn't sure about Lou either. But I was keeping an open mind because I felt he might provide a juicy underworld story I could use in one of my newspaper columns.

'Yes, I'll talk to him,' I told Teddy and took the receiver.

'Hi, Eamonn, dat you?'

ht: Eamonn, as a toddler

w: As a young boy

Eamonn with his mother outside the house he bought her

Grainne, the young 'Liz Taylor'

Left: Eamonn in his late teens

Below: Early days in Dublin, commentating

pposite above: At school in 1930, amonn aged eight (third from the ght in the back row)

pposite below: With Synge Street chool friends (centre of the back ow)

Eamonn with his mother outside the house he bought her

Grainne, the young 'Liz Taylor'

ht: Eamonn, as a toddler

ow: As a young boy

Above and right: Eamonn and Grainne on their wedding day, 1951

Above: Happiness in Chiswick: Grainne, Eamonn and baby Emma

Left: Early married life

Below: Eamonn, the cook, serves lunch to Grainne at home in Dublin

Right: With 'Quiz', the poodle
Eamonn lost while Grainne was in
hospital

Below: At home in Chiswick with,
from left to right, Emma, Niamh
and Fergal

The Happy Family:

Above: Emma has Mum taped during one of Grainne's dressmaking sessions

Left: Cuddles for baby Fergal

Below: Lunch with Emma and Fergal

Above: Proud Dad with Emma, Fergal and Niamh

Right: Eamonn, Grainne, Emma, Niamh and Fergal leave for a family holiday

27, Maitland Court,
Lancaster Gate,
London. W.2.

Dear Mrs Andrews,

This is to let
you know that life without
you is dull and colourless.
I can't stick it any longer, so
I'm running away.

I'll love you
always

Eamonn

P.S. I will of course be back
tonight.

Darling

If after 25
you don't know that
your nails set
on edge   maybe
after 25 yrs   you
don't know that your
presence sets me
on fire!

Love
E

FRI...

TELEMESSAGE LXP
MRS GRAINNE ANDREWS   HATS
2 WINDSOR HOUSE
HEATHFIELD GARDENS
LONDON
W4

DEAR MADAM,

THIS IS TO INFORM YOU THAT NOT ONLY HAVE I REMEMBERED OUR
WEDDING ANNIVERSARY OF TODAY BUT TO REMIND YOU OF OUR DATE TO
GO SHOPPING AND OF MY EVER INCREASING AND ALMOST UNBELIEVABLE
DEVOTION TO YOU. NOT ONLY THAT BUT I SUFFERED THE EMBARRESSMENT
OF DICTATING THIS MYSELF.
YOUR LOVING ANNIVERSARY SHARER
HYMIE.

Loving messages from Eamonn to Grainne

ght: The first British *This
Your Life:* Ralph
dwards, creator of *This Is
our Life,* surprises his first
British victim – Eamonn
Andrews

Below: Ralph Edwards
with an emotional Eamonn

Above: With great friend, bandleader Joe Loss

Left: Eamonn with distinguished guest Cardinal Heenan

Below: With *What's My Line?* mystery guest Trevor Howard

above: Eamonn with (left) Muhammad Ali, Lucille Ball and Noël Coward (right) on *The Eamonn Andrews Show*

right: Eamonn sees the joke on *The Eamonn Andrews Show* with guests Bob Hope and Bing Crosby

opposite above: Left to right: Grainne, Mickey Hargity, husband of Jayne Mansfield (right), and Eamonn

opposite below: Eamonn and Spike Milligan

Above: With great friend, bandleader Joe Loss

Left: Eamonn with distinguished guest Cardinal Heenan

Below: With *What's My Line?* mystery guest Trevor Howard

ght: The first British *This Is Your Life:* Ralph Edwards, creator of *This Is Your Life,* surprises his first British victim – Eamonn Andrews

low: Ralph Edwards with an emotional Eamonn

Left: Bob Hope, Bing Crosby and Eamonn in reflective mood on the golf course

Below: Fergal, Grainne, Emma, the Irish Prime Minister Charles Haughey and Niamh at the unveiling of the bronze of Eamonn by Marjorie Fitzgibbon, ARHA, at the RTE headquarters, Dublin, September 1988

'Yes, Lou. How are you?'

'Yeah, foine, foine. Now, lissen, Eamonn. I thought I'd just remind ya, t'day is a Holy Day of Obligation. Don't forget ta go ta Mass.'

I think the lesson he taught me was not to judge a book by its cover.

Lou was my first real taste of the American fight-game characters, and he brought me into contact with many more. He introduced me to one promoter who had an office in Madison Square Garden, and I had many a session sitting in on his conversations with a never-ending stream of colourful Damon Runyon characters who popped in just to chew the rag. It was fascinating, seeing and hearing for myself that the great American writer had not built the characters up any – just translated them and their talk straight on to paper.

Lou Indago died a few years later. I liked him and owed him a lot. He was one of the names I always prayed for.

When I went to the Goodson–Todman office to discuss *What's My Line?*, I discovered I had a lot to learn. What had struck me as a fairly simple, straightforward, one-shot guest appearance was treated by Mark Goodson and Bill Todman as a matter of great importance. It was typical of the meticulous professionalism with which they treated their work. They were not going to allow me on the screen until I'd been thoroughly briefed on how the show was run and the kind of questions that should be asked, as well as the different terms used.

As it was, I nearly brought the house down when I asked a mystery guest if he made gramophone records.

Gramophone records! Panel and audience nearly collapsed at this prehistoric naïvety. As far as New York was concerned, the gramophone record went out with the ark. Discs, platters, tapes, yes – but, please, not gramophone records.

And thank goodness I didn't ask a London taxi driver a question that was on the tip of my tongue. I had a hunch he was a cabbie, most of whom seem to be Jewish. I thought it would give me a clue to his job if I knew whether he was Jewish or not – but Goodson told me afterwards that I'd have closed down the network if I'd asked that question, on racist grounds.

By the time wer were due on air, I was very nervous; and the fact that my fellow panellists seemed very distant and aloof didn't help. But my tension eased as the programme's host, John Daly, introduced the first challenger and I discovered how difficult the panellist's task is. When the celebrity guest came on, I didn't have a clue who he was and I was none the wiser when I took my mask off and was told he was Peter Lawford. I knew him by name, of course, but not by sight.

I got through the programme, and after Daly had made a short goodbye speech to the audience, I stood up with the rest of the panel and prepared to leave the stage. Well, it was over. It seemed to have gone well. I lit a cigarette. Suddenly, I had a strange feeling I was alone. When I looked round, I discovered I *was*. Had I been that bad that everyone should vanish as if I had some disease?

Assuming everyone had gone to a room for the customary after-show drinks party, I asked a scene-shifter where I should go.

He looked at me as though I were daft. 'Everyone's gone, bud,' he said. 'They've all gone home.'

I must have been terrible; so bad that they couldn't tell me; they'd bolted to save embarrassing me. I was standing there, feeling desolate, when Gil Fates, the producer, came down with the director, Franklyn Heller. I tensed, waiting for the axe to fall.

But Gil said: 'That was fine, Eamonn.'

That didn't cut any ice with me; I'd heard all the showbiz platitudes. But he was saying: 'Yeah, great, great. Can you do another one next Sunday?'

Suddenly I felt young again.

A few nights later, I was watching Jimmy 'Schnozzle' Durante in cabaret at the Copacabana club when I saw in the programme that Peter Lawford was on the bill. I felt I may have insulted him on *What's My Line?* by not recognizing him, so I decided to redress the balance. I asked if I could see him. I was told I couldn't. I wrote a note, saying: 'Sorry I didn't recognize you the other night, Mr Lawford. Come and have a drink.'

He didn't come. He probably had no idea who I was.

15 THE FIGHT GAME

After the Robinson–Olson fight, I stayed in Los Angeles to take a close look at the movie industry. The great film capital of Hollywood was beginning to change: studios that had been empty and silent started to buzz again, not for the cinemas, but to feed the growing baby – television.

Everything about a programme, I quickly discovered, was 'the greatest'; there could be nothing conceivably wrong with the show, its star or the product it plugged. It could be that the production team got the sack. If that happened, the *next* show to employ them would become 'the greatest'. It was an attitude that was to put the United States so far ahead of the rest of the world in television.

A big star at that time was a singer with a wonderfully deep voice named Tennessee Ernie Ford, who was very big in England, too; indeed, his chart-topping record, 'Sixteen Tons', was my own favourite for several weeks. I was delighted to be given a guest spot on his TV show and some time before the live show was due to go out, I suggested to an assistant that I met him to go over the ground we would cover.

The bright, efficient middleman replied: 'Guess you may not be able to see him right now. In fact, you may not be able to see him at all before the show. We're very busy getting ready.'

I realized that, I said. But as we were to talk in front of millions of viewers, it seemed commonsense to at least meet each other and have a brief chat.

'You don't have to see him,' the young man said. 'All you gotta do is sit on a stool and when Tennessee sings this song, he'll sort of drift over and say: 'Hi. An' who are you?' and you can say who you are. Or, maybe *he'll* say who you are. But, eh, what'd you have in mind to talk about?'

I didn't mind, I said. And between the two of us we came up with a few ideas.

'Any funny stuff?' the assistant asked. 'I mean, like have you a little anecdote you wanna tell?'

There was some slight story he agreed would fit in nicely. And then I asked again if I could speak to Tennessee for, perhaps, thirty seconds.

The assistant shook his head. 'You see, it's this way,' he said. 'Mr Ford never prepares for this sort of thing. But don't worry, he's the greatest. Relax. It'll come off and it'll be OK. Mr Ford never prepares, but when it goes on it'll be great, so just relax.' He clicked his finger and thumb. 'Mr Ford'll think of sumpin', just like that.' And then he was gone.

When my spot in the show came along, I was perched on a stool in a lonely space on stage. Tennessee's warm voice filled the theatre and when he finished the song, he wandered over to me.

'Hi,' he said, in a voice that came up from his bootstraps. 'Folks, this here is Eamonn Andrews.'

He started asking me questions. I was surprised, and not a little impressed, at the homework he must have done. But then I caught sight of a little blackboard being held just under the lens of the camera shooting us. On it were all the points I'd covered with the middleman – including the lead-up to my funny story. So much for Tennessee Ernie Ford always being prepared.

I quickly reckoned that my spot would be over before we got to the story, so I telescoped three or four answers, hardly giving Tennessee a chance to read the cue card and got into my anecdote in double-quick time. We met at a party later and had a laugh about it.

One of my favourite TV stars at that time was James Arness, who played a marshal, Matt Dillon, in a very successful western series called *Gunsmoke* in America and *Gun Law* in Britain. I did not know why it was re-titled and nor did Arness when I met him on the set and asked him. But he was thrilled that his series had taken off in Britain.

'Waal, waal, waal,' he said in that long, slow drawl so familiar to me through the show. 'And you say they like us over there? Waal, waal, waal.'

Looking at his 6 ft 5 in, sixteen-stone frame, he reminded me of John Wayne and I was to find out that the legendary cowboy actor had indeed signed Arness for a film called *Big Jim McLain*, then released him for *Gunsmoke*.

'I admire him,' Wayne said. 'He's a man's man, unaffected – and he can act.'

What Wayne probably liked, too, was that the toughness the rawboned Arness showed in his screen roles was not entirely fictitious. He was wounded on the Anzio beachhead and spent a year in hospital. But he shrugged off any talk of heroism with: 'I was too big a target to miss.'

Matt Dillon's sidekick in the series – the limping Chester – was Dennis Weaver, who went on to star in several major movies, notably the Steven Spielberg truck thriller, *Duel*. I learned he only just failed to be selected for the 1948 Olympics in the decathlon event. When I talked to him about the popular Chester, he said: 'I guess I'm like the gal known for her figure who gets a chance to act as well.'

Probably the most lovable character in the series was Doc, played by Milburn Stone, a serious man, but with a quiet, warm charm. While I was in Hollywood, Milburn's home was burgled and valuable property stolen. They might have got away with it, but for the influence of TV on the little boy next door.

The lad was a fan of *Gunsmoke* and a popular crime series called *Dragnet*. When he saw two suspicious-looking men leaving Milburn's house, he went into action on the lines of his favourite programmes. He wrote down the colour of their hair, what they were wearing, the way they walked . . . and the registration of the car they were driving. Twenty-four hours later, the men were picked up by the police.

I wonder how that effect of TV on the young mind fits into the sociologist's reckoning!

Before I left the *Gunsmoke* team, Arness urged me to take the short plane trip to Las Vegas and arranged for a fast-talking Hollywood publicist named Norman Greer to fix me a free room at the New Frontier Hotel. Greer was a great guide to the gambling capital. 'You can have the cheapest holiday in the whole of the United States here,' he told me. The hotel room charges were lower than anywhere else to encourage people to go there and spend their money on the slot machines or crap or card tables.

'One guy last week left with $50,000,' he said.

My mouth hung open. 'No!'

'Yeah,' said Greer. 'Mind you, he arrived here with a million.'

I spent only two nights in Las Vegas because I had to get back to Hollywood for a business appointment. I asked Norman to use his influence to get me on a 5 A.M. flight.

'You'll be OK,' he said. 'I rang them.'

'Did you get me a seat?'

'No. But you're on the waiting list.'

'That's no good,' I complained. 'I must be back early. I can't break this appointment.'

'You'll get on the plane,' Norman said calmly.

I wasn't convinced. 'This waiting list,' I said tensely. 'Am I near the top?'

'You're thirty-ninth.'

'*Thirty-ninth!*'

'Don't worry, pal, you'll be on that plane all right.'

I felt my stomach tighten. I didn't live my life this way. I wanted my mind put at rest that I would definitely be in Hollywood for my appointment.

'Norman, how can you be so sure?'

'People who book up always wait for just one more go. One more roll of the dice.'

It didn't make sense to me. But I had no choice. I went to the airport at dawn the next day, still sceptical. How could I hope that all thirty-eight people would miss their flight waiting for just one more roll of the dice?

Well, I did make my appointment. I got on that plane just as Norman told me I would. And as we taxied to the runway, I counted six empty seats. Amazing, isn't it, how tightly a gambler is held by one more chance?

Shortly after that breathless jaunt to Las Vegas, I found myself in a city that could not have been more different in just about everything – Moscow. The purpose of the trip was to cover the first post-war visit of an English amateur boxing team. I got behind the Iron Curtain in the end, but what an adventure!

Before the trip, Grainne and I were to go on holiday to France for two weeks, and when we were due to leave I still hadn't got my Russian visa. To make matters worse, I had an Irish passport – and Ireland didn't recognize Russia. The tourist thaw hadn't started and the Russians were taking their time deciding whether I was going to get a visa or not. My passport, I was told, needed to be in London in case the Russians needed to use it. Which was rather inconvenient, since I needed it to get into France. I don't know what laws were broken, but as soon as Grainne and I landed in Paris, somebody collected the passport from me and whisked it back to London.

Everything was fine all the time I was in France, but we teamed up with Teddy Sommerfield and his wife, Dorise, and they suggested going to San Sebastian in northern Spain. How I managed to get past the Spanish border, I never found out; a temporary document of identification I'd got from the Irish Embassy in Paris was printed in Gaelic – and I spoke no Spanish. The border guard and I shouted at each other a few times and, finally, he got fed up and shrugged his shoulders and stamped me through.

After another piece of cross-channel smuggling, I got back to London. To my delight, my Russian visa had arrived – but there were more problems ahead at Moscow airport.

The boxing party was greeted with smiles and handshakes and the fighters and officials presented with garlands. But after an hour's delay, frowns replaced the smiles: there were twenty-five in the party, but only twenty-four passports. Had anyone not handed in his passport? No.

Finally, I solved the mystery. The immigration official counting the passports had come across a strange-looking green booklet with a harp on it – and tossed it aside. My poor passport was still causing me trouble: it hadn't figured in the count. When I pointed out what had happened, all was well and we got on our way. But I felt like a marked man the rest of the trip. Siberia for me.

I found Moscow a city of contradictions and paradoxes: there was an odd mixture of excitement and sadness, happiness and drabness; and, on many sides, an intense desire for friendship.

Those seven days in Moscow were an eye-opener and I returned to

London enlightened. Two surprising sights stayed with me: at 2 A.M. one morning I watched as a gang repaired tram lines with picks, shovels and pneumatic drills. Nothing amazing about that . . . except that all but two of the workers were women! One of the men simply held a chisel while a woman swung at it with a sledgehammer. The other was a supervisor.

The other long-remaining memory was of a woman begging in the underground. In the capital, there is practically no begging at all, but this woman was sobbing, her hands extended for alms, and hardly one person passed her without giving her something. Our guide explained that Muscovites would give if someone begs because, to be reduced to that, the need must be great indeed.

The great American heavyweight, Floyd Patterson, fought Sweden's Ingmar Johannson for the world title three times. I was privileged to be able to cover the fights for BBC radio and apart from the fisticuffs themselves, I had reason to remember each occasion for years afterwards.

On the night of the first fight, I was at the Madison Square Garden ringside, waiting for the action to start, when Frank Butler, *News of the World* sports editor, asked me if I knew who was sitting behind me. Discreetly, I turned round and glanced at a fat man, wearing thick, steamed-up glasses.

'No idea,' I told Frank.

'Ever heard of Jack Liebling?' he asked.

'Not A. J. Liebling?'

Frank nodded. 'That's right. A. J. Liebling of *The New Yorker*. That's him in the glasses.'

I was a fan of Liebling. He'd written *That Sweet Science*, one of the best boxing books ever written, and, to me, he was one of the best writers in the business. I stole another glance round and looked at him with interest and admiration. Then Frank introduced us; I probably behaved like a fan at the stage door.

The big fight began – and ended dramatically early. Against all the odds, Patterson was knocked out in the first round. Pandemonium.

I had to do some quick thinking. In Britain it was 3 in the morning;

millions had waited up to hear the fight. With the fight over in just a couple of minutes, I had to try to get them a little more value for their sleeplessness. I fought my way through the mayhem in the ring for some interviews, then looked around for some celebrities. John Wayne was working for ABC Network and he helped me out with some drawling knowledgeable comments. Then I got a few words from Ralph Edwards, my *This is Your Life* friend. Suddenly I remembered A. J. Liebling. What an opportunity. 'I have with me one of the world's greatest boxing writers – A. J. Liebling,' I told Britain's listening millions. 'What do *you* think about that fight, Mr Liebling?' I handed him the microphone and sat back to enjoy the polished prose of the master.

But all the great man said was 'Shocking surprise' – and handed the mike back.

I was dazed and deflated, and hurriedly looked around the bustling ringside for someone else to fill the empty air-time. I had the feeling *The New Yorker* paid Liebling by the word.

When the two fighters met again, I secured a fine exclusive, but no one ever heard it. This time Patterson won by an early knock-out and the Swede was still recovering when I jumped up and told Frank Butler: 'Carry on talking – I'm going into the ring to talk to Floyd.'

But that was easier said than done. The ring was packed solid with well-wishers and police with truncheons were trying to restore order. As I climbed under the ropes, a truncheon arched towards me. 'BBC,' I screamed, holding up my microphone. The noise was deafening and Patterson was engulfed in a mass of congratulators. But I managed to get a few words from the new heavyweight champ.

Then I noticed Johannson, sitting in his corner, head down, lonely, desolate, stripped of the glory that had been his for a year. It was a sorry sight, but a poignant story: the half-conscious ex-champion, now ignored by everyone. I moved towards him, through the excited officials and photographers, pulling anxiously at my microphone lead. Suddenly, I felt it go slack. 'Oh, no,' I said, 'my cable's slipping.' But then it felt all right again and I got to Johannson's corner.

I gave it the full treatment: the forgotten man slumped on the lonely stool; vintage human interest stuff. I even roused the dazed Swede into speech. I got a few comments from his manager, Eddie Alquist, too. I was delighted. I knew it was good, probably the best piece of the night and I rounded it off happily: 'And now, back to you, Frank Butler.'

I fought my way back to the commentary position, feeling good. The sound engineer was sitting close to Frank. 'Everything OK?' I asked him.

'Sure, sure,' he replied. 'We had the problem of having only one sound channel, you know, so when you said, "My cable's slipping," it was a perfect cue for me. I faded you out and took Frank in.'

I stared at him in disbelief and disappointment. Millions had heard the triumphant joy of the new champ, it was true. But my impromptu exclusive on the heartbreak of the loser was lost for ever.

The third and final contest was held in Miami in 1959 and afterwards I teamed up with the comedian, Jimmy Edwards, who had flown from Jamaica for the fight. The heavens opened and we dived into the nearest bar, drenched to the skin. Over a drink, Jimmy suggested we went to a nearby hotel where Schnozzle Durante was performing; Jimmy said he'd worked with the piano-playing comic in London and knew him quite well. When we got to the hotel, however, we could not get in to the show. He was a big enough draw on his own, but Floyd Patterson was the hotel's guest of honour and the place was overflowing. No amount of persuasion could get us past the door so we went to a nearby café for a meal. Jimmy penned a note to Schnozzle, telling him what had happened and where we were.

Eventually, someone did come with an invitation to join Durante in his dressing-room. And when we went in, I thought I was going to fall down laughing at the sight that greeted us: Schnozzle was pacing up and down the centre of the room smoking a cigar. Apart from a hat pushed back on his head, he was stark naked. He was so hot after his act, apparently, that he had stripped off to cool down. He'd always been funny on stage, but nowhere near as funny as he was that night.

We were introduced to four other people in the room, at least one of whom I recognized. One of the names, though, could not have meant a thing to my pal, Jimmy.

'Well,' Schnozzle asked him. 'What'd you tinka da fight? What's dis about a low blow or som'p'n? Was it low?'

Jimmy launched forth as if there was no doubt about it. 'Absolutely ghastly! Patterson should never be allowed to get away with it. No wonder they booed him. Hit the Swede when he was down.'

There was no stopping Jimmy: he went on and on, having a real go at the world champion until I could stand the embarrassment of it no longer.

'Excuse me, Jimmy,' I interrupted. 'You didn't catch the name of this gentleman here, did you?' I motioned towards an unassuming quiet gentleman in the corner. 'This is Cus d'Amato. He's Floyd Patterson's manager.'

A lesser man would have fled, but Jimmy bluffed it out; I think Cus was so fascinated by his huge handlebar moustache and commanding English accent that he would have forgiven him anything. Besides, his boy had won and was still champion of the world. All was well as we enjoyed a celebration drink then marched out into the warm Florida night.

I was to return to the States again – to make a television commercial. For someone used to measuring his life in minutes, it was an amazing experience for me. To have a lady with a stop-watch come up and murmur 'That was great, but you were half a second under – we'd better do it again' was as near as I'd come to looking over the edge of the world towards heaven . . . or hell.

The subject was toothpaste. And after fourteen months of negotiations and indoctrinations, I was satisfied that the product was good enough, and flew to Dallas for three days to do what proved to be the first of several shoots. During a short stop-over in New York, I was taken to the International Hotel, and was mesmerized by the first automatic phone I'd seen: no communication with the switchboard; a number for everything one could possibly want. I marvelled at the efficiency and made calls I didn't need. Within half an hour, though, I began to feel lonely for an operator's voice. I felt that I could stay in that room for ever and no one would ever know; that I could control the world from it; live and grow old and bearded in it, dialling number after number on a gold-coloured circle.

When the phone finally rang for *me*, I jumped as if a man from Mars had landed. Someone was on the way to take me to the airport. Destination Dallas. The fun was about to begin: I was about to learn how it was possible to say and shoot the same four lines 400 different ways until, suddenly, the world ceases to exist beyond the lights and the silent, sinister camera.

I was introduced to the director of the commercial, a small, thick-set balding man with large, sad eyes, named Bernie Rubin and asked him why we had to shoot the ad in Dallas and not New York. The reason, he said, was the weather. He was shooting outdoor approaches to a drugstore and needed plenty of sunshine. The New York climate was too unpredictable.

That first night we worked inside the drugstore, moving one pace to the left, one shuffle to the right, nodding forward instead of back, crouching instead of standing, then standing instead of lounging, adding one second here, taking off one half second there. Then doing it all over and over again: being shot at from under, then over, the counter; being peered at by men with light meters and lenses and dabbed by a make-up artist who told me he had returned to America to make his name as a sculptor after studying in Italy, but could find no other work than chiselling tombstones.

And there was Sascha, the girl with the stop-watch; a gentle English expatriate concerned with continuity and time and nothing else. She would murmur to Rubin that the last take was fine, but we needed to save half a second. When we did the re-take, I was aware of her pulling me over the speeding hand of her watch and felt a sense of personal triumph when she told me I'd made it. She and her colleagues were superb professionals. Somehow they persuaded me to do it 'once more' without making me feel I had done it a dozen times already. And even if I had, they managed to convey the delicious thought that the only purpose of the re-take was to give themselves the joy of seeing such a brilliant performance all over again. It was two o'clock in the morning when the last re-take was shot. I dropped off to sleep in my hotel bed, memorizing my opening line for the next day's outdoor shoot: 'We are now in Dallas, Texas, where the sun is shining.'

At eight o'clock I stepped out of the lift . . . into a full-scale, pale-faced conference. There was some disaster of which I was not aware. The script was being frantically rewritten. My opening line, it appeared, was out. I now had to say: 'We are now in Dallas, Texas, where, believe it or not, it's snowing . . .'

I walked to the swing doors. It *was* snowing.

We flew to Natchez, with its plantations, cotton, drawls – and money. Shots stepping off the plane; shots outside a magnificent pillared house and interviews with the beautiful woman who owned it. It should have been a graceful opening to the commercial: a shot of the huge house, a brief scene as I introduced myself, the woman telling me what the toothpaste had done for *her* daughter then inviting me in with a seductive Texan drawl. But when the company's salesmen in London saw the sequence, they found it hilarious. The woman sounded as if she was making the wrong sort of invitation.

On to Ohio. The makers of the commercial were so concerned with the integrity of every detail they would not hear of me speaking against a back-projection in London. A DC3 flew us to Cincinatti for fifteen seconds of filming – or less – in which I said: 'Here is our laboratory in Cincinatti.'

Just over two hours later, we were heading back to New York. The two days had been exhausting but I read something in a newspaper that was to make my tiredness vanish. The world heavyweight champion, Floyd Patterson, was about to sign that day to meet Sonny Liston; and, since I had a three-hour wait for my connection to London, I had time to get a scoop. On landing at Idlewild Airport, I rang the BBC and asked for a mobile recording unit to meet me at the Manhattan hotel where the signing was due to take place. We got there in time to intercept Patterson's manager, Cus d'Amato, coming out of a lift and he agreed to an interview. We plugged the recording equipment into a socket in the hotel hallway and, with no more formality than that, got the background to a contract on which the ink was barely dry. With the time difference on my side, I had a hot news item for *Sports Report* the next day almost before the newspapers had printed it.

Droning back over the Atlantic, it hit me that, although my three days in the States felt like three exciting weeks, I was only halfway through the commercial. I would have to return in little over a week.

On Monday another sleek car arrived at the television theatre and I was New York bound again – via Manchester. When we landed there, a young man in uniform dashed up the steps and asked if I was getting off. He seemed disappointed when I said I wasn't. 'We don't often see you here,' he said. 'We'd like to offer you the hospitality of Manchester.'

I felt embarrassed because I wasn't drinking, but I said: 'Fine. I'll get off.'

We raced across acres of tarmac, in a side door and hurried down endless nightmarish corridors, all the time chatting about Manchester and television and television and Manchester. Eventually we emerged in a dining room. It was deserted, but the young man motioned to me to sit down. He disappeared behind a door and came back, crestfallen.

'The barman's gone,' he groaned.

I was relieved. It saved me explaining I was on the wagon.

But then three laughing women with buckets and brooms came into the room, bounding round our table, and screaming, 'Crackerjack.' One of them, an Irishwoman, produced a bottle of beer, which brightened my crestfallen escort. Determined I should have a drink, he started pouring it into a glass. I was saved by a loudspeaker announcing the departure of my flight. I jumped up, leaving the beer where it was, and hurried back along the never-ending corridors, across the windswept tarmac and up the steps of the plane. I collapsed into my seat, feeling as though I'd been in a race.

We had to make a second stop, at Prestwick Airport, and the steward told me it had a duty-free liquor store.

'Oh, yes,' I said, non-committally.

'You can get whisky or anything else, cheap as dirt.'

I murmured some sort of nothing. But the obliging young man was not to be put off. 'I'll arrange for you to get a bottle or two of something,' he said.

'Not to bother,' I urged him. But as I stepped down into the dark Scottish air, a uniformed gent said: 'Mr Andrews?'

'Yes.'

'This way for the liquor store!' he boomed.

As we approached a small building, he spotted a girl in uniform and called out: 'Take Mr Andrews to the liquor store.'

'Certainly,' she replied. 'This way to the liquor store, sir.'

By now, the whole plane was aware that Mr Andrews was looking for a liquor store. And minutes later I was the owner of a bottle of whisky I didn't want.

A crowd of cheery Scottish women, presumably part of the ground staff, had gathered outside the duty-free shop window and were shoving bits of paper through the cracks for me to sign. I signed them all, convinced I must have looked like a refugee from Alcoholics

Anonymous, locked away from the world with a bottle of whisky, marked in red: NOT TO BE OPENED IN FLIGHT.

We took off for New York with a new crew, and, beyond an anxiety that I might be forced into having a large dry Martini, all was well. But we had to stop a third time – at Boston – and we were herded into a bare smoky room for an Immigration check. A man next to me with two children told me how he'd emigrated to Canada six years before and never dreamed of returning to England. Could I guess what his job was?

It was four o'clock in the morning and I was shattered. But I had to play *What's My Line?* with him. Sleepily, I asked him questions. After three, I asked him if he was a policeman. Yes, he said, with a look of amazement.

It was nothing to the amazement I felt. If it had happened on air the cynics would have said it was a fix.

I felt very smug, but tried not to show it.

I was met at Idlewild by the toothpaste company's advertising account executive, who was handling the commercial. For all I knew, he owned a distillery, but when we reached the hotel, I presented him with a bottle of whisky, marked in red: NOT TO BE OPENED IN FLIGHT. I'd bought it specially for him at Prestwick, I said. He was very touched.

Filming was easier this time. All the shooting took place in New York or New Jersey, so there were no charter planes across the country. By the third and final day, I was blasé: I knew when to consult Stopwatch Sascha, when to be available for the tombstone chiseller, when to be guided by director Rubin.

I thought New Yorkers were too hardboiled to be interested in film cameras, but a great crowd gathered as the crew started arranging their equipment at the edge of Central Park. I walked up and down, mumbling the lines to myself. My audience nudged each other, speculating who this great actor was. Some continental star, no doubt!

When filming began, a little fat man crouched down out of shot with a boom microphone. I walked into camera shot. The crowd surged forward, eager to catch my words. Suddenly a brittle New

York accent brought me down to earth: 'Aw, gee, he's only talkin' about toothpaste.'

I wanted to catch the cynic by the throat and explain what an important toothpaste it was. But I couldn't be sure who he was. Anyway, what Sascha had to say pleased me more. I'd done my bit in seven and a half seconds. Which was perfect.

My first and last US commercial was over.

17 A GREAT PUBLIC SCHEME

One day in 1960, Michael Hilliard, Minister for Posts and Telegraphs in the Irish Government, asked me if I was interested in becoming Chairman of an independent body which would launch television and take over radio in Ireland. It was the most exciting, challenging, frightening question I'd ever been asked, and I was to think about it deep and hard over the next few days. In the end, I decided I didn't have a choice. It wasn't as dramatic as the soldier going to war, but it had the same undertones of duty: I strongly believed that Ireland must have its own television service. I decided to accept.

I went to see the Minister. 'I have a phone call waiting,' he said. 'Is it yes or no?'

'Yes,' I replied.

He picked up the phone and dialled. 'The man we were talking about is here and is prepared to consider it,' he said. 'We'll be over straight away.'

Ten minutes later I was being ushered into the Taoiseach's office in O'Connell Street. Suddenly the enormity of the task came down over me like a black sheet. I was frightened; and I wondered how men of state cope with nerve-breaking problems every day of the week. Here was one comparatively tiny problem – and I felt overcome by it before we'd even started. The Taoiseach, Sean Lemass, was calm and reassuring, but as I left the office I couldn't help wondering how one dealt with millions of pounds of other people's money and not lie awake at night. I was to lie awake many nights!

I was made chairman of an advisory committee, and my fellow members were business executive E. B. MacManus, newspaper proprietor Commander George Crosbie, and a gentle lawyer named Paul Wilkinson. After the Act was passed, we were to be joined by Theo Moody, a professor of history from Trinity College; Ernest Blythe, director of the famous Abbey Theatre; Charles Brennan, a distinguished insurance broker and patron of the arts; Fintan

Kennedy, a wise and experienced trade union executive; James Fanning, a newspaper proprietor and leading light in Ireland's amateur theatre movement; and the only lady in the midst of us all, a charming schoolmistress named Aine Ni Cheannain.

We were to get to know each other well through long, smoky, but seldom acrimonious board meetings. We were to know the pressures from people who thought that running a television service was as simple as entertaining your friends to dinner; who felt it should be run one way and not another; who didn't want it at all; who felt they were the answer to any television board's prayer, and who knew even before we started, that we were going to do it wrong anyway.

In England I was showered with offers of money from people who had heard television was a goldmine and wanted me to invest their savings for them. I had a hard time explaining that I was doing the job for just £20 a week, and that I wasn't going to make any profit. I even had to stop my own Radio Éireann broadcasts because some people were prepared to pretend that I got those programmes only because I was chairman! But this was a good thing, really, and I resolved not to appear professionally on Irish radio or television so long as I was chairman of the authority.

Soon, blank sheets of paper began filling up with sketches and drawings as we aimed to build the most modern television studios in the world. There was one advantage in being a late-starter: we could learn from the mistakes of the pioneers. We found a beautiful, twenty-five-acre site at Montrose, Donnybrook, just outside Dublin, and architect Michael Scott started shaping his plans. It was a breathtakingly exciting time and, one sunny afternoon, I stepped on to that field and looked around. The cows were grazing and munching; the old house that was to be the source of much argument later, about whether or not to preserve it, looked shabby and neglected. Indeed, there was already what seemed like some Machiavellian plot by the Department of Posts and Telegraphs as to how we would acquire the field – it was already Government property – and what strings might be attached to the green grass and the chestnut trees, already dropping their spiky-covered conkers.

I felt a thrill, and yet a disbelief, that Ireland was, at last, going to have its own television service; and that it was going to spring up in this magic field. Surreptitiously, I pocketed a few shiny chestnuts and took them across the Irish Sea to Chiswick that night and planted them in pots. I had a vision of planting some of them in front of the house, and some in the back, so that later I could tell my children, or my children's children, if I were lucky: 'These chestnut trees are the same age as Irish Television.' Unfortunately, I gave them too much water and they moulded away in the pots. They were not an omen, thank heavens. A superb television service grew and grew, on that green field.

We were given helpful advice from the BBC and some of its top engineers travelled to Dublin to meet us. Posts and Telegraphs had long had a relationship with the Corporation and, over the years, I, too, had made some very good friends in Engineering, as well as Programming. During one discussion, a sobering point emerged: the old Shepherd's Bush Empire, that I knew so well, had since become the BBC Television Centre and it emerged that the BBC had already spent as much adapting it to the needs of television as we had available to build our entire station.

At that stage, a highly technical point not understood by many was whether to launch the new service on 405 or 625 lines. The BBC were already broadcasting on 405 lines and the forest of aerials proved there was already an Irish audience with sets capable of receiving 405. Anyone who remembers the East Coast at that time will appreciate Jack Benny's joke about there being so many aerials that even the fog came in shredded.

Initially, it would have been less expensive to go 405, but there were strong indications that Britain would be switching to 625 in the near future. It was a decision that would have to be taken at Government level and no one was prepared to give us hard information. Fortunately, I had a slightly better than nodding acquaintance with a mercurial Tory Minister called Ernest Marples, who was the British equivalent of our own Minister of Posts and Telegraphs. Ernest was a colourful character who had his own vineyard and rode around London on a bicycle. He agreed to see me at his home, off Eaton Square, and to my utter surprise the Postmaster-General was there, too. We had a charming, but useless, discussion for some time before the PMG excused himself and left. I told Ernest that if I knew which way the British Government was going to move over the linage question I could save my country countless thousands of pounds, which was vital because of our low budget. He crossed a leg over a knee, put his hands behind his head and said that an election was coming up and that very question could be thrown up as a political bone. He was not prepared to commit himself but he was prepared to tell me, confidentially, that the decision would be 625 lines. He did warn me, however, that if I ever mentioned that he had told me, he would deny it. I had no problem trusting him and felt cock-a-hoop. I went back to my colleagues and said: Let us go 625. We did.

The search for staff began. Speed was top priority – and we were determined not to be bogged down with red tape and too many of the formalities, inescapable in such an organization. Applications for the director-general's post poured in from all over the world and it was a tremendous job, attempting to judge at a distance, and at speed. We were deliberating a short list with little optimism when a telegram arrived from Mexico City.

It said: HOLD ANY DECISION UNTIL YOU READ MY APPLICATION – EDWARD J. ROTH.

I was attracted by the assurance and confidence of the cable and we arranged to see Mr Roth. He was flown to Dublin amid cloak-and-dagger security. He was young and dynamic and had been in radio and television even before he left university. He got the job of director-general.

Roth turned out to be a dedicated enthusiast, who talked and read and thought television from noon till night. I was now spending three days a week in Dublin and we lived in each other's pockets for two years.

Roth was dismissed by many who should have known better, as merely 'an unknown and relatively inexperienced American'. But there was much more to Roth than that: he was full of innovative ideas and quick to grasp the many contradictions and conflicting interests in Irish society. I never believed in having a dog and barking myself, but I had to tread warily with Ed because he was a total stranger to the scene, and some things one discovers only by experiencing them. We never had a serious conflict, but I had to stay closer to his work than I would have wished.

People in similar positions to Roth – particularly in broadcasting and newspapers – tend to become power-crazy. But he never did.

The go-getting pioneer spirit, the sense of being in at the beginning of something that would eventually be great, moulded the talents of craftsmen and artists, technicians and technocrats, and produced a team spirit that was catching and headily encouraging.

Roughly three-quarters of my waking hours were spent on RTE and the other quarter keeping abreast of my programmes for the BBC. One advantage was that I didn't have time to socialize and so come under the pressures that were out there waiting for me. Ed Roth, however, was an easier target and they got to him in many different ways. He was stronger than he looked, though, and dozens of times asked me to mark his card when he suspected somebody was trying to bend him. I was, for instance, well aware of the presence of Archbishop McQuaid, but managed to evade a confrontation until the day the programmes went on air. Outside one of the studios, he turned to his secretary, Canon McCarthy, and said, with all the charm for which he was so well-known: 'Do you think, Canon, the Chairman might honour us some evening by coming to dinner – or would he be far too busy?'

Eventually, I did accept the invitation and had a delightful, unpressurized evening. The Archbishop, of course, had been arguing that because the studios were in his diocese, they were his responsibility. We tried – and, for the large part, succeeded – in pressing the responsibility towards the benign Cardinal Dalton up in Armagh, and ended up with two very reasonable and understanding men as our link with the Bishops – Archbishop Morris and Bishop Conway.

The stories about Archbishop McQuaid's devious interference in matters secular, as well as religious, are legion and I tended to discount most of them – well, at least half of them! I defended him frequently, because I knew some of the raconteurs who spread the stories were incapable of resisting the creative urge. Indeed, I remember one very quiet, respectable dinner party in actor Richard

Harris's home when he was still married to Elizabeth. Her father, Lord Ogmore, was there and so, too, was a jolly clergyman, who was introduced to us as the Chaplain of the Tower of London.

Richard talked about how J. P. Donleavy's play, *The Ginger Man*, had been picketed at the Gaiety Theatre at the instigation of Archbishop McQuaid and how he – the Archbishop – had personally put pressure on the proprietor, Louis Elliman, to stop the play going on. I pooh-poohed this personal intervention angle and said it was almost certainly some holier-than-thou who had taken it upon himself to anticipate the Archbishop's disapproval. Harris flew into a rage. His face was cracked with anger, and I thought he was going to jump on the table. He shouted at me that he had actually seen the Archbishop's representative priest come into the theatre.

Later, I came to the conclusion that Dickie was right. Thankfully, on that particular night, he wasn't drinking; otherwise, I doubt if I'd have left his house in one piece.

As 1961 wore on, the studios were beginning to grow on the grass at Donnybrook. But not fast enough: people were arriving to take up jobs almost before the jobs existed. We made plans. We scrapped them. We made them all over again, and then, in one moment of exquisite madness, we said we'd get a picture on the air before the end of 1961.

With only months to go, Michael Barry resigned as the BBC's Head of Drama, and joined us as Programme Controller: it was an almost impossible task, but he was warmed by the enthusiasm he found around him, and it wasn't long before he was telling us that the impossible would, after all, be possible. Everyone was working round the clock and I secretly worried that some might not last the pace. A much hoped-for Christmas launch was now out of the question, but we set our hearts on New Year's Eve – the latest possible moment we could leave it and still say we had opened in 1961.

During November, I was having a drink at the BBC's Television Centre with that captivating singer and actor Paul Robeson. A taxi was waiting downstairs to take me back home to Chiswick. Fog was beginning to come up. I was anxious to get home, because I had an early morning in Dublin the next day, but I couldn't resist the magnetic personality of Robeson. Unknown to me, King Hussein of Jordan was being shown round the studios by the biggest of big nobs, prior to a sumptuous dinner to be held upstairs. The King and I had got on very well when we'd met on a *This is Your Life* programme honouring Sergeant Major Lord – and he remembered it. He asked Tom Sloan, then Head of Light Entertainment, if I was around. Tom discovered I was in the bar and summoned me to the royal presence. I was flattered, delighted, but slightly on the wrong foot. The King and his influential hosts had stopped on the way upstairs, waiting, it seemed for me. As the King walked to the lift, he motioned me to walk beside him. I stopped at the lift, but he nodded me into that as well, then nodded me out upstairs. The dinner table was set and gleaming. The staff were poised and when we entered, pre-dinner drinks were swept in arcs under noses and into hands.

'You must stay for dinner,' muttered His Highness, in that slight, musical, but guttural, accent of his. I could feel *and* see the freeze among the big BBC nobs around me. I tried to say that my taxi was waiting; tried to indicate that he was putting my life, if not my whole career, at risk. No matter what I thought of, it would have been *lèse-majesté*. Somehow a chair was found and somehow, God help us, I found myself sitting at a large table, next to the King. The conversation, for the most part, is a blur. My producer, Leslie Jackson, and other lesser mortals downstairs were obviously not allowed to make contact with me. I hoped to God the taxi-driver would stay.

The big boss man, Kenneth Adam, icily asked me to tell His Majesty about progress in RTE and my position as Chairman. I told him as much as I could think of, and asked him why Jordan hadn't got television yet, although his answer vanished from my mind as the drink continued to flow. Countless glasses of wine later, I asked him if he would consider giving a greeting to Irish Television, which was due to open at the end of the year. He said he would indeed consider it. Suddenly, I noticed the clock. It was five past midnight. Before I could stop myself, I slurred out the information to His Majesty: 'Good Lord, it's my birthday. It's the 19th of December.'

The King stood up. My fate, if it had not been already sealed, now looked irretrievable. He hammered the table for silence, announced that it was my birthday and forced everyone to their feet to wish me a happy one.

Oh, Lord! I thought I'd never get out of the building.

When I did, the fog was thick but, amazingly, my taxi was still there. Somehow the driver made it through the pea-souper to Chiswick. Grainne's worried face was pressed to an upstairs window. She met me at the door.

'What happened?' she said.

'I was having dinner with King Hussein.'

Full marks! Grainne never said a word, just told me to get to bed. At seven o'clock, I woke up, head throbbing and phone ringing. It was King Hussein's aide-de-camp.

A cheerful RAF voice bubbled: 'The King will be delighted to record a greeting for Irish Television, provided you have the cameras here before eleven o'clock, when he must leave for Jordan.'

My stomach dropped. 'Certainly,' I said.

I quickly got Tom Sloan's home number.

'You got me into that last night, Tom,' I said through parched lips. 'Now you get me out of this.'

Such was Tom's respect for his distinguished guest, that he said he would somehow arrange for a camera crew to be at the Dorchester before 11 A.M.

Ninety minutes after that phone call I was sitting with the key members of our television team in Dublin. Just before lunch, I got the news I was dreading: 'King Hussein recorded. Tape will be despatched to you as soon as possible.'

Before we broke for lunch, I told my team the news of King Hussein.

'Very good,' said Michael Barry. But his eyes were so glazed and his face so pale, he clearly didn't mean it. There were murmurs of 'Great', 'Unusual', even, possibly, 'Wonderful'. However, the comment of the day was yet to come. As we headed for the door, Jim McGuinnes fell into step beside me. Without even turning his head, he said: 'Jesus, Chairman, you've cost me every bit of Jewish advertising I've got!'

Well, of course, we could not have King Hussein on his own; so all hell broke loose and our slim resources started stretching out towards Heads of Governments – Adenauer in Germany, Nehru in India . . .

We made that New Year's Eve deadline. But on the big day – a Sunday – a big freeze paralysed Europe and most airports were closed. Many guests coming from all over the world got in before the shut-down; the others – including Grainne and myself – had to travel to Dublin by boat.

Our cabin was freezing and we arrived at Dun Laoghaire at six o'clock in the morning, stiff with cold; Grainne said she was convinced she was going to die of frostbite! Even at that time, and in those conditions, I couldn't imagine Sunday without Mass and although Grainne grumbled because she was a little ragged, we went off in search of a church. She said I probably wanted to pray for the opening, at the Gresham Hotel that evening, to be a success!

Divine help or not, the début of Irish television *was* a success. And it struck me as amusingly ironic that the momentous pictures that evening showed real snow falling on the joyous crowds singing in O'Connell Street. For many months the fringe TV receivers in Ireland had been fuzzy with rather a great deal of electronic snow!

At that inaugural ball, I kept what they call a low profile and rightly left the formal opening speech to Ed Roth: I hadn't got into the venture for television exposure. The hotel was jammed for the launch party. It could have been filled ten times over by those who wanted to be there and those who felt they should have been there. Hand on my heart, I refused to have anything to do with the invitations.

It had been a bruising, exhausting two years. On a tiny monitor, I saw, and barely heard, Cardinal Dalton sending us on our way. I thought I heard him mention my name. What was that? 'He said he thought Eamonn Andrews was on the side of the angels,' Grainne informed me.

I settled for that.

With the job done, I thought that was the end of the road for me. But many of the problems were only beginning and I was pressed to stay.

Edward Roth, however, came to the end of his two-year contract and accepted an offer of a top job with ATV in London – flattering confirmation of our judgement.

Finding a new director-general was now an even tougher job. The shape was there and we needed a dynamo of executive business knowledge to weld the organization into a smooth-running machine. We found the man all right – an exiled Irishman named Kevin McCourt, who had distinguished himself in the field of commerce with the giant Hunter-Douglas Corporation. He accepted our challenge and by the beginning of 1963 was at the helm.

The problems continued – some big, some small, all urgent. A journalists' strike almost closed the station; one of the worst winters for generations held us up for months. And criticism poured in from the most unexpected quarters.

When we were being attacked for something totally unavoidable, Kevin sent me a quotation from Edmund Burke:

> Those who carry on great public schemes must be proof against the worst fatiguing delays, the most mortifying disappointments, the most shocking insults and, worst of all, the presumptuous judgements of the ignorant upon their designs.

The quote gave me a smile when one was needed, whether Burke meant it to be amusing or not.

It wasn't long before I had another odd example of Archbishop McQuaid's intervention; odd because I took it for granted that what I heard was strictly true, although, afterwards, I wondered if there had been some creative, political colouring added. Anyhow, on one of my fairly rare trips to Government Buildings to give an account of myself to the Taoiseach, we finished a fairly amiable conversation with a reference to the good Archbishop himself. Apparently he was most unhappy about two of our successful TV performers – Justin Keating, who talked about farming matters, and Proinsias MacAongusa, who was bilingually covering a multitude of subjects. Lemass did not spell it out, but he gave me the idea that the

Archbishop felt these should be seen and heard no more on the national station because there was much more than just a left-wing slant to their performances.

I was quite shocked. Lemass was quick to soothe me; he was not asking me to do anything, he said – he was merely passing on a message. I said I would have to have much more information before I even thought of doing anything about it; in fact, I felt there was nothing at all I could do, unless the Archbishop made a direct and uncovert approach to us on the subject, or the Taoiseach made a specific request. That was the last I heard of it.

Ironically, when I resigned from RTE, Proinsias MacAongusa wrote a scathing and hurtful article, saying that I had invented my reasons for leaving and had no intention of staying, in any event. I was so incensed by the injustice and the untruth of it that I took legal advice. That wise old solicitor, the late Desmond Collins, listened to counsel's opinion, then told me I clearly had a case against MacAongusa. He added, however, that very few people would have read the obscure paper in which MacAongusa's piece had appeared but legal action would make certain it was seen in every national paper in the country. Enough said.

At the beginning, of course, I didn't need any pressure from Archbishop McQuaid, or anyone else, to know that we needed a chaplain at the station. There are good arguments against the appointment of a chaplain, the best being that it tends to put religion into a cubby-hole, soothes the conscience of the governing body and spikes any number of meddlesome clerics. Anyhow, there was more to be said in favour than against and we ended up with a wonderful Dominican priest named Emanuel Dodd. It was a natural sequence of events, then, to have a Church of Ireland representative and the Reverend Day joined us. Immediately, he was known as 'the man who got even with Dodd' – a play on *The Man Who Got Even With God*, a very popular book in Ireland about an American Trappist monk. At one of the receptions on opening day, I met that delightful character, Archbishop Simms, and told him the joke about his man Day.

'Ah, yes,' he murmured, 'Every Dodd must have his Day!'

Not a man to get fazed easily, Archbishop Simms. Spike Milligan once told how, after a very good lunch in Dublin, he was bounding around Hanna's bookshop when he spotted this character with the Roman collar browsing over a book.

'Bless me, Father,' said Spike, in one of his terrible Irish accents, 'for I'm a Catholic!'

'I'm very relieved to hear it,' said the Reverend, as Spike became aware of the purple beneath the collar of good Archbishop Simms.

The drafting of the Television Bill had very little to do with the Authority, because it was a *fait accompli* by the time they were appointed. There were what amounted to almost furtive discussions with the Committee when Leon O'Brion himself – or some lesser Civil Servant – would bring in sections of the drafting, making it clear that it wasn't really our bailiwick (which it jolly well was), and then snatching the documents away like a shady solicitor who doesn't want you to see too many details above a signature he has asked you to witness. Besides, there was no way we were going to move the subsequently dreaded Section 31, which, then, had little more significance beyond the fact that the Minister could say no to anything at all. So far as I was concerned, it kept a very big stick in the Posts and Telegraphs cupboard at the GPO. Besides which it seemed pretty reasonable that the Minister had to have some power and we were of the belief that public opinion would keep the exercise of that power within the bounds of common sense and fairness.

Questions were being continually asked in Dáil Éireann about television: some of them were constructive, if critical, but, for the most part, it seemed that as soon as politicians realized that any question got newspaper coverage there was no stopping them. We were at once the destroyers of the national heritage, the national music, literature, sport, culture, the enemy of churches, the breaker of families, the weakeners of moral law, the money-grubbers, who buy Mickey Mouse instead of Finn McCool and the adventures of Rambo – had he then existed – over the heroics of Cú Chulainn.

Lemass was wonderful during most of these criticisms, even, and especially, when he agreed with some of them. He'd nod his head and smile and twinkle and mutter something along the lines of: 'Well, I suppose you know what you're doing.' Mind you, he believed that television should, in effect, be an arm of the government; and it must have been most frustrating for someone at my level of unimportance, but momentary power, to disagree so fundamentally with him. It must have been a great relief to Lemass when my friend, bluff old Tod Andrews, succeeded me as chairman and agreed one hundred per cent with him.

I learned one interesting tactic from Lemass: if he had to answer a justified criticism, he invariably asked me if there were any other skeletons, so to speak, in the cupboard; and, if there were, to let him have the lot and lump them all into the one basket, the one answer; it avoided painful moments dragging on and on with supplementary heel-snapping.

The only time he was really annoyed with me was when his second Economic Plan was published and it was rightly and quickly – and detachedly – dealt with on RTE. He sent for me post haste: he was in something of a rage. How dare these so-called experts deal with the plan without them, or, indeed, the nation having had time to think about it? What did they know about it anyway? And why should they presume to criticize something that had been put together by experts who knew a great deal more about running the country? I didn't placate him fully, but he did cool down. I told him it would have been impossible for the station to ignore the Plan, and that the only way to off-set his criticism of hasty thinking on the part of *our* experts was to extend the embargo period to give them time to study it fully. Obviously, the man in the street was not going to take in all the nuances of so important a document, but television just couldn't let it lie there. Lemass huffed and puffed and he said, all right, but, in future, make sure these kind of things are treated with the care and respect they deserve. Certainly, sir.

We remained friends until the day he died: a fine man, who did much for his country; a politician who could be tough without being bitter.

In those sixties days, I have a blurred recollection of being in a small licensed restaurant somewhere round the back of Trinity College in Dublin. It was more a club than a pub; more a man's joint than mixed, with figures hunched conspiratorially over tables, munching, gulping and gossiping. I was with a tough-guy, gravelly-voiced actor who ordered two more drinks after the bar had closed. To my surprise, they came without demur or sleight of hand. I expressed mild, but hopefully sophisticated, surprise.

'It's OK,' growled my companion. 'Charlie's over there.'

'Charlie?'

'Charlie Haughey.'

Charlie was Minister for Justice and still a drinking man (he gave it up in the seventies).

My actor pal and I finished our drinks, paid the bill and left the shadowy hostelry.

'See,' he said, nudging me with an elbow, and indicating a squad car parked discreetly and darkly a few yards down the street.

I have no idea whether Charlie really was inside that restaurant. Indeed, rumours flew around Charlie like moths around a bulb. Which is the reason I'm writing about him, because I was involved in an astonishingly persistent one.

I first became aware of it in the early sixties. Someone came up to me and said: 'I hear you thumped Charlie the other night?'

'And what the hell did I do that for?' I asked, highly amused.

'The way I heard it, he made a pass at your wife.'

The next time I heard it, my informant had had it first-hand from someone who said they were actually present.

'Where did it happen?' I asked. At Charlie's home, I was told.

The next time, it had been witnessed at the Gresham Hotel. And, soon after that, at Jury's, on the other side of the city.

Outside a boxing ring, I've never thumped anyone in my adult life; indeed, anyone who has boxed knows you're more likely to damage your fist than your opponent's head. Nevertheless, I started racking my memory to see if there was any possible area, any possible happening, that might have given rise to a sliver of a story that would tempt the colourful embellishers who reside in my native city.

I could unearth only one clue.

I had visited Charlie's home for the first time, thanks to a Harley Street doctor named Vincent Sullivan, who dreamed of setting up a World Research Hospital which would achieve all sorts of magical medical breakthroughs. He got me on his small, but influential, committee whose task was to find a suitable site with Government backing. Vincent, an Irishman, was on fire with the idea and no disappointment, no setback, deterred him for long. Why not try Ireland? The climate might not be what he'd had in mind at first, but it was mild enough and there were still many beautiful and unspoilt areas left.

A meeting was set up with Sean McEntee, the then Minister of Health, topped off with a cocktail party at Charlie's lavish new home in Grange Road. Charlie then held the all-important post of Minister for Finance, and several important people were due to be there.

He was always a charismatic man who could charm the birds out of the proverbial trees. Women adored him. He had the ability, one was given to understand, to make a woman feel as though she was the only one in the room when he talked to her. His way was to put his arm round them and flatter them. He tried it on with everyone – probably even Mrs Thatcher, Grainne used to say later, when he became Prime Minister.

That evening at Grange Road, Charlie received us personally and graciously, as is his wont. And he did make an innocent pass at Grainne, who was looking particularly fetching. Both she and I would have been somewhat peeved had he not. But it was hardly the sort of pass to warrant a punch on the nose.

The rumour died. That was that, I thought, and forgot about it. I was extremely busy with my own career in London and the very demanding job of Chairman of Irish Television.

But then I got a call from Kevin McCourt, who was now the station's Director-General.

'Can you talk?' he asked. 'Are you alone?'

He was very concerned. He had just had a confidential telephone call from Tony O'Reilly – the famous rugby international, then head of the Irish Sugar Company – who had heard how, *only three nights before*, I'd had a blazing row with you-know-who and had knocked him down – in the lounge of the Hibernian Hotel.

Kevin couldn't believe it when I started to laugh. I don't know if he believed me when I told him the truth. I don't know if O'Reilly did when *he* told *him*. But there it was, back in full force, this time with a version that Charlie had insulted my children. There were hints that someone was trying politically to smear him. It was incredible but not very funny.

Several taxi-drivers told me about it in the years that followed. To those who didn't like Charlie, I was a hero, and I disappointed more than one of them by telling them the story wasn't true. One driver, not allowing me to interrupt, spoke to me with great respect and said how, on a long trip to the south of Ireland with the self-same Charlie, he so resented the orders he was getting, he was tempted to stop the car and do what I had done. I lost my courage then and didn't tell him I hadn't done it at all!

There was one weird side-effect. One Christmas, an outbreak of foot-and-mouth in Britain was so serious that emigrants were asked not to come home for fear of bringing back the disease. Various well-known Irish exiles, such as Dave Allen, made public appeals, but no one asked me. A year later, I met a representative of the Fleet Street agency who'd handled the campaign. Not standing on modesty, I asked him why he had not chased me to help in the appeal.

His reply staggered me: 'The Department in Dublin told me you were *persona non grata*. Something or other about having had a fight with some minister or other.'

And so it rolled unbelievably on. When Charlie became Taoiseach, the rumour took on more serious connotations. One or two newspapers rang me to ask if there was any truth in the story. I let them know quite forcefully that there was not. One newspaper did not ring me – the *News of the World*. You can imagine my reaction when I saw this headline blazing at me: EAMONN HITS PRIME MINISTER.

I wondered how Thames Television would feel about having an

interviewer who went around bopping prime ministers – and realized that I would have to put a stop to the rumour. I had been tempted to sue a newspaper more than once, but had always cooled down and drawn back. This time, I went ahead. After a bit of bluffing and blustering, the *News of the World* settled for a few thousand pounds and an apology in open court.

On the day of the court case we were invited to dinner by Bryan Cowgill, managing director of Thames. It was an informal get-together on a boat he keeps at Teddington for such occasions. The chairman of Chelsea Football Club was there with his wife and, to my happy surprise, Eric Morecambe and Ernie Wise and their wives. Finally, in strolled Sir Larry Lamb and his wife. I remembered that Larry was editorial director of the Murdoch Group that included the *News of the World*. He drifted over, drink in hand, whispered in my ear: 'You cost us about 5,000 quid today,' and drifted on. Not another word was said about it and he chatted up Grainne most of the evening.

Back in Dublin, I rang Charlie: if he liked to come over Sunday morning, with family and friends, I'd get a case or two of champagne to celebrate.

'OK, I'll come,' he said, 'provided it's Dom Perignon!'

It was. And he did.

I bought sixty copies of the 'offending newspaper' and made a carpet out of them from the doorway in.

Charlie, who had recently given his first official interview as Prime Minister, looked at me with those hooded eyes and the unexpectedly innocent-looking smile.

'Guess what the first question was?' he said.

I didn't have to. I had not stopped the rumour, but, at least, I'd slowed it down to a gallop.

19 CLOAK-AND-DAGGER BABY

Although we were happy in the flat at Lancaster Gate, we wanted a house, a place of our own, with a bit of seclusion and a garden. The sort of home I had in mind was a modern one in a wood, with lots and lots of glass, and Eamonn was happy to let me try to find it. Over the years, we must have looked at scores of houses, but they were either too expensive or not what we wanted. In the summer of 1961, however, I came across the house of my dreams. It wasn't in a wood and it didn't have lots of glass, but it did have a garden at the front and half an acre of garden at the back that stretched down to the Thames.

What it also had, sadly, was a price tag of £20,000 – around £8,000 more than our limit. Eamonn was horrified and said we couldn't afford it. But he fell in love with the house the moment he saw it and told me to ask our accountant if we should buy it. The accountant thought we were mad, but said, 'Go ahead', and on 29 September we became the proud owners of 61 Hartington Road, Chiswick, in West London.

Unfortunately, Eamonn was away on that day and our housekeeper Alice Szonn, Quiz and I moved in without him. The celebration had to wait until the next day. I immediately threw myself into the taxing, but immensely rewarding, task of turning the house of our dreams into a home, and as our tenth wedding anniversary approached, I had it just the way we wanted it.

We were sitting chatting one night when Eamonn brought up a subject that had been on our minds more than ever since buying the house – children.

Both of us were disappointed that a baby hadn't come along in ten years. We had been for all sorts of separate tests and were told there was no reason why we shouldn't have children; but it was something that just didn't happen. Throughout all those years, we kept hoping – and praying. A relative sent me a novena to St Jude, the patron saint of hopeless causes, and night after night I prayed to him that we would be blessed with a child. Eamonn was devoted to Our Lady and prayed to her night after night. But, sadly, no one was hearing our prayers. I was worried for Eamonn, although tests had shown that there was nothing wrong with him. We kept hoping, but nothing happened, and as the months rolled into years we didn't talk about it any more and kept our sadness and disappointment to ourselves and just hoped, privately, for a miracle.

Shortly after moving into the house, however, it seemed pretty clear there were not going to be any miracles and Eamonn brought up the subject of adoption. I was not at all sure about it. Eamonn was very keen, and seemed very well informed about how to go about it. Later, I discovered why. We talked it through and I said it was such a huge decision, I needed time on my own to think about all it would entail.

It was Fate that gave me that time. On the night we should have been celebrating our anniversary, Eamonn had to go to a BBC dinner and I spent the night alone in the house. I had plenty of time to think. I thought back over all that we'd done in the ten years we'd been married, and I had to be honest: Eamonn and I were set in our ways and, frankly, selfish with each other; we loved travelling and, with no ties, were free to do anything, go anywhere, whenever we wanted; a baby would make a drastic change to our lives and I wasn't sure I wanted that. I thought long and hard that anniversary night and, in the end, I decided that if Eamonn wanted children so much it would be selfish of me not to agree. When we next talked about it, I said: 'Darling, if it's what you really want, let's go ahead and adopt.'

Before I could blink, Eamonn had invited a priest to dinner and we were sitting at a table talking about what it would all entail – and whether we wanted a boy or girl. Suddenly it dawned on me that Eamonn had been talking to this priest and other people about adoption behind my back, in the hope of persuading me.

Eamonn didn't mind which sex our adopted baby was, so he allowed me to have my way, not only with a girl, but also the name we gave her. I chose Emma after one of my best friends at school. I've always loved that name.

On the day we were due to collect her, Eamonn was doing the current affairs programme, Today, so I went with my sister, Susan, who was on holiday from America.

It was a nerve-tingling emotional moment and I admit I was terrified of that tiny baby when I held her for the first time. On the way home, I told our driver to stop, and I changed Emma into a new white dress and bonnet I'd bought. I wanted her to look her prettiest for her Daddy.

Eamonn got away from the studios as fast as he could that evening. As he came into the living room, I picked Emma up and put her gently into his arms. He stood there, still with his overcoat on, looking down at her lovingly. Then he looked at me and grinned and I could see the tears of happiness filling his eyes. I put my arm round him as I felt my own tears coming. Then Susan started to cry. It was a big moment for all of us.

Emma saved her own tears for night-time: they started the moment we went to bed and didn't stop all night. She had colic and cried every night for months. I got up to see to her because Eamonn needed his sleep, but he was never a good sleeper and I'm sure he went to work a little ragged in those days. There must have been some tension between us, but neither of us admitted to it: that would have been disloyal to Emma.

We were totally engrossed in that child. We doted on her, unashamedly. She was everything we'd ever wanted, and when she did something particularly amusing we would find ourselves looking up and catching each other's eye, with no words necessary to show how happy we were.

Eamonn would hurry home in the evenings: he wanted to see Emma have her bath, not hear about it from me; he wanted to say goodnight, not just be remembered as a sort of disembodied benediction; and he even changed her nappy. He was in a tense, worrying business, but he would come in and take Emma on his knee, and watch her wiggle and giggle, and say she was better than any tranquillizer. I had only to look at the joy she brought to his face to know that adoption had been the right decision.

He was a little put out, of course, that suddenly Emma, not he, was the centre of attraction. In the past, if he was going out alone to a dinner or some other formal function, I would lay his suit out, with a handkerchief in the top pocket, and his patent shoes and black socks.

Now, with a baby to look after, I didn't have time for such pampering, and Eamonn would march about the house, getting his things together himself, tutting: 'Things have changed around here.'

'You're right, they have,' I would say.

Emma was a cloak-and-dagger baby. I was longing to take her out in her pram, to show her off in all her pretty new clothes, but I couldn't. She was not legally ours yet and, if someone told the press that TV celebrity Eamonn Andrews had a new-born baby, Emma's natural mother might put two and two together and try to claim her back. In the event, the Daily Express did find out and a *reporter spent days on our doorstep trying to get us to give him a scoop; he even tried to open the door of our moving car to ask questions. I'll always be grateful to the editor of the day because he could have run a story, but chose not to.*

Those six months were very tense, but finally the natural mother signed the necessary papers, and early one morning, I went to a local magistrates' court to collect the documents that made Emma officially ours. It was a magical moment I will never forget.

The same day, Eamonn and I went to a Catholic church in Chiswick High Road for Emma's dedication, and then we organized an intimate party for all our close friends who had been guarding our secret so loyally for so long. We didn't invite any newspapers, but did a story with pictures later, when our pride and joy could not be taken from us.

Eamonn the proud father could not wait to show off Emma to other friends back home in Ireland, so we rented a house in the village of Howth, just outside Dublin, and threw a big garden party.

The star of the show, however, was less than ecstatic about making her début on her parents' home ground: she was in the soundest of sleeps and refused to wake up for ages. We were desperate to show her off, but forced ourselves not to rouse her in case she cried her way through the introductions. It was worth the wait. Emma woke up with a huge smile and a happy gurgle and behaved beautifully all day. We were so, so proud of her.

For years, I had been pestering Ronnie Waldman to let me do a late-night talk show along the lines of those in the States which had cleared the way for King Johnny Carson to become an arrogant, smiling, talking millionaire. At one stage, Ronnie told me – in all seriousness – that it would not be politic to have such a late-night show in Britain as it might keep the work-force up so late at night they would not clock in the next morning! Two better reasons, of course, were the runaway success of *What's My Line?* and *This is Your Life*. Since, in addition to these, I was hosting *Crackerjack* and *Playbox*, the point was easily made that it would be impossible to do yet another programme, and ridiculous to cancel such winners in favour of the unknown.

The opportunity to do a chat show, however, did come – in a most unexpected way. First, Donald Baverstock decided to drop *What's My Line?* without warning or consultation. Till then, I had been sailing along happily with the BBC. I had got to know their ways and their prejudices; I knew most of their unspoken rules, and I liked most of the people I worked with, from stage staff to directors. The atmosphere was good, possibly too comfortable: a creeping, but happy, paralysis that seems to affect all organizations where the dreaded profit motive doesn't seem to apply; where no one worries about pencils or paperclips or trips to far-away places that take three weeks, not three days.

Baverstock wasn't even aware that Teddy Sommerfield had put a clause in my contract, calling for consultation or compensatory payment in default. Baverstock probably would not have cared anyway. And it was cold comfort to me, since I have always put programmes way ahead of the rewards that go with them. This is not some piece of pious artistic junk; it is just a matter of commonsense. If you're going to survive, the viewer doesn't care what you are paid, but what you do. Somewhat like a friend of mine who always tries to restrain me on the racecourse by pointing out that it really is better to have a winner at two-to-one on, than a loser at a hundred to one. Anyhow, Baverstock's ploy made me uneasy. There were lots of changes happening at the top in the BBC and, at last, they were becoming aware of the competition threatened by the hungry boys at ITV.

The 1964 summer break was coming up when I was asked to go to Television Centre to discuss the future with Baverstock, the steely-eyed Michael Peacock and Steward Hood, the droll Scot I had known from his days as news editor at Broadcasting House. I had a feeling I wasn't going to enjoy the meeting and I was right. After the usual shadow-boxing, they came to the point: they thought it was time to rest *This is Your Life*. I was very annoyed and felt the only reason I was being told at all was because I had kicked up a fuss about the other programme.

For the first time, I began to have serious thoughts about leaving the Corporation. What a comfort we now had ITV. However, I chided myself, silently, not to be hasty and to remember how much I enjoyed the whole ambience of the BBC, and how it had become so much part of my world, even if I had not proportionately become a part of its.

Perhaps they would have something interesting to offer. I waited. I liked Stewart Hood immensely; he was an off-beat character, but, I felt, thoughtful, sincere. Bouncing Baverstock I enjoyed hugely, but felt no warmth from him; one sensed an ego as big and bleak as a Welsh mountain. Michael Peacock I never did understand; a man of recognized talent, he was distant, suspicious and somehow patronizing.

Baverstock switched on the charm. Of course, they would give me a new contract. Of course, I would be guaranteed some presumably enormous – by BBC standards – sum of money. And, of course, they would think up wonderful programmes for me.

I told them I *had* two wonderful programmes, both of which were now being cancelled; and that I was interested only in the programmes they had to offer, not in the money. They probably did not believe me about the money, but I never did or did not do a programme because of the price tag attached to it. I always said I would like to do this or that, then let my agent worry about the money.

'We have lots of ideas that would take you around the country and give you some fun as well,' Baverstock said. He had one idea, for instance, of taking a huge auditorium in Cardiff and have Huw Weldon one side of the stage and me the other, and rivet the audience. Ho, ho, ho. Everybody chortled, but, devoted fan as I was of Huw – later Sir Huw – I couldn't for the life of me see what we could do together.

There was nothing more practical suggested. Clearly, the object of the exercise was (a) to say they were not going to do *This is Your Life*; and (b) to offer me a three- or five-year contract. I repeated that programmes were all that mattered to me and that I would think it all over.

At this time, one of the BBC's executive stars, Brian Tesler, had been lured to ABC Television, the weekend contractors, as Programme Controller, and Teddy Sommerfield had gently been sounding him out about the possibilities, should I ever consider leaving the BBC. Brian, an old pal of mine, expressed a very heartening interest, because the then ITA considered ITV's weekend sport a disgrace and he was under pressure to do something to improve it. He told Teddy he was planning a Saturday show to be called *World of Sport*, but needed a presenter of stature, authority and appeal to give it any chance of success. Who better than Eamonn Andrews? he said. I was flattered, particularly when Brian threw in the bait of my own live weekly chat show, and I left that meeting with the BBC bosses in a daze, knowing deep down that I would not be going back.

The negotiations for my defection were carried out like some Le Carré spy plot. To ensure absolute secrecy, Brian would arrange to meet Teddy and me in a leafy London square and talk through the financial details in the back of a huge black Mercedes with tinted windows. When I shook off the nostalgia and annoyance and the fear of the freelance, I recognized Tesler's offer for what it was: a very exciting and challenging moment in my career. And, in the summer of 1964, I was being photographed with Brian and ABC's managing director, Howard Thomas, having signed a three-year contract.

What a year that was! Grainne and I adopted our second child, a boy we named Fergal . . . and I even received a Papal Knighthood for services to charity.

In fact, I was to do *World of Sport* for twelve gloriously happy years, and one person who was responsible for making them so enjoyable was the editor, John Bromley, who went on to become head of ITV Sport. How worried was young John that August morning when he walked through the gates of Teddington Studios into, for him, the unknown world of television. He had been a Fleet Street sports reporter and the shock to the system was dramatic. Setting up *World of Sport* was no fun: there were rows about facilities, about content, about staff – about almost everything – and John admitted to me that he feared he had made a mistake, and that he should get back into the comparatively sane world of newspapers before it was too late.

He was to say later that it was my kindness, patience and gentle cajoling that persuaded him to stay in the business; I was his TV 'guru' and if it had not been for me he would not be enjoying the sporting life of television. Certainly we would meet at midday every Friday at my Chiswick home and talk through the problems he felt he was having putting the show together. But gentle encouragement was all he needed. One did not need to be a genius to see that he had the drive, the ability and the talent to become just what he did – one of the most dynamic, discerning and likeable operators in the world of television. For my part, I was delighted to help launch such an illustrious career, as well as form a deep, lasting friendship.

Throughout my life I had always tried never to look back or go back. When I left the Hibernian Insurance Company I never stepped across the door again. I didn't try to analyse it, but it was probably a mixture of shyness and fear of not being wanted again; and of trying to avoid sentimental hurt.

I wasn't going back to the huge BBC Television Centre either. I'd never really warmed to its immobile vastness and I didn't know if I'd be welcome there, since many of my colleagues must have suspected I'd changed channels for filthy lucre and nothing else.

Soon after starting on *World of Sport*, one of my regular Chiswick minicabs arrived to take me to the Teddington studios. Throughout the journey I was reading a script and some research material and was totally absorbed. Suddenly I heard the driver announce: 'Here we are, sir.' I was about to get out when I realized where he had taken me – BBC Television Centre!

'Drive on,' I hissed. 'Wrong studios!'

The world of Independent Television was tougher and tighter – a world with no cosy, lazy corridors. The first meeting for the *Eamonn Andrews Show* took place in ABC's administrative offices in Hanover Square, in a makeshift sort of room, with borrowed chairs around a reasonable-sized conference table. A grizzled, but young, bearded red-headed Canadian with a ready smile balanced by cold blue eyes was executive producer, representing the company at the early meetings. His name was Lloyd Shirley, who later became a luminary in Euston Films. The producer in charge was a former Fleet Street photographer, Malcolm Morris, who was brimful of ideas and eager to tackle his first major TV assignment. Renée Bloomstein was secretary and Jeanne Lachard researcher. And then there were Roy Bottomley and Tom Brennand, two characters from Oldham, down to try their luck in the hostile South. They were described as writers, but there was comparatively little writing to be done, only introductory links and little more. They were mainly ideas people, who would devise ploys to catch the eye and ear of the viewer, help to balance the programme and generally niggle at the bits and pieces to get the best overall effect.

Tom, hunched and growling over the table, gave most people who thought they had a 'good idea' a pretty tough time. His partner had that other quality essential to good television, never mind life itself: bubbling, bright-eyed, undefeatable optimism. They were a formidable pair, with a thoroughness and doggedness essential for pushing ideas through.

At an early meeting, Tom wasn't happy about something and was beefing away, head swinging from one side to the other. Lloyd Shirley stopped him in mid-sentence with his soft, but deadly, Canadian drawl: 'Tom, if you wanna bleed, go out to the toilet and do it there!'

I had left the BBC all right.

It was a harder, headier, more dangerous atmosphere than at the

BBC. One felt people could be fired for doing a bad programme, whereas at Television Centre the most that would happen would be a belt of a memo, or a long period of contemplation in your office away from the studios.

Two other things I noticed at ABC: I was meeting more Jewish people who seemed to have a special flair for the Arts, and for entertainment in particular; and there were more women – seemingly fragile creatures, many of them with university degrees, who were capable of battering open the most tightly closed door and afraid of no one when it came to berating the high and the mighty. And they all seemed to be freelances, living from one series to another, confident that their talents would keep them in demand.

When Malcolm Morris was lured away by a plumb executive post with Tyne Tees Television, I had two other producers: the dizzily flamboyant Bryan Izzard, and Gordon Reece, a fascinating little character with rimmed glasses, and impeccably coiffured hair and a plummy rolling upper-class English accent that must have sounded like a nail on a glass to Tom and Roy. Gordon, who exuded charm and warmth would arrive smoking a cigar almost as tall as himself; I felt that if the mortgage was overdue, and he was down to his last five-pound note, Gordon would use it to light the next cigar. They always seemed to be available from a huge box I imagined must have ben part of a legacy from some well-heeled officer uncle in the Indian Army. Gordon probably felt I supported Tom and Roy too often against him; and it is always difficult joining a team that is already started. Anyhow, he did just the one season with us and, some years later, was credited as 'the man who gave Mrs Margaret Thatcher her television election-winning image'.

The team would have two morning meetings at my home: one in mid-week, to make hopeful decisions about the content for the following Sunday; and the second one on Sunday morning, to put the final touches for that night's show. One young researcher called Andy Allan came straight from university, hoping to make a go of it in television.

He was so impressive we signed him up at once. But when he was due to attend his first meeting there was no sign of him. That was the end of it, as far as I was concerned; the programme couldn't afford a cavalier approach. I prepared a little speech, telling him he was being fired: I felt the lesson might do him some good.

An hour and a half later Andy came loping along the path. And before I could utter one word of my speech, he said: 'Remember, you asked me to investigate that book on yoga?'

We all nodded.

'Well,' said Andy. 'I took it out late last night because I knew you would want to know about it. I read this section on self-hypnosis. You know, it works. I put myself to sleep, and came to just half an hour ago.'

It was the most outrageous ploy I'd heard and he stayed with the show. Now, he is Managing Director of Yorkshire Television.

There are some things in show business nobody can teach you. No one can teach you, for instance, to be a good disc jockey, a really good sports commentator or a talk show host. I guess I made all the mistakes on the *Eamonn Andrews Show*: telling jokes I didn't believe in; reading scripts when I should have been free-wheeling; keeping to a question line when I should have taken off into the unknown; listening to my next question instead of the current answer; forgetting that nine out of ten guests are more nervous than their host.

Gradually, it became more fun, more relaxed. The super Teddington Studios, the eager audience, the swish, rich sound of Bob Sharples and his orchestra, the whole team concentrating on that one world of the show itself, as if nothing else mattered outside.

It is part of the magic and part of the danger of show business. It is one of the reasons why you have so many crazy film actors and actresses around; why marriages go bust and restaurants are wrecked. The unreal world has for them become the real world.

We didn't go quite that far on the *Eamonn Andrews Show*. And if we *were* ever in danger of going too far, the press were always ready to give me a kick up the other end to remind me I was just one of them. Nevertheless, it was an exciting and separate world and some of the most famous names in the outside world were knocking on the door to get on the show. Of course, some wouldn't come on for love or money.

Around this time, there was one moment when I would have loved to have been a fly on the wall. My mother, who, remember, thought I was the best thing since two thousand years ago, was staying with us for a few weeks. She and Grainne went shopping and ended up for lunch in a colourful little restaurant off Oxford Street called The Old Vienna. The tables were very close together and Grainne realized they were sitting next to a charming, non-malicious journalist, Barry Norman, who had recently interviewed us for his *Daily Mail* column. His guests that day were that moody song-writer Lionel Bart and his agent.

The two ladies pricked up their ears when they heard Barry say: 'You've never been on the *Eamonn Andrews Show*, have you?'

'Nah,' said Bart.

'He's been asked several times,' said the agent. 'But always refused.'

'What does Andrews know about life?' asked Bart, dismissively. 'What does he know about anythin', except his wife and kids. He don't go anywhere.'

With my mother fingering the butter knife, Grainne decided to finish lunch early. But she could not resist pointedly bidding Barry good afternoon as they left. Barry blushed. It was a good sign. Anybody who could still blush in our business can't be half bad.

The *Eamonn Andrews Show* hit the air live at five past eleven on Sunday 1 October 1964. My first guests were Sugar Ray Robinson, that aristocrat of the boxing ring, Willie Rushton, Terry Thomas and the svelte actress, Honor Blackman. We had a group called the Nocturnes and Sandie Shaw, pop singer, who was climbing up the charts with no shoes. The show was well-received, except for a few pressmen who felt I'd spent too long talking to Honor about her fear of spiders.

Sugar Ray was a prince among fighters, with a style more balletic than pugilistic. Towards the end of his career, he boxed Britain's Terry Downes, an ex-Marine world champion and roustabout Cockney.

That night at Wembley, Sugar Ray was surrounded in his corner by more seconds than he could probably afford, and had what looked like oxygen supplied to him between rounds.

'Blimey,' said Terry from the opposite corner, 'it's like boxing in *Emergency Ward Ten*.'

Afterwards in promoter Harry Levene's hospitality room, I met the late Godfrey Wynn, the eminent writer who had been taken to his first professional fight by the then editor of the *Daily Express*, Bob Edwards. The whole setting seemed out of joint for the tennis-playing Godfrey. I asked him if he had enjoyed the experience.

'Yes, indeed,' enthused Godfrey. 'Sugar Ray Robinson was wonderful, wasn't he? But who was that other fellow who looked as if he had just rushed in off a building site?' It was a gem I always treasured.

For the next few weeks my chat show went smoothly enough. But it was not long before the balloon went up, however, and it would be headlines all the way. The show that did it was one on which we had cricketer Freddie Trueman, actress Diana Dors and comedian Jimmy Edwards as guests. Four days before, Trueman had arrived back in the country following a tour of Australia with Yorkshire. Seemingly without contacting his wife, Enid, he went on to Jersey, and, on the morning of our show, some papers hinted that his marriage was on the rocks.

On the show, I introduced Freddie, then turned to Diana and said: 'Di, have you anything you would like to say to Freddie on his return from Australia?'

The blonde bombshell barely batted an eyelid. 'Yes,' she said. 'When are you going to ring your wife?'

Freddie let fly along the lines that it was 'nowt to do with thee' . . . and we were in the headlines with: FIERY FRED SKITTLES THE GOSSIPS.

The critics claimed Jimmy Edwards made me blush with some of his heavy-lidded *doubles entendres* and, without being immediately aware of it, I was being built up as a very shockable character who shouldn't really be asked to mix with such horrible guests. The inevitable side-effect, of course, was that many a guest shouted the equivalent of 'Knickers', possibly in the hope that I would rush off in horror, but more in the stone cold certainty that it would make the headlines.

I was often told that I should exercise more discipline, more authority. Later, ABC began to lose its nerve, lest any action on the show should jeopardize their position in the re-allocation of television licences due for consideration by the Independent Television Authority.

A clincher came when that extraordinary, ambitious, single-minded and talented actor Laurence Harvey came on. He was giving a swaggering performance in *Camelot* and was full of confident charm. Off-stage, Larry fancied himself as a raconteur, a story-teller of droll, captivating talent and, on air, he said he wanted to tell a story. I was wary enough to head him off, but he did something no one had ever done before: he got out of his chair, walked over to the orchestra and called a camera towards him.

I couldn't abandon my other guests, Harry H. Corbett, of *Steptoe and Son*, and Petula Clark among them; and even if I could, I had no hope of getting close enough fast enough to do anything about it. Harvey told the most tasteless joke about a camel and the Foreign Legion – and jammed the switchboard.

I was surprised, because I would have judged Harvey too clever to have misjudged his audience. Anyhow, all hell broke loose and, as a direct consequence, it was decided that, in future, the show would be recorded an hour or so earlier so that there would be a chance to edit or bleep. I was greatly disappointed; I love live television and I didn't believe it when I was told viewers didn't know the difference.

The first of the taped shows had the famous photographer David Bailey on board. I can't remember who else was there, but I do remember David uttering the immortal line: 'I think that's a load of crap.'

The building trembled. The bleeper was applied. When the show went out, however, the bleep cropped up in the wrong place and the nation heard the offending word, which was followed, a few seconds later, by a bleep. Naturally, viewers assumed that since 'crap' had stayed in, David must have been guilty of a much more heinous offence at the point of the bleep.

We had another run-in with the bleeping concept while talking about drugs with the lovely, lonely, ill-starred Marianne Faithfull and the portly, silver-tongued Lord Boothby, an old friend of mine.

Boothby admitted, as only he could, that he had tried pot and found it boring and useless. Malcolm Morris and I had a raging battle that night, but the bosses supported Malcolm and Boothby's confession disappeared.

No talk show is complete, of course, without an occasional visit from Spike Milligan. And no talk show host should ever agree to it without checking with his doctor that his heart is sound and blood pressure more or less normal. For there is no way one can know what Spike is going to do, or not do. Fortunately, he is a lovable rogue and you forgive him almost anything.

He made one dreadful appearance for me in a chat show from the Sportsman Club in London: he talked all sorts of gibberish, mostly about putting the Pope on the moon and to keep taking the tablets. I was annoyed and when we came off the air I told him so. He looked me straight in the eye and said he thought he'd been chatting during the commercial break. Believe it or not, I believed him.

He gets up to all sorts of things, such as locking himself in his room and sending a telegram to his wife downstairs, telling her what he wants for lunch. He played one beautiful straight-faced trick on me. One morning he rang up my secretary and dictated a letter to me in my time, on my paper, then asked her to type it and sign it per pro Spike and deliver it to me across my own hall.

Spike gave us a big problem – although he didn't know it – with the comedian Woody Allen, who made his first British appearance on the *Eamonn Andrews Show*. Woody agreed to do the show on one condition: he was the only comedian on it. This was not a problem, since the balance of the show usually required only one recognized comedian anyway. But at the last minute a guest dropped out and we had to find a replacement. We had bitten the dust with several much-heralded Americans and couldn't take the chance that Woody would fill out the extra time.

At that time Spike was appearing, very successfully, in a play called *Son of Oblomov* – a straight play given the zany Milligan touch.

The day before the show, Woody rang to see if there had been any changes. He was told somebody had dropped out, and that an actor called Milligan, who was appearing in a Russian play, had been brought in. Woody had no fears; straight actors, one imagined, he could eat before breakfast.

Woody was already on the set when Spike came on; he was wearing a floppy hat he wore in the play and proceeded to lay about Woody with ad libs and slightly acid humour.

After the show Woody was none too pleased, but bore no grudges. He took a bit of tuning into that night, but, for those who got on his wavelength, he was devastatingly funny, acidly witty and fast as light. He should have stayed that way, perhaps, instead of becoming an actor with a message!

As you can imagine, there were a few heart-stopping moments.

The Dubliners and the late, great, hell-raising American actor Lee Marvin, for example, aged me a year or so one night. For all the impression you might have that some of the Dubliners drink the Liffey dry from time to time – the Guinness Liffey, that is – they are a truly professional group. Nevertheless, there is an excellent pub close to the studios, and I was slightly nervous, particularly since Marvin hadn't exactly been depriving himself of nourishment.

I got on with the show, hoping for the best. Unfortunately, the little waiting room behind my set was far from soundproof and as I talked with my opening guest, I could hear one of the Dubliners and Marvin booming in deep conversation. One sentence came over clearly and struck terror into my heart: 'Why don't we go next door and have a pint?'

I could feel the show dropping around my ankles. I hit the commercial break as fast as I could. I got the Dubliners assembled to open the second part. Then I ordered some sustenance and armlock to be brought down for Mr Marvin. It was quite a night.

Shirley Bassey gave me the same feeling of dread another time. She is a pretty temperamental lady at the best of times; artists who give so much of themselves with such intensity usually are. With her husband, Kenneth Hume, adding fuel to the rocket it was a case of . . . outer space here I come!

Hume said he wasn't happy with the sound balance in the studio. Nothing Bob Sharples or the sound engineer did pleased him or her. Shirley went back to the hospitality room, and literally minutes before the show started decided she wasn't going on. Worse, she told a fellow guest, the American actor, James Garner, that she was not appearing because everything was second class.

In a grandiose and noble gesture, Mr Garner said: 'If you're not going on little lady, then I won't either.'

Pandemonium! No amount of pleading, it seemed, would make them change their minds. The show was falling down around us. The next day's headlines filled my mind.

Finally, just when everyone was at desperation point and tempers were boiling, Tom Clegg, the director, got down on his knees to Shirley and somehow, miraculously, made her relent. Garner followed suit and the show was saved. Just.

There was some sort of crisis most weeks, but we had our moments of triumph and one of the nights I treasured involved that great boxer, Muhammad Ali, who became something of a friend of mine. I first met him when, as Cassius Clay, he won the Olympic title in Rome. It took me a long time to learn to call him Muhammad Ali and when he came on the show he publicly rebuked me for making the mistake, not once but twice. He balled a fist, but, needless to say, never threw it.

On that show, I came to realize just how fast a talker he was. An invitation to appear on the show had been sent to his dressing-room at Arsenal's football ground after he'd beaten Henry Cooper for the second time a few nights before. I wasn't at all sure he would remember to turn up. But he did, and joined some astonishing competition in the persons of Lucille Ball, Noel Coward and Dudley Moore.

Ali dominated the show; admittedly, it was by way of being a no-contest and the Master smiled his Buddha-like smile as if he were presenting his own protégé. Ali was in bouncing form and came up with a classic I never tire of repeating. For the first time, I had got from him the origin of his famous claim: 'I'm the greatest.' He had copied it from a home-town wrestler, thinking how well it suited his own dreams to become a champion. I argued that he had achieved everything and didn't need to go around shouting 'I'm the greatest' any more. And I reminded him he had even painted out the one blemish inflicted on him by Cooper who had knocked him down the first time they fought. Fresh from his latest victory, would Ali stop irritating people with this brash and now unnecessary claim?

He pondered the question for a moment.

'Well,' he said, finally. 'I guess I'll keep on saying I'm the greatest – but more modestly!'

He brought the house down.

I was hugely flattered when I was told how Muhammad used to react when meeting British visitors in the United States while at the peak of his career.

'How is Henry Cooper?' he would yell. 'And how is Eamonn Andrews?' Being bracketed with Henry Cooper was an added bonus, not the least diminished by realizing that, once Ali got any reaction, he would repeat the names, parrot-style, for as long as there was any mileage in them.

My cup of ego balm overflowed when I discovered that on a well-publicized BBC Television feature about the champion, on which they had spent oceans of money, Ali kept shouting messages to me – a form of televisual sacrilege, since I was working for a rival channel. I never got around to asking my old friend Harry Carpenter, that most meticulous of broadcasting journalists, why those greetings never made it to the screen.

The Eamonn Andrews Show often frightened me. Many critics said it frightened the life out of them, too. But the fact is it would have run for many more years had the ITA not changed the style of contracts so that ABC died. Thames Television was born, and I became a weekday man instead of a weekend one. I loved a cartoon at the time, showing two old gents chatting in front of a newspaper poster which read – BRITAIN CAN TAKE IT – with a caption underneath: *Eamonn Andrews Show* to run three times a week.

I seldom met my guests beforehand. I wasn't sure that was a good idea, but it was felt a pre-broadcast chat might destroy what we hoped was the spontaneity of the show by, perhaps, going over the same ground twice.

It was interesting to note that fear struck at even the mightiest. Maybe fear is a strong word, but it is more than just nerves. Whatever it was didn't always show itself as such. I began to recognize it in bad-tempered demands for this, that and the other: more light, less light, make-up change, water, whisky, telephone. Aggressiveness. Hearti-ness. Sullenness.

I got a great kick then – and years later – noting the people whose manners improved when the programme was over. I recognized that nerves or fear or whatever had, once again, played their part and forgave them everything that went beforehand.

One of the most bizarre things on that late-night show concerned the extraordinary, contradictory and talented ex-diplomat, ex-politician, and university lecturer, Conor Cruise O'Brien.

The programme appeared under the banner of the Philip Jones empire, known as Light Entertainment Department. But that did not preclude moments of seriousness. One weekend, we were playing the usual jigsaw game of trying to put the pieces together, to balance talk with music, when one of the researchers said a literary agent had been on to suggest a suitable guest might be O'Brien, who had just published a very serious book about the United Nations.

I had never met him, but knew enough to realize that, apart from the book, he had an interesting tale to tell, not least of all concerning the late-lamented US Secretary Dag Hammarskjöld, who had been killed in a plane crash.

'Why not?' I said. 'It'll be something different.'

There was not much time to read the book, but I had a brave try, although it was heavy going. Came Sunday night. No sign of Conor. It was approaching air time and the guests and I assembled behind the set as the orchestra got ready to sweep us on screen with music. Just then, Conor arrived, puffing, and apologetic; he had been delayed at a dinner party. I shook hands with the good don, noting that he did not seem the most amiable of characters. His eyes began to expand – or so it seemed. He looked as if he had seen a ghost. I followed his gaze. He was staring at one of the guests, Arthur Askey, the diminutive comedian, who was wearing a ludicrously funny hat and over-long scarf.

'Is this a light programme?' Conor wanted to know, his voice hoarse.

I pretended to mishear.

'Not very late. We'll be off the air before midnight and you'll be last on, which will give us the chance to discuss your book separately and seriously. It's very interesting.'

I had added the platitudinous bit as I saw his eyes continuing to extend and widen. Then I was on. First commercial break over and I was heading, as we talked, towards the second, after which I'd be introducing my author. Suddenly, my eye was caught by the floor manager. He was holding a piece of cardboard above his head. I read it and felt the familiar tingle of panic.

It said: NO O'BRIEN.

Security was very tight at Teddington, but O'Brien had fled, presumably terrified, past all the guards and into the night. It was several years before I saw him again.

At the time, I burned with indignation, and I wrote to him, bitterly accusing him of not having played the game, or some such fairly fatuous remark. He replied, briefly and snootily, saying that since he wasn't part of my game he didn't have to play to my rules.

He went on to become a very courageous politician and, years later, I interviewed him on the *Today* current affairs programme. Remarkable how politics can change a man; how the pursuit of votes can produce infinite charm.

'I shan't run away this evening,' he said. And we both laughed – fairly heartily.

Early in the seventies, when Eamonn was doing both This is Your Life and the Today show, we decided to extend our home in Portmarnock, which was ideally situated near the sea, golf course and airport. It was a thirty-year-old, single-storey, flat-roofed building, perched on the edge of a disused stone quarry. Dublin architect Sam Stephenson's first reaction was to demolish the existing house and start from scratch, but this proved unnecessary and we ended up including the house in a huge extension, with a two-storey addition in the old quarry.

Sam found the old rock face of the quarry the most interesting feature of the site, and felt the house should integrate with it by descending in several levels to the quarry floor, which became a semi-enclosed garden. A new swimming pool and waterfall from the rock face gave the garden unusual features. Much to Eamonn's delight, Sam designed a circular window, glazed with a bubble dome, which gives a spectacular view of the garden from Eamonn's study. In 1978, House and Garden magazine said this must be 'one of the most dramatic vistas open to any house-owners in Ireland'.

Certainly it was our ideal home – the house of our dreams – and Eamonn could not wait to get back to it and us, particularly as our latest addition, Niamh, was a cheeky rough-and-tumbling three-year-old who couldn't wait to leap into her Daddy's arms and listen to the latest tale of Eamonn's creation, Larry the Leprechaun.

Those weekends were wonderful and the children and I looked forward to them with a passion. He always said it was like a holiday, returning to Dublin on Thursday after three days in London; and, in a way, it was for us, too. While he was away, I ran a little dressmaking business at home, but this had to stop when Eamonn arrived back: he was very supportive because he knew I enjoyed it, but he was somewhat bored by it, really; and he certainly hated it encroaching on our time together. In the end, we compromised: I worked while he was in London and put away the needle and thread on Thursday morning to dedicate the weekend to whatever he wanted to do.

Understandably, he did not want to do much more than just be with us.

After the pressures of This is Your Life, *and whatever else he was doing, he just wanted to relax in the company of loved ones, who were not going to make demands on him. This does not mean he flew in, and sat around doing nothing until it was time to fly off again. Oh, no: although those weekends were like a holiday, he tried to cram in as much as possible, and that meant taking me out, making up for lost time with the children, pottering around in his garden, playing golf, cooking for the family and entertaining close friends.*

He felt life was precious, and wanted to be doing things most of the time he was awake. Even in his leisure time, he was a workaholic.

Having such a hectic schedule in London, Eamonn might have been forgiven for just thinking of himself; but nothing was further from the truth. Emma, Fergal and Niamh – as well as me, I hope! – were seldom off his mind, and when he walked through the door, his heavy 'Gladstone' bag would be weighed down with gifts for all of us, plus two bottles of duty-free champagne. He was a caring husband and father, and knew what interested us; and he would always bring home cuttings from newspapers and magazines on subjects close to our hearts. If one of us had been raving about a book review, for instance, you could bet your life Eamonn would have bought the book as a present. When the children were younger, I suppose it was like Christmas Day every Thursday. But if Eamonn sounds like Santa, with a guilt complex for being away so long, that's wrong; he was just plain thoughtful.

Thursday afternoon was a ritual we had enjoyed since moving to Portmarnock: I had my hair done in Malahide and Eamonn picked me up in the green Mercedes, and took me to lunch at the King Sitrick, by the harbour in Howth. I always felt it very romantic. And even though we talked about the usual husband and wife things over our meal, it always came home to me how much I loved him and I would feel a thrill, a tingle of excitement, like being on a first date. Afterwards, we would walk out to sea on one of the two long piers, like two carefree lovers, and I would feel the warmth and strength and kindness of Eamonn and realize how much I'd missed him; how much we'd all missed him. Those romantic reunions were to have a poignant, but tragic, significance to me one bitterly cold windy October day as Eamonn paid the price for his obsessional dedication to work.

For all children, Friday is the best day of the week, but for Emma, Fergal and

Niamh, it was even more enjoyable: their Daddy drove them to school. It was a novelty they looked forward to all week, and Eamonn enjoyed it, too. In fact, he gave up doing the Today show on Fridays so that he could give the school-run a second go.

Having led such a hectic life in London, Eamonn liked to take things slowly and would never exceed the speed limit. When the children were younger, this had amusing repercussions, which the children talk about even now. On Saturdays, he often took them to see his mother at the house he'd bought her at Tevenure, and she would cook steak and kidney pie, which Eamonn adored, followed by apple pie and custard.

Eamonn would take the longest possible route home, dawdling along at the legal limit and generally irritating other motorists who wanted to get a move on. He wouldn't give a you-know-what that he was leading a queue; and, in fact, if the driver immediately behind started hooting or flashing his headlights, he would get the children to kneel on the back seat and make ugly faces through the window. He didn't want them to be rude, just to stop the angry driver giving him any more trouble.

Eamonn, you see, hated cars clogging the city; he felt they should be left at the outskirts, and transport restricted to horse and cart. For a while, he was quite serious about having a pony and trap for our trips into the village, but it was a question of who would look after it and none of the children was keen.

This calm relaxed approach to life was reflected in the clothes Eamonn wore during those weekends. I liked to see him in a suit, but he was always in some old jumper or cardigan and trousers. If he hadn't been on television, I don't think he would have possessed a suit; we never talked about clothes as some couples do, and if I did buy him something, he would say: 'That's nice', but he'd never know whether it was new. I got away with murder.

When he changed to smoking cigars, he was forever letting the ash fall off and burn his shirts and jumpers, even his trousers. I embroidered over the holes each time in bright pink and purple to send him up, but he didn't care, and would walk around the golf club without any shame or embarrassment whatever. If people did question his multi-coloured gear, he'd just say: 'Oh, that's Grainne, reminding me that I burn holes with my cigars.'

Certainly, the bright colours didn't seem to bother Eamonn. And three years before his death we discovered why. He was always putting on clothes that clashed appallingly, and the children and I put this down to extreme bad taste.

But in 1984 he came out of a medical check-up and said: 'I'm perfectly fit, but they've discovered I'm colour blind.'

We all laughed and forgave him. That explained everything . . . all those times he'd put on a mauve tie with a bright green shirt under a red jumper and say innocently: 'How do I look?'

Boxing was Eamonn's first sporting love, but his favourite recreation was golf and he would always have at least one game a week with his close friends, Dickie Duggan and Az Guirey, at Portmarnock golf course. Although I'm sure he tried his hardest to win, Eamonn was not seriously competitive although he did have a respectable handicap of eighteen.

Unlike many people I'm sure we've all met, Eamonn was not a golf bore. He got a hole in one at Portmarnock a few years ago – the joke of the year! – but never bragged about it. He would rather talk about what a lovely day it was than describe his golf strokes.

He would have loved to have been a better golfer, but it takes practice and lots of lessons to get a low handicap, and Eamonn never had the time. Ironically, he was making time for lessons just before he died.

To illustrate what Eamonn thought about his golf, he wrote about a meeting with Gillie Potter. The eminent raconteur-cum-writer had just written a one-upmanship book on golf and the Today producer thought it would make a good idea for the programme. Eamonn wrote:

Instead of having a plain staid studio interview, the producer decided to set up cameras at the nearest available golf course and persuade Gillie to be photographed one-upmanshipping me over a few holes. It was great fun to begin with. Unfortunately, I hadn't been given the opportunity of explaining just how bad my golf was. Gillie became more and more frustrated, as, indeed, did the camera team.

I presume that, in effect, my golf was so disastrous that it could go no further in that direction, and all Gillie's ploys could have no effect, or at best, the opposite effect to the one intended.

This seemed to be the case. Where my ball should have sliced into the rough or nested in a tree, it would soar down the middle. Where it should have exhausted itself well short of the hole it just galloped on and plunged into it with a rattle that became embarrassing. The more I tried to fail, the better I played. Social conversation ceased. I never met Gillie again.

With his keenness to make the best out of things, I'm sure Eamonn would have loved to have been a do-it-yourself expert. But the sad truth is, like most journalists, he was not very good at anything practical or the least bit technical. He couldn't mend a fuse – and even setting the TV video was beyond him. As Emma said, he was pathetic at things like that, and would leave them to Fergal, whose mind works in that way.

But Eamonn did have an excuse for one of his DIY failings. At our first flat in West Hampstead, I asked him to hang some curtains I had made for some very high windows. He refused point-blank and asked if I'd mind him holding the ladder for me instead. I didn't want to, because I am short and the ladder was too small, but Eamonn was adamant, so up I went. I thought he probably did not want to hang the curtains, but his refusal was far more profound than mere bloodymindedness, and, in years to come, I was to have proof of it at the Eiffel Tower in Paris and the Empire State Building in New York.

Eamonn suffered from a fear of heights.

To millions, Eamonn must have come across as a city man; but he was a country boy at heart with a consummate love of nature.

One Sunday morning, we came home from Mass to discover one of our labradors, Jilly, had started giving birth to pups. She was standing by one that, sadly, had died, and was obviously about to have more. Eamonn and Emma quickly got Jilly to the boiler house where it was warm, and stayed there watching the puppies being born.

Emma was not particularly moved by the scene; she had been to farms and seen animals being born many times. But when she looked at Eamonn, he had tears in his eyes. She realized it was the first time in his life he had seen anything born and it was an emotional, almost mesmerizing, experience.

He talked about it for weeks afterwards, Emma told me. And he was still talking about it just before he died – 'that wonderful day when the puppies were born'.

Nature would feature in the beautiful letters – always in green ink – Eamonn would write and one, in particular, is treasured by Emma. He wrote

*to her while she was away at a retreat and described, in colourful detail, what
was going on at home in her absence. The letters were so vivid, she said, she
could almost feel the air running through the house.*

*Eamonn loved pottering around in his greenhouse at the end of the garden,
trying to grow plants and vegetables. He did not have much success, but it was
not for the want of effort and determination.*

*When we bought The Quarry, we kept on a gardener and handyman, Jack
Lowry, who had worked for the previous owners. One day, Eamonn told him
he wanted to grow some melons from seed. Jack, who knew a bit about
gardening, advised him to buy melon plants grown in heated greenhouses
because the temperature in his greenhouse was not right and the seeds would
take too long – if they would grow at all. Eamonn listened carefully, but said he
wanted to try anyway.*

*Jack turned out to be right. For two years Eamonn tried to grow his seeds in
a little pot but, just when they looked as if they would make it, they dampened
off and died overnight. Jack tried to persuade him to buy plants, but Eamonn,
his determination shining brightly as ever, said: 'I'll give it one more try.'*

*But nothing happened; reluctantly, he gave in and planted four melon
plants. They grew and bore little fruits, but never developed. Eamonn was
bitterly disappointed. Jack consoled him that there was a lot to know about
melons, which they didn't, and said things might be different the next year.
Even Eamonn's faith was wearing thin by now.*

*One morning, the following summer, Eamonn was in the kitchen when Jack
came up from the greenhouse. He was holding three small melons the size of
eggs. Eamonn couldn't believe it. He and Jack looked at each other, a sort of
pride in their eyes, not able to decide who should try one first. In the end, Jack
told Eamonn to go ahead. Eamonn said he'd never had a tastier melon in his
life.*

*Before the house was built, the land was very wild and Eamonn was fascinated
by the birds it still attracted: whenever he spotted one, he would go through
book after book trying to discover what species it was. One day Jack found a
nest with four tiny birds in it and asked Eamonn if he wanted to take a
photograph. Jack warned him he might miss the opportunity, because the birds
were ready to fly. Eamonn said it would have to wait until the next day as he*

was busy. The next morning they went to the nest . . . and the birds had flown. Eamonn was very disappointed.

He was always sad, too, when trees had to be cut. He and Jack planted dozens of trees on the edge of the lawn when we moved in fifteen years ago and Eamonn refused to let them be trimmed. In the end, they grew so tall they had no foliage at the bottom. Eamonn finally gave in. If there was a storm the first thing Eamonn would ask Jack the next morning was: 'Is anything down?' And his relief would show if everything was all right. Even if a tree had come down, Eamonn needed a lot of convincing before he would let it be cut away; he always thought it might be able to grow, if straightened and supported. He loved the garden and Jack knew he had to cut everything back gently, not hack at it.

He had a go at growing cabbages in the garden. Jack warned him it was no use because the wood pigeons would eat them, but Eamonn said he'd try anyway. When the cabbages started growing, Eamonn thought he'd cracked it – but the pigeons were only waiting until they were big before scoffing the lot! Eamonn took it philosophically with a grin, but again, he was disappointed because he would have liked to have grown and eaten his own vegetables, rather than buy them in a shop.

Don't get the impression Eamonn was a penny-pincher, though. Frugal, yes, but certainly not mean or stingy: he had been brought up to make the best of things, to make something out of nothing. He would seldom throw away anything from our meals, for instance. He would use what was left over to make something else for another day. I can remember him scraping a leg of lamb and making Monday Pie with pastry and frying potatoes left from lunch into a hash with onions, and they were twice as delicious to him, not only because they tasted delicious, but: waste not, want not. He hated waste. If I or one of the children went to rip the twine on a package, he would say: 'Don't cut it. We'll open it and use it again.' He would take his time undoing the twine carefully, and put it away in one piece, and, sure enough, we'd use it again. That sort of thing was normal in Irish families years ago, and Eamonn never forgot.

The same with the fire. He had all these tricks he had learned when poor in Synge Street, and he was forever trying to use them in the house. If we had to go out, I would simply put a guard in front of the fire and remake it when we got back. But Eamonn hated the idea of it burning away while no one was there and he would try to keep the fire alive by banking it down with ashes. In theory the fire was asleep, not cold and dead, and he would wake it gently with a firelighter when he got back. If his system worked, Eamonn would be pleased. But most times it didn't, and he'd have to use one firelighter after another and, eventually, more coal to get it going. That didn't stop him banking and banking that fire, though: he had seen his mother and father do it expertly when he was a child and he felt he ought to be able to do it, too. I had to laugh one afternoon. We were all waiting for Eamonn to finish banking before we could go out and Emma said, impatiently: 'For God's sake, do we live in a tenement?'

Eamonn's frugality stretched even to fruit. If he took the children for a walk along the coast road to Malahide on Saturdays, for example, he knew that they would get peckish. And, unknown to them, he would slip tangerines or apples into his anorak. He would work the conversation round to eating, and enjoy their surprise and delight when he pulled the apples or tangerines from his pocket. But it would be only half a tangerine or half an apple each: he always felt the children should have a little and want more, rather than too much and not appreciate it. He loved them enjoying simple pleasures; he could not bear the idea of them being spoiled.

He may have wanted me to cut down on things. But he never asked me – because he knew I wouldn't! There was one amazingly trivial incident, however, and it makes me smile, even now, to think of it. Eamonn had read an article by Prince Charles about how one should squeeze toothpaste from the bottom of the tube, and he – Eamonn, that is, not Prince Charles – started inspecting the basin after I'd cleaned my teeth. If any toothpaste had dropped off my brush, old hawk-eye would spot it.

'You're putting too much toothpaste on,' he said one day.

'So?' I replied.

'How can you waste it like that?'

I said I didn't give a damn; it was unimportant to me. But it was important to Eamonn. He mentioned it several times after that and, eventually, wrote about it in one of his Catholic Herald articles. That reminds me: I must get a pump-action tube – the plastic tubes don't roll up like the old ones used to.

Although Eamonn was serious about the toothpaste, he would have seen the funny side, too; and although I can't remember them now, I'm sure he would have made a few wisecracks in case he thought he'd upset me. He wasn't a practical joker, but there was always a lot of laughter in the house, mainly from verbal banter. Eamonn had a quick wit – and, I have to admit, an acid tongue – that saw the humour in thousands of situations and people. He would rib me mercilessly, but he could take it, too.

He was not a moody person. He had his highs and lows, like anyone, but the lows were most often connected with work, rarely the family. I've heard him get het up a number of times and the person on the receiving end was always Malcolm Morris, the This is Your Life producer.

In Eamonn's 'Gladstone' bag with the champagne and presents would be the script for the following week's programme. Eamonn would read it either on Friday or Saturday morning in bed with a cup of tea. And he'd speak about it with Malcolm on the phone. The show was so important to both of them that calls often got heated, with both of them arguing and shouting – sometimes swearing – at each other as they tried to make their point or get things done a certain way. These rows were never personal: both men were the best of friends and loved each other dearly; it was just that they cared for This is Your Life with a passion and wanted it to be right. I never sat and listened to Eamonn, because I always had other things to do, but I do know he gave Malcolm a rough time many weekends. Whether he always got his way in the end, I don't know.

Eamonn was never a screamer, a ranting, raving, let-yourself-go type: in all the years we were married, he rarely lost his temper in front of me. Certainly he never lifted a finger to anyone – not even Charlie Haughey! He often raised his voice to Niamh, however, when he was trying to teach her something and she wouldn't concentrate. He could swear, of course, and we did use some choice words between ourselves – not in temper, but in conversation, for amusement, mainly. Actually, to say he was not a ranter or raver is not strictly true. Eamonn was known to shout and scream all right – but on his own! Niamh would come running into the sitting room, late at night, worried that we were having an almighty row . . . only to discover it was Eamonn getting all steamed up at a soccer or boxing match on TV. And Emma would say she cringed in her bedroom at the thought of this grown-up person getting all upset and bellowing all by himself. She used to think: I must turn off this match or fight, or my father will have a heart attack and will be dead on the floor. But that was Eamonn: he knew and loved most sports and would get totally involved. As a former boxing commentator himself, he was particularly irritated by

ITV's boxing man, Reg Gutteridge, who apparently makes a point of talking a lot during the fighting. This used to infuriate Eamonn and he would shout at the screen: 'Shut up, Reg. I want to watch!'

One hears a lot of people say 'I hate this person' or 'I hate that thing'; it's part of our everyday language. But it wasn't for Eamonn. The word 'hate' was anathema to him and he would not stand for it from the children; he wouldn't allow them to use it, even as a joke. Emma and Niamh, particularly, might come in and say: 'Oh, I hate so-and-so,' and Eamonn would make a big point of it and say: 'Do you really hate them?' Of course, they didn't, so Eamonn would suggest using 'dislike'.

And he used to infuriate the girls by always seeing the side of the person they 'hated'. They would come home from school looking for support and understanding after an argument; but, instead of him standing up for them, he'd take the other person's side. 'Maybe they were having a bad day,' he would say; or: 'Maybe they don't have as much as you.'

If one of the girls said the other person had twice as much, he'd just say: 'Well, maybe their father is giving them a hard time.' Emma and Niamh would complain that, even if they were clearly in the right, he would always see the other person's side, and they would end up feeling guilty for having the row.

In rows himself, Eamonn had a marvellous way of always coming out on top – even if he lost. He would bring an argument to a close by simply saying: 'You could well be right.' He did it with viewers and listeners who wrote to disagree about something he had said. That one sentence – 'You may well be right' – would infuriate them. He wasn't backing down but he wasn't continuing the discussion. He liked to aggravate and rankle people like that, for it left them no satisfaction. And no comeback.

22 BODY – OR SOUL?

Something that rankled with me was Eamonn's obsession with punctuality. The Irish are notorious for being late for everything, but Eamonn was an exception: he was never late for anything. At dinner parties, first nights or premières – any formal function, in fact – I did not like being the first to arrive, but it didn't bother him. While we were getting ready at home, he'd say: 'How long do you think it will take to get there, darling?' I'd say, twenty minutes, half an hour, or whatever, and he would immediately double it, to be on the safe side.

The prospect of being late, quite frankly, terrified Eamonn and he would get very excitable and hyper, telling me to get a move on. Of course, we'd arrive indecently early, and have to drive round the block to kill time. I'd be looking smug and Eamonn would say: 'You were right – you bitch.'

It all sounds funny now. But it used to drive me mad at the time. For Eamonn's anxiety only served to get me in a state myself. After all, no woman likes to be rushed, does she?

That need for punctuality, plus his quest for perfection in everything he did, or tried, made Eamonn quite demanding at home. And at no time was this more evident than when all five of us assembled around the kitchen table for the Sunday Lunch. It was a big event, not only for Eamonn, but for the children and me, too, for it was the only time in the week we were all together. Eamonn looked forward to sitting down with us all; and since he always cooked, he insisted on everything being organized. If he'd told us lunch was at 2 P.M., it had to be two on the dot – not five past – because he wanted to serve immediately the food was ready and couldn't stand being kept waiting. He had this thing about hot food and would not start until everyone was sitting down.

We had the most wonderful Sunday lunches. And the most appalling.

The good lunches came later when the children were older and more in the mood to do what Eamonn enjoyed most, which was having a chat. But when Emma and Fergal were in their teens and Niamh was a small child, those long-awaited Sunday afternoons often disappointed Eamonn and left him very upset. The problem was, I think, that he expected too much from them because he had been away most of the week, and, as Emma said, tried to cram the whole family life into that one Sunday – that one lunch! He saw the afternoon as special, and wanted it to be perfect, but to the children it was just another day; they were pleased their Daddy was home, of course, but, like any normal children growing up, they wanted to do their own thing, see their own friends, and Eamonn never really understood that. His own childhood had been vastly different.

It would tear Eamonn apart to see the children fighting. It would mean nothing to them, but Eamonn took it very seriously and it would distress him so much he sometimes cried. That would set me off, too. After it was all over, I would say: 'They've forgotten all about it, darling.' But he was rarely convinced. He had never consciously encouraged them to express their emotions and I don't think he ever really understood how and why they did.

Most fathers appreciate that bickering between kids is normal; something that is over and forgotten in a matter of minutes. But, because Eamonn saw those lunches as idyllic, he would get terribly hurt if something had happened to spoil them. And while the children wouldn't remember what the squabble was about after half an hour, Eamonn would worry about it all the way to London.

I was a stickler for manners. Emma had three years start on the others and was no problem, but Fergal launched into every meal as though it were a race and Niamh would eat with her mouth open, never resting her knife and fork down on the plate. I would tick them off for bad manners, then Eamonn would tick me off and before we knew it the children would start bickering among themselves and the lunch was on its way to being spoiled.

Eamonn would be wounded; and he would plead with the children to stop arguing, saying: 'This is my Sunday – I'll be gone tonight, or in the morning . . .' But, of course, they were children and they could not suddenly stop being themselves, and fit into the role he wanted them to play, for just one afternoon.

Emma would be the one to benefit when Fergal's urgent pleas to be excused were granted and Niamh got down to play with her toys. Emma would gleefully rush off and grab her poetry books and ask her Daddy to read to her, usually chunks of T. S. Eliot. When she was older, Emma would tell me she knew I was bored stiff; I was sometimes – but it was lovely hearing those beautiful words being spoken in Eamonn's wonderful, resonant voice, knowing Emma was enjoying it so much. Sometimes Eamonn left for London on Sunday evenings and, despite his passion for punctuality, he'd be at that lunch table, reading poetry just an hour before take-off. But then, he and Emma were kindred spirits, with a love of words, and reading to her was a labour of love in every sense. He could have read anything – even the Irish Times editorial – and Emma would have sat there enthralled.

As the children got older, the Sunday lunch became more what Eamonn wanted, which was simply a good, relaxed meal with lots of interesting conversation to follow, and it was not uncommon for us to still be sitting at that table at five o'clock. We covered many subjects. One of them, believe it or not, was death. Not the sort of topic usually discussed over roast beef and Yorkshire pudding, but then the Andrews family always had a catholic taste in conversation: Eamonn never believed in shoving any point under the table if one of us wanted to talk about it.

One day death came up. Eamonn said he felt I was more likely to die before him and I said I did, too. The children would say: 'Oh, Mummy, don't go before Daddy!' And Eamonn would say, lightheartedly, but somewhat seriously, too, that if he lost me, he would go into a monastery.

Remembering how he had once considered entering the church, I wouldn't have bet against it.

And another subject was women – Eamonn's Other Women.

Before tongues start wagging up and down the country, I must say that it was all a family joke. To my knowledge, Eamonn never had any affairs; but the children found it hiliariously funny that certain women might fancy their Daddy, and they ribbed him unmercifully.

Joanna Lumley, for example, was a running joke for ages. One day, Eamonn mentioned she'd invited him to lunch – made a pass at him even – and the children, Emma and Niamh mainly, picked up on it at once. After that, he had only to mention he was lunching with someone the following week, and the girls would say with knowing looks: 'Who is it – Joanna Lumley?'

Eamonn loved the children winding him up like this and would deliberately let slip names of women who, he said, fancied him. Susan George and Jilly Cooper are two names that spring to mind, but before either of their husbands raise their eyebrows, I must stress that this was Eamonn's idea of a bit of family fun, and is not to be taken too seriously. Having said that, I gather Jilly told a number of people – including Malcolm Morris – that she fancied Eamonn. She was on the panel when What's My Line? was brought back and went to Eamonn lots of times for advice about a book she was writing, called Rivals. When the book was published, Jilly sent a copy to me, saying that there were shades of 'your darling Eamonn' in the hero Daniel, whose every other word seemed to be that colourful Anglo-Saxon expletive. I wrote back saying that there were 'no shades of my darling Eamonn in your focking Daniel'.

Eamonn never gave me reason to be jealous, but a famous singer in Hollywood made me see red, much to Eamonn's amusement. Her name is Eartha Kitt, a slinky, feline-type whose career was not hindered in the slightest when Orson Welles labelled her 'the most exciting woman in the world'. I never did find out whether Eamonn agreed with the great man, but I do know that the lady found it necessary to run her fingers sensuously down his back at a Beverly Hills pool party. We were living in Hollywood then, taking a three-month look at the place, before deciding whether Eamonn should accept a TV job offer.

The party was warming up under the Californian sun. Steaks were sizzling on the barbecue. Iced cocktails were being served up – and guests' inhibitions were coming down. I was chatting to one interesting gentleman in the film business when it suddenly occurred to me I'd lost sight of Eamonn. I wasn't unduly bothered: there were several glamorous women around, but, although we'd been married about seven years, the traditional 'itch' was not something I'd ever thought about with Eamonn. However, I glanced around to see where he was – and I spotted him, stretched out on a sun-lounger, chatting with Eartha Kitt. She was running her hands along his back and, no doubt, purring into his ear.

I was furious. And I told Eamonn so later.

'But I couldn't see what she was doing, darling,' he said, with a grin.

'You could damn well feel it, couldn't you?' I snapped.

He laughed. 'Well, yes . . .'

Whether the cat-like temptress wanted to know if Eamonn had the seven-year-itch, then scratch it for him, I never found out. Eamonn was flattered by her attention, because she was so famous. But she was not his type and he found the whole episode – particularly my jealous fury – highly amusing.

Eamonn himself never once got jealous – even when a President of the United States made it obvious he was as interested in my body as in anything Eamonn had to tell him.

It happened in the summer of 1963 – a few months before President John Kennedy was assassinated in Dallas. Eamonn and I were having lunch with Ireland's US ambassador, Freddie Boland, in New York. When we mentioned that we were going on to Washington to visit my sister, Susan, Freddie said he would ask a journalist friend to try to arrange for us, and Susan's husband, Peter Mooney, to meet President Kennedy at the White House.

Eamonn and I were thrilled a few days later when we got a phone call at Susan's apartment to say that the meeting was on: we had to be at the White House at 9 A.M. sharp the following day and Kennedy would give us twenty minutes or so in the famous Oval office. The early hour didn't appeal to me, but I was as excited as Eamonn and the next day we arrived at the White House more than a little early – as you would have expected with Mr Punctuality – for our 'audience'.

I suppose I should remember what was said at that, for me at least, momentous meeting. Unfortunately, I can't. Perhaps I was too nervous or excited; more likely, a combination of both. But, apart from hearing that Kennedy was looking forward to visiting Ireland in the near future, the only thing I can remember is how he mentally undressed me as we were introduced. I was in my mid-thirties and hardly naïve, but it was somewhat unnerving, if a little flattering, I can tell you, and I'm sure I must have blushed.

The President's helicopter brought our meeting to an end, as if on cue, after precisely twenty minutes and we left, arranging to have lunch with Peter later.

Of course, in 1963, there were no rumours then of Kennedy's big sexual appetite and womanizing ways, and I wondered whether I'd imagined his over-friendly interest. But no sooner had we all sat down to lunch than Peter brought it up. Modestly, I said nothing, but Eamonn said he had definitely picked up on it, too, but would not have said anything if Peter hadn't. With it out in the open, we all laughed, none heartier than Eamonn.

Kennedy, I have to say, was by far the most exciting man I have met. After the big fellow, of course.

I am the type who likes to look, but not touch and two other men I could have admired all night were Harry Belafonte and Sean Connery. Eamonn introduced me to Belafonte when I flew to Las Vegas to join him after he had covered a world boxing title fight. I was excited anyway after winning the jackpot on an airport fruit-machine, but when later Belafonte stopped to talk to Eamonn in the hotel, I breathed in deeply and thought: My God, what a gorgeous man! He was sensuously exciting and I was attracted to him. When I told Eamonn, he was a little surprised, because, for me, a relationship is more about the mind than the body. But Belafonte's body – as Joan Collins observed in her autobiography – was rather special.

Sean Connery is the only other man to have any effect on me physically. I met him for the first time at a party in Rome, then again at the Dorchester Hotel in London, and I could feel the attraction just standing beside him.

Throughout our marriage, however, I never had any evidence of adultery, nor suspected it. Being in London on his own so much, Eamonn could have had affairs every week, but I'm convinced he didn't. He had no time! Anyway, it is not the time, it's inclination and I honestly don't feel it was there.

Maybe I should have thought more about it, but we were in a very happy situation and I felt deeply loved. When Eamonn wasn't seeing me, he was phoning or writing romantic letters and notes, or sending intimately cheeky telegrams, and when we were reunited there were always those thoughtful gifts that said as much as anything about his feelings. Unfaithfulness never once crossed my mind.

Before he gave them up, Eamonn loved a Havana cigar after lunch. He was furious at the cost, but he enjoyed them so much he had a humidor at a cigar importers in Dublin. He had always smoked cigarettes, but stopped when he first became ill. When he took up cigars, he smoked them like cigarettes, sometimes ten or more a day. But I'm sure he didn't enjoy them as much as some smokers; they were more of a prop, really, something to do with his hands.

In his cigarette days, he was so addicted he would smoke in the street on the way to lunch, although he was embarrassed enough to hold the cigarette down so that people he knew wouldn't see it. It was the same with cigars; he would light one before dinner as well as after, and happily smoke it in the street.

Once, in Paris, celebrating our anniversary, this rebounded on him, causing a certain amount of annoyance. The doorman of the George Cinq Hotel had summoned a taxi to take us to dinner. Eamonn had a cigar going and when the driver saw it, he refused to take us. Eamonn was livid, because the cabbie looked down his nose at him, and at the cigar, leaving us in no doubt what he thought of cigar smokers.

Another taxi was summoned. Eamonn held the cigar down out of view this time, and we got in. After one puff, however, the driver got a whiff and pointedly slammed the glass behind his head – a sort of smokescreen between him and us! Then he kept turning round, giving us dirty looks. Eamonn didn't have much time for French taxi-drivers after that.

He had another embarrassing moment when we were on holiday in Barbados. He was enjoying a large Havana after dinner when someone complained to the maître d'*, who asked Eamonn to put it out. Reluctantly, Eamonn obliged, but he was blazing. We knew who had objected and Eamonn muttered to me angrily: 'Who the hell does he think he is!'*

I think it might have comforted Eamonn somewhat on his memorable Comet trip to New York that even the great Sir Winston wasn't allowed to light up a Churchillian cigar in flight!

As Eamonn's breathing difficulties got worse, he smoked fewer and fewer cigars and, finally, saw the sense in giving them up altogether. He missed them greatly, though, and the Christmas before he died he relented and lit up a huge Montecristo.

He gave one to Fergal and I took a fun picture of them puffing away. Eamonn got a kick out of that and he planned to do the same the next year. Sadly, it was a present he wasn't around to give.

For some reason, Eamonn's behaviour around the place started to change when he stopped smoking cigarettes. Before, he liked the house to have that lived-in look: he loved newspapers lying around and would tell me off if I put them away in cupboards where he couldn't find them. It never bothered him if the children left anything in their rooms; they could always clear it up or put it away in due course. He would leave the electric carving knife out in the kitchen after Sunday lunch and it would drive him mad if it was put away. Full ashtrays could stay full; and if he or one of the children knocked one over, so what? He wanted our home to have what he called a 'casual air' about it. I wasn't sure I did, however, and we often clashed because I'd always been neat and meticulous and liked to see things in their place.

And then, quite dramatically, our roles reversed. Overnight, it seemed, Eamonn became a fusspot; all the things he hadn't considered important would really worry him. He'd see six mugs in one of the children's bedrooms and say to me: 'This is disgraceful. What are we going to do about it?'

I'd tell him: 'It's simple. Don't go into their rooms.'

He'd be really upset, and want to do something. But I'd say that if all my years of nagging hadn't worked, there was no point in telling them anymore. He saw the sense in that because he thought one person nagging was enough.

But he didn't approve of it. He didn't like me missing the brush with toothpaste either; it wasn't just the waste – it was the untidiness. With all the things going on in his head, it seemed so petty – and I told him he should have better things to think about. Eamonn's attitude to newspapers changed, too. We had most of them delivered and he'd go mad if the children left them all over the place, particularly on Sundays when the quality papers had three or four separate sections. He would methodically put the sections back in their right place so that the paper looked as if he'd just bought it. Before, he wouldn't have dreamed of doing that.

Eamonn was not the only one who changed. As the children got older, their taste and moods naturally changed, too, and they disappointed Eamonn by bringing an end to a ritual he'd relished for years: the Great Sunday Breakfast. You'd have thought that preparing lunch would have been enough cooking for one day, but Eamonn got a big kick out of serving up huge fry-ups, plus his speciality – pancakes – at between 8 and 8.30 every Sunday morning. When the children were very young, and in bed early on Saturday night, they loved those breakfasts and would get up for them eagerly. But the older they got, and the later their Saturday night activity, the keener they were to stay in bed.

'Oh, no, Dad,' they would groan, burying sleepy heads under their pillows. 'Not breakfast this early!' Eamonn took it philosophically, but you could see he was hurt. He would, I'm sure, have been happy for them to stay young children, enjoying those breakfasts, for ever.

Looking back, it hits home to me how easily Eamonn was hurt. You would have thought that someone who'd survived in such a tough business for so long would be thick-skinned and a little cynical. But Eamonn saw only the best in people, always had a positive approach and took it badly if he was let down.

Eleven o'clock Mass on Sunday morning, for example, was another ritual we'd enjoyed as a family all our lives. But with age, the children went off this a little, too, and sometimes would go only because Eamonn made them feel guilty. It was not so much what he said, more how he looked. He'd be so down in the mouth at the prospect of going to church on his own that they would get up and go with him.

Once, he wrote to Emma from London, telling her how hurt he was that Fergal had not gone to Mass one morning. Fergal was about eighteen at the time and somewhat rebellious. Eamonn was willing to accept that the boy had his own ideas and feelings, but, at the same time, he was hurt. Eamonn would write about only those things close to his heart, so we knew this mattered to him.

Often Eamonn would go to church on his own, but sometimes he would go for a jog round the streets or just do exercises in another part of the house. Always, though, he would be out of bed between 6 and 6.30. In my half-sleep, I would hear him getting ready, but I could never work out if he was putting on a shirt and trousers for Mass or a tracksuit for his work-out.

He would come back around eight o'clock and kiss me on the cheek, waking me gently, beautifully. I would want to know if he had been running or to Mass, and I'd reach out and touch his shoulder, asking: 'Body – or soul?'

Eamonn would laugh, because the answer was always in his clothes. Even the most fervent churchgoer does not work up a sweat on his knees praying to God!

That was a little joke Eamonn and I shared for many years. Emma reads more into it than I: she says the body was Eamonn's outward public persona, the TV personality; and the soul was his spiritual, private self, the part of him the family saw and worshipped.

Whatever it means, I miss those early morning awakenings with an ache I never thought I would be able to bear.

Eamonn was such a believer. It is hard to describe. He was so kind and understanding, so keen to help, not only within the family, which would be expected, but outside, too. Once, Emma wrote to him in London, apologizing for something she said in a row with him. He wrote back a compassionate reply, explaining that he understood, and that she should throw his letter away, as the matter was forgotten. He then went on to encourage her to help other people, because she had so much goodness in her, telling her not to worry about being taken for granted because doing good would make her feel better herself.

I knew the Catholic religion meant a lot to Eamonn, but he nevertheless surprised me one day when he revealed that he had seriously considered becoming a Christian Brother. He was seventeen at the time and his mother took him for an interview with the Christian Brothers. I can picture him now, a scrawny teenager in his white knitted socks, and his mother in her black mac. I asked him what had happened to make him change his mind, but he never told me. Maybe it was because it was then he became aware of girls and didn't fancy a life of chastity!

Ironically, Emma seriously thought of becoming a nun – also at seventeen. She came back from retreat for her birthday and was full of it. I was very worried because she was so intense, but Eamonn, who had always encouraged religion, was calm about it and very tolerant. He would have been delighted if she had chosen to enter the church, but he would not have tried to force her. His mother gave Emma a card for the Devotion to Our Lady of Good Counsel and told her that she would pass her school exams if she prayed every night. Emma did – and duly passed – with flying colours.

One of his school pals called Eamonn a 'Holy Joe', because of his obsession with going to Mass. He was anything but that: he was never offended by doubles entendres *or* risqué *comments and often made them himself.*

And he loved gambling, though not in a serious way: you would never have seen him in a betting shop or a casino. Every Grand National day, he never failed to organize a family sweepstake which the children enjoyed. He just liked the idea of a bet and wager on anything – even two flies running up a wall!

Once, on holiday with some friends, Archie and Miriam Moore, on the Irish coast, Eamonn wanted us all to go in the sea, but it was a bitterly cold day and the water was freezing. The four of us talked about it for a few minutes, then Eamonn said: 'Archie and I will bet you a bottle of champagne you won't go in.' Never one to turn down a challenge, not to mention a bottle of bubbly, I persuaded Miriam to brave one of the coldest summers on record – and we inched our way in. Brrr . . . did we earn that champagne!

When it came to sex outside the privacy of one's home, however, Eamonn was a bit prudish and quite easily embarrassed.

We were celebrating our anniversary in Paris in 1972 when we discovered Last Tango in Paris, *with Marlon Brando, was showing. It seemed an appropriate movie to see, so one afternoon we went along, not really knowing what to expect. Well, anyone who has seen the film knows that there is one sequence involving Brando and Maria Schneider that is explicit and somewhat perverted. It didn't particularly offend me; I was quite happy to accept that it was a necessary part of the story, and to see the film through to the end. But I could sense Eamonn's discomfort next to me; he was tense with embarrassment. He sighed audibly a few times, then whispered to me that he felt we ought to leave. I had no intention of leaving and told him so. He sat there watching Brando's performance for a few seconds, but then sighed again and said we really ought to leave. With that, he edged past people and walked up the aisle to the exit. I was convinced he would return in five minutes when the steam had gone out of the scene, but he didn't and I ended up watching the rest of the film on my own. At the end, I felt sure he would be sitting in the foyer waiting for me with a funny expression on his face. But he was nowhere to be seen, and I ended up having to walk back to the hotel. I would have got a taxi, of course, but I didn't have a penny – or, rather, a franc – on me. I got lost a few times, but, thankfully, I knew the name of the hotel. Eamonn, surprisingly, wasn't worried because he knew I'd find my way back; in fact, when I finally turned up, he was amused by the whole episode. Apparently, he walked out of the cinema, convinced I was behind him. When he realized I wasn't, he thought of going back in, but he told me he'd have had to buy another ticket and his pecuniary caution got the better of him.*

Eamonn turned to his religion for support even in helping him start the car, finding parking spots – and even in finding things he had lost. The car was a very hit-and-miss affair. The children and I lost count of the times it broke down – and Eamonn was no mechanic. He would lift the bonnet and fiddle around, as though he knew what he was doing, but, really, he didn't have a clue; if it did start, it was pure luck, not pure genius. Usually, his answer to the problem was to tell the children to say their Hail Marys, then rock the car backwards and forwards, fingers crossed. We nearly always got it going eventually – and Our Lady got the credit. He would rely on the Hail Marys when anything went wrong.

For parking spaces, he would pray to the Holy Souls, the dead people waiting outside the gates of Heaven for a space inside. He believed that if he prayed to them to find room for the car, they would do so. It never seemed to fail, either with the children or alone, and Emma does it even now.

Eamonn prayed to Saint Anthony to find things. He told the children they had to make a pledge to give him money, as much as they could afford, and to give the cash to him.

Emma was dubious about that one. 'Surely you don't have to give money to a saint!' she said, incredulously.

'Yes,' Eamonn replied. 'Saint Anthony needs the money for some good for others.'

Emma thought about this for some time and did some research. She found the telephone number of a convent, who told her there were lots of boxes around town where she could deposit money for Saint Anthony.

When she lost something she would pray and promise to pay a certain amount, but she never got around to it. One day she lost something and was at her wits' end when she couldn't find it. She told Eamonn who said it was because she hadn't paid up in the past. And, typically, he used the experience to impress on Emma a valuable lesson of life: that you must honour your commitments, keep your promises.

Emma and a friend once compared men to doors. Some, they decided, were like a trap door: one minute you feel safe, the next they're gone from under your feet and you're left trapped. Others can be like French doors: interesting but not very stable. And so on.

Emma always compared her Daddy to an oak door: strong, sturdy, totally dependable. And she would say – as Niamh and Fergal did – that his door was always open: he was always ready to listen to any ideas and suggestions, and he always treated them with respect. And his judgement was always wise. No wonder Fergal said his Daddy seemed to have all the answers.

We were always learning from Eamonn, me as well as the children. He was my teacher and professor; he educated me in so many ways and helped me to grow up and become my own person. I learned from listening. Eamonn had the gift of the gab: he loved words and was a great conversationalist, with a great vocabulary and command of the English language, and we all could not help but learn from him.

He was an academic at heart and would have loved to have gone to college or university as a youngster if his parents could have afforded it. One of his big regrets was not having a high qualification in English language or literature, or even another Arts subject. He didn't have a chip on his shoulder about it, but I think he would have liked to have had a degree in the drawer, just for himself. Fergal's girlfriend was amazed at Eamonn's knowledge of literature. She was taking a Masters Degree, part of which was on espionage novels and she had long conversations with him about spy thrillers and their authors.

There was definitely a touch of the schoolmaster about Eamonn. The children would show him their homework before he left on Sunday and if it was obvious they'd hurried something – like a map – and got it wrong, he'd be cross. He would tell them if a job was worth doing, it was worth doing well. His father had impressed that on him as a child, and he'd never forgotten it. Eamonn did not have to work too hard with Emma, who was intellectually very close to him, or Fergal, who was gifted technically; but he had many a ding-dong row with Niamh, who never found swotting the easiest of pursuits.

He wanted her to get her leaving certificates from school and was always telling her how important it was to study; he knew how difficult it was because he'd gone through the same agony himself, but he was determined she would succeed. It wasn't an easy time, and things would get so heated between them that I would walk out of the room because I couldn't stand seeing them so upset. Eamonn's refusal to give up and Niamh's hard work paid off in the end, though: she got her leaving certificates. So, full marks to both of them!

Eamonn was so proud of Niamh. She was never an academic type, but at one end-of-term presentation she picked up prizes and Eamonn pointed her out to everybody he met, beaming: 'That's my daughter.'

Eamonn would walk around the house in a blue 'Henry Higgins-type' cardigan, looking very much the schoolteacher. Niamh called him the

Professor. She has that cardigan now, and treasures the memories it holds of how much her Daddy cared for her.

If a university degree was one ambition Eamonn failed to fulfil, acting the part of a private detective like Raymond Chandler's famous Philip Marlowe was another. The nearest he got to it was dressing up in a 'Marlowe' hat and mac and posing with three gorgeous girls for the cover of TV Times. In the early days he longed to be an actor. His voice was terrific, but he didn't move well and, deep down, I'm sure he knew he wasn't good enough. It never bothered him, though. And, much later, he told the children stories against himself of when he took acting lessons under the stage director, Ria Mooney, at the Gaiety School of Acting.

In one play, Eamonn had to say a line with the word 'cushion'. He pronounced it 'cusshen', which appalled the demanding Miss Mooney. 'It's Cush – on, Andrews,' she would roar, during rehearsals. 'Not Cush – en!' Eamonn was mortified: he felt his accent betrayed his modest Dublin background. With typical application, he practised saying that one word night after night, until it sounded as if he had been pronouncing it 'Cush – on all his life.

The night of the play arrived. Keyed-up, Eamonn waited in the wings: 'Cush – on . . . Cush – on.' Oh, yes, it most definitely was going to be all right on the night. His moment came. Eamonn walked on stage and spoke his line with great confidence and pride. Pleased with himself, he smiled at Ria Mooney in the front row. But she wasn't smiling. Nor were the rest of the cast. They didn't know what to do. The production was in chaos. For Eamonn had been so keyed up about the damned 'Cush – on' that he had come on five pages too early. He should have been asking for tea!

His dreams of acting stardom began to fade after that and his life took a different course. But he never lost his interest in acting and was fascinated by some of the actors he met. Even in later life, if someone had approached him to play Marlowe I'm sure he would have jumped at the chance.

I never did find out why Eamonn had such a passion for private eyes. I knew he liked mysteries by Agatha Christie, Mickey Spillane and, later, Elmore Leonard; and Columbo was his favourite TV cop series. But he never explained why the interest was so deep. He loved escapism – something far removed from the real-life stories that consumed his working life. Maybe it was simply that: a need to switch off and enjoy a different, less demanding, world, while still exercising the brain.

I wonder if he would have written *a detective mystery or spy thriller?*
Certainly he wanted to write – not only his autobiography, but a novel, too –
and poetry – and I'm convinced he had the talent and determination to do so.
Mind you, like many writers, he would find excuses not to tackle that daunting
blank page. Eamonn had a beautiful study overlooking our swimming pool,
which was some distance away from the hustle and bustle of the kitchen and
family room, and ideal for writing. But he would complain that the phone kept
ringing every five minutes and disturbed his concentration. I solved this by
saying I would take the calls and tell people he was busy. But Eamonn would
shake his head and say seriously: 'I'd still be aware of what's going on. I need to
be out of it.'

And so the idea of a tower was born. It would be 100 feet high, Eamonn said,
with four windows, looking out in all directions. He could escape to the peace
and quiet and look out to sea and be undisturbed, and create. I'm sure Eamonn
would have loved to have built that tower; and that he would have written up
there. But, at the same time, I think it was a pipedream; a romantic notion that
was really a convenient excuse not to get down to actually writing, which, of
course, is an extremely tedious, arduous, lonely business, demanding strict
self-discipline, more than peace and quiet.

A clue to the inner battle Eamonn was having with himself even while
writing this book is contained in the start of an unfinished chapter:

It should have rained today so that I could get on with this story.
Instead the clouds push westwards and the birds are calling me
outside. In my mind's eye I can see the golf club less than half a
mile away green and challenging, a world of its own stretching
along by the salt sea-waves.

I don't think a tower, however high, however romantic, could have helped
him overcome that little bit of writer's block.

Having said that, when Eamonn became ill, I did say, quite seriously: 'Why
don't you give up television and build your tower and become a writer?'

He sort of laughed and said: 'Not yet.'

I would have loved Eamonn to develop his talent for poetry. He had a lovely
turn of phrase and simple poignancy, and wrote so many beautiful poems over

the years that, one day, I might try to compile them in a book. It would be lovely for them to live on.

Emma, too, had a talent for poetry and, when she was seventeen, Eamonn would take her to readings at Dublin's John Player Theatre. Emma adored those readings, and understood how difficult it was for Eamonn. 'Poor Dadda,' she would say. 'Standing around with a coffee and me, and everyone wanting to speak to him.' Many people were surprised to see Eamonn at such a reading, but his poetic talent was not something he had ever shouted about, so few people outside the family knew of his interest.

Around this time he and Emma shared a moving, if bizarre, experience: they each wrote a poem on the same subject at the same time – without knowing it.

One day, after Eamonn's mother died, Emma was rummaging through some of her things when she found a very old brown envelope, with the words Kevin's Caul in her grandmother's handwriting. Inside the envelope, Emma found a piece of skin that looked like a piece of very, very old chicken breast. Shaken, she showed it to Eamonn.

'My God,' he said. 'How strange. I didn't know this existed.'

They were both moved by the discovery because it was rather like finding a bit of a dead person. Eamonn told Emma to put the envelope back where she had found it. She went to her room, filled with morbid thoughts. Eamonn went to his study.

That evening, Emma went up to Eamonn with a poem she had written: it was about Kevin's caul. Eamonn read it, then pulled a piece of paper out of his pocket.

'It's weird you should write that,' he said. 'Have a look at this.'

Eamonn had written about the caul, too.

The experience moved Eamonn deeply. For Kevin was a brother, who had died when he was nearly a year old. Eamonn was only a toddler himself and was not told how or why Kevin died; but he remembered, vividly, finding out and running to an aunt's house and locking himself in a bedroom and crying and screaming because his heart was broken.

Neither Eamonn nor Emma mentioned Kevin's caul again.

Eamonn's favourite work was 'Adlestrop', a poem about a station, by Edward Thomas. He never told me why he liked it so much, but a friend, the late Tomara Issacs, had given it to him years before and Eamonn carried it in his wallet for years.

Emma would love hearing Eamonn talk about a certain book, then surprise him with it for his birthday or Christmas. After he died, she got all these books back – a poignant, if terribly sad, reminder of the literary joys they shared.

Although Eamonn was phenomenally successful in what he was doing, he thought television was an awful career, and he didn't want any of the children to try to follow in his footsteps.

I didn't realize until years later that, in terms of thinking what she was going to do in life, Emma had an awful time growing up. She believed that because her Daddy was famous, she would have to be, too; and she used to worry herself sick because she didn't know what she could do. It was such a relief for her when she went into her first job – public relations – and realized she could just work like everybody else, and be ordinary.

Before that first job, however, she did secretly fancy following in her father's footsteps – and without telling him went to RTE for an interview as a continuity announcer.

She wasn't surprised in the least when she didn't get it. 'I must have been out of my childish mind, putting myself up for such ridicule,' she told me later. 'I hadn't a clue. I couldn't even speak one word of Irish!'

The last thing Emma would have wanted is for her Daddy to fix it that she got a job in radio or television. She would have wanted to do it on her own or not at all, and Eamonn would have appreciated and understood that.

He was tolerant and understanding in everything they wanted to do. But he put his foot down when Niamh told him she wanted to become an actress. He made his point by saying that for every successful actress who landed a starring role there were hundreds, if not thousands, drawing the dole. Niamh quickly dropped the idea and took up looking after children instead. Now she is an air stewardess – with Aer Lingus, naturally.

If Eamonn had had his way, we would have been surrounded by children. In fact, when a nun rang us, offering twins for adoption shortly after Niamh arrived, Eamonn's eyes lit up at once. I went into total shock at the prospect of having any more, but I was terrified I might be persuaded by Eamonn, who adored being with children and playing with them. Fortunately, he understood that enough was enough, and adoption was never mentioned again.

It was a shame for Eamonn, I suppose, because he had an inborn talent for getting on with children; a magical way of looking at them which made them *take to him immediately. He was able to communicate at their level without being childish and they always fell for him.*

He always talked to children and would perform tricks with coins, or mime or make rabbit's ears, which never failed to make them laugh.

At home, he would think nothing of crawling around on the floor with our three, letting them clamber all over him. He was their friend as well as their Daddy, and they adored him. When Niamh was a child, they were always running around the house, roaring and screaming, and hiding from each other. It was a game that went on for years and when it was over, when Niamh had grown up and didn't want to hide any more, Eamonn felt sad, as though he had lost part of himself with the passing of her childhood. He came in one day and, spotting Niamh in another part of the house, immediately went into hiding. He waited and waited, expecting Niamh to discover him. But she didn't and a good twenty minutes later he emerged to find Niamh curled up in a chair, reading a magazine.

'Hi, Dad,' she said.

'Didn't you wonder where I was?'

Puzzled, Niamh said: 'What do you mean?'

'I was hiding. Weren't you looking for me?'

'No,' said Niamh unconcernedly and went back to her magazine.

And that was that. The hiding game was over for ever.

Niamh was always a Daddy's girl, however, in a different way from her sister. Whereas Emma would just want Eamonn to read to her, Niamh would leap into his arms for kisses and cuddles. She was still doing it at eighteen years old and nine stones when Eamonn was losing strength and barely able to hold her.

Much as he loved seeing children playing and having fun, Eamonn did not like the idea of them thinking war, even a game of cowboys was fun. He hated guns and everything to do with them, and he did not even allow Fergal to have one as a toy. I didn't agree with this because it was harmless, and all Fergal's little friends had toy guns. But Eamonn was obsessed with it. We didn't argue; it would have been stupid for me to insist Fergal was given a gun; and anyway, the boy had most other things, so not having a cowboy pistol was no big drama.

Eamonn not only worked hard, but he played hard, too, and on summer holidays he would switch off and throw himself wholeheartedly into having a fun time. Since he was away from home so much, the summer break was vitally important to us all and we had some memorable, magical times. When the children were small, we travelled the world – to Jamaica, the Bahamas, Portugal, Corfu and Majorca and other sunny spots – either as a family on our own, or with friends and their children. Usually, we rented a house or a villa. Eamonn was always keen to have a holiday in Ireland, though, and we would also find time to go to Cork or Galway or Kerry or other picturesque spots on the beautiful west coast, for a week or two.

For several years when the children were growing up, we also hired a launch for a sailing holiday on the Shannon, Britain's longest river. And out of all the wonderful times we spent together, our very first boat trip is by far the most memorable. How can we forget it? As a holiday, it was not so much a comedy of errors as a series of dramas.

For a start, our skipper – Eamonn, naturally – had never steered a boat in his life. I didn't know the ropes either and ordered too many provisions, with disastrous results. And, to cap it all, a doctor had to be called to Emma – thanks to a dead fish. Oh, yes, and Fergal fell overboard!

We were so excited the morning of that first boat trip: it was an adventure; we were literally sailing into the unknown. My job was to ensure that the one thing we didn't do was run out of food or drink, so I went crazy, ordering all sorts of provisions to cover every conceivable situation. That was mistake number one: I ordered so much stuff there was no room for it all in the tiny galley and I had to find space for it wherever I could in other parts of the boat.

The booze I'd bought was a problem: where was I going to put that? Our bedroom – the captain's cabin – was the answer, but all the cupboards and drawers were jam-packed, if not with clothes, with tins and jars of food. The only place I could think of was a sort of dressing-table: not ideal, but it was any port in a storm, if you get my nautical drift.

Sadly, for me, that was my second mistake. For the moment Eamonn switched on the engine and we set off, there was this almighty crash, as though we'd smashed into some rocks. And I discovered that the bottles of booze had promptly skidded along the dressing-table and on to the bed. A whisky bottle had broken, with its contents soaking the only blankets the cabin possessed. It rained throughout the trip, so the blankets had no chance to dry out. Have you ever tried sleeping in whisky-sodden blankets for seven nights? It's enough to put one off the stuff for life.

Our trusty skipper managed to steer us safely to our first port of call, where Fergal promptly fell in, fully clothed. Someone – I can't remember who – fished him out and Eamonn ordered us all to wear lifejackets. Come to think of it, he didn't bother to wear one himself.

The next casualty was Emma: she found a dead fish, which she looked on proudly as some sort of trophy. She stuck a finger in its mouth, as young children are wont to do, and unfortunately stabbed herself on a sharp tooth. Predictably, perhaps, on that accident-prone holiday, it gave her an infection and she was so sick we had to leave the boat to find a doctor. He was called Davy Jones, as was the plumber we had to call to pump out the loo when it broke!

Despite the set-backs and the dreadful weather, we made the best of it, however. We had some lovely lunches and dinners – and, of course, Eamonn the ever-willing chef was in his element frying massive Irish breakfasts for us all in that tiny galley. Lying in that sodden bed with the gorgeous smell of sausages and bacon thankfully overpowering the now familiar stench of whisky is a memory that will never leave me.

Later, Eamonn and Fergal did some fishing. One day they were so excited, we all felt they had caught a whopper. But it turned out to be an old sock. It seemed to sum up the holiday.

For a man who made a living from surprising people Eamonn was not that keen on surprises himself. Apart from the two This is Your Life shows, he was surprised only one other time – by me. And the secret arrangements were so nerve-wracking, the whole thing left me wondering how the This is Your Life team go through such tension week after week.

It was Eamonn's birthday: nothing special; not a recognized milestone like fifty or sixty – sort of in-between – but I just felt like springing something different. I confided in Eamonn's accountant, Conor Crowley, and asked him to set up a meeting with Eamonn that would keep him out of the house until 7 P.M., by which time all our friends would be assembled.

It was an arrangement that could have ruined a good friendship. Eamonn, assuming the meeting had been called for an important reason, was on time as usual – probably early. But Conor, who knew there was nothing to discuss, didn't bother turning up until half an hour after the scheduled time. Eamonn was steaming. He was just about to leave when Conor walked in. Somehow Conor covered the reason for calling a meeting and then they drove to The Quarry. Eamonn thought they were picking up Conor's wife, Pat, and me to go out for dinner, but, of course, when they arrived the place was full with friends wanting to wish Eamonn a happy birthday. Eamonn enjoyed it, but I felt totally drained by the suspense of it all, and I vowed: no more surprises. The most amusing part was chatting about it afterwards and hearing Eamonn tell how mad he was at being kept waiting for a meeting he didn't know didn't exist.

He threw a surprise party for me to celebrate our twenty-first wedding anniversary – and it was a disaster. Twenty-one is nothing special, but Eamonn, in his sweet innocence, thought it was like the personal birthday milestone, and arranged for a gathering at my favourite Chinese restaurant, Fu Tong, in London. He was working on the Today programme at the time and told me he would meet me at the restaurant after the show. When I arrived, I asked for a table for two on the ground floor where Eamonn and I usually went, but the restaurant manager started taking me upstairs. I didn't even know there was seating upstairs and was flabbergasted to see Eamonn sitting down with eight of our friends. It should have been a memorable night, and it was – for the wrong reasons. One of the guests, the actor Rex Harrison, behaved so badly, he was an embarrassment.

Eamonn, always the perfect host, had ordered everything. The food kept coming in typical Chinese fashion and the drink was coming out of our ears. But Rex wasn't satisfied and he kept clicking his fingers at the waiters for more and more wine. He was so rude, so dreadfully bad-mannered that for me he ruined what should have been a fun evening.

He was only there because he had married Richard Harris's ex-wife, Elizabeth, who was our friend. The next day Elizabeth sent me some flowers, with a note apologizing for her 'horrible' husband.

I appreciated the gesture. But I felt sorry for Elizabeth. There was only one person with the need to apologize . . . and it wasn't her.

I was not really surprised at Harrison's bad manners. He had behaved in a ghastly manner one evening before their marriage when Elizabeth invited us to his flat for dinner with the playwright, John Mortimer, and Imogen Hassal, the actress, who years later, tragically died.

I can remember the evening only for its awfulness. The flat looked like the set for A Streetcar Named Desire; there were cobwebs all over the place, as though it had not been cleaned for months. And Harrison was so arrogant and selfish, it made me wonder how and why poor Elizabeth got involved with him.

One faint memory moves hazily out of the mists of time: Elizabeth's record player went wrong and she was doing her best to fix it. Harrison was most irritated and started moaning at her.

We were all embarrassed and I remember telling him, as politely as I could, to shut up. 'It is Elizabeth's after all,' I said.

'Yes,' he snapped arrogantly. 'And she should damn well know how to use it!'

To the world who saw My Fair Lady, Harrison was the cultured Higgins, who taught Eliza etiquette. To me, he was the one in need of lessons in good manners.

Surprises were out, however, when it came to birthday and Christmas presents for me. Eamonn wouldn't risk buying something I didn't like, so he always played safe by asking me in advance what I wanted. He always hated going into shops but he went to Gucci because they sent him a catalogue and he could order something by phone and pick it up later. He did try a couple of surprises in our early days, but was put off because I didn't like them. One present was a big Gucci stole, which wasn't me, and I exchanged it for a blouse; the other was a black and brown bag, which I gave to Emma, since I didn't possess one thing that was brown.

He didn't have much idea about hats for me, either. At Easter one year we were going to a lunch and I needed a new hat, so Eamonn said he would buy me one as a present. Normally, I would have chosen it myself at the shop in London where I had been buying hats for ten years, but, for some reason, I couldn't get there. Without hesitation, Eamonn said he would choose one himself. Well, you should have seen it. It was a pudding-basin shape, very old-fashioned and it sat on my head like a potty. I couldn't bring myself to wear it to the lunch – or, in fact, anywhere!

He was always buying flowers and in the early days bought me lots of lovely jewellery. He stopped jewellery gifts later because he felt they might attract the attention of the wrong sort of person – and because he thought I had enough anyway!

Eamonn's last two presents will have an everlasting memory. One was some flowers he bought me to thank me for looking after him during an attack he had in Dingal: his 'Florence Night-and-Day-agale,' he called me. The other was a coat. Eamonn had been worrying about what he was going to buy me for Christmas, so I pointed out the coat in a Dublin shop and he ordered it. By the time Christmas came, Eamonn was dead and I wasn't interested in presents, but the shop rang anyway – discreetly, I must admit – and asked for the money. Eamonn's probably laughing that the final joke was on me . . . because I'd picked a particularly expensive present and had to pay for it myself!

It was supposed to be a momentous occasion. The quayside was packed. A band played Dixieland jazz. The gangplank was lined with everyone who was anyone in Dublin high society. All eyes were on me as I stepped forward and took the champagne bottle at the end of the rope. Nervously, I pulled my hand back, ready to let the bottle swing out and smash against the side of the ship in the traditional way. The band stopped playing. The crowds hushed, expectantly, preparing to cheer. Forcing a smile through my nerves, I let go of the bottle. It swung out towards the ship. I tensed, waiting for the sound of glass smashing against steel; for the cheers that would herald the launch of Eamonn's latest enterprise.

But nothing happened. The bottle missed the ship and the rope brought it swinging back to the quayside. Someone caught it and handed it to me. A flush of embarrassment tingling my cheeks, I pulled my hand back again, further this time, and let go. But, once more, the bottle missed the ship and came swinging back, impotently.

No one seemed quite sure what to do. I thought of picking up the bottle and chucking it at the ship; it would have smashed then; but I suppose I would have ended up in the Liffey myself. In the end, I was told simply to smash the bottle on the gangplank itself – which I did, successfully, I'm happy to say.

The next day, the Irish papers were full of the story. My bad luck with the champagne that day in July 1984 was a bad omen, they said. And they were right. The floating restaurant and disco aboard the MV Arran, the project on which Eamonn and his business partners were pinning all their hopes, was to sink just seven months later. Significantly, perhaps, the last nail was banged into its coffin on January the thirteenth.

The trouble was that Eamonn's business interests, which he and his partners had nurtured carefully over nearly forty years, were sinking slowly in a financial quicksand and they needed the Arran to take them to safer waters. If the project had taken off, captured the public's imagination the way everyone envisaged, Eamonn, I'm sure, would have been alive today. As it was, the business disaster, and its messy aftermath, was the beginning of the end.

Eamonn had nothing to be ashamed of: the idea of a restaurant and disco on a boat was a good idea, if a little ahead of its time, and he made sure no one but himself lost money. But, as a well-known TV personality, he was up-front, the one who made the headlines, and the pressures caused him a lot of stress. And that, I'm convinced, started the illness that was to kill him.

People thought that Eamonn earned a fortune from his Irish business interests. Nothing could be further from the truth. In all the years since he and Dermod Cafferky formed Broadcasting Company and watched it grow into Broadcasting and Theatrical Productions, none of the partners – except Fred O'Donovan – had taken out a penny in salary. Both Eamonn and Dermod had other jobs that paid the bills; so they ploughed back whatever money was made, as an investment for the future; a sort of pension plan.

In the early days, Eamonn regarded his business interests outside British television as a hobby. But this changed when Broadcasting and Theatrical Productions became Eamonn Andrews Studios, and Fred O'Donovan was paid a salary as chief executive, responsible for the day-to-day running of the company. Eamonn saw the long-term potential of what they were doing and always took a deep interest in what was going on, what decisions had to be taken.

He was fully behind the decision to take over Dublin's Four Provinces Ballroom and turn it into the Television Club. And when it was suggested that the Dolphin Hotel, which had been closed for four years, could be turned into something new and spectacular, Eamonn was all for it; as he was with the suggestion later, to buy the Portmarnock Country Club.

In looking for the moment it all started to go sour, when a wrong decision was made, it is hard to ignore what happened involving the Gaiety Theatre. For some years, the company had been producing summer shows and pantomimes for the theatre's impresario, Louis Elliman. But then, in 1967, Louis died. With no outlet now for its shows, the company negotiated to buy the theatre from the man who owned it – one Joseph Murphy. His asking price was £120,000 – not a small sum, but one that could easily be raised from a bank, since the company's various enterprises were profitable. One of the company's financial consultants, however, advised against buying. It was better to rent, he said, because the company was in entertainment, not the property business.

The advice did not appeal to Dermod, who felt it would be better for a theatrical company to have its own theatre. But the consultant's figures made sense to Eamonn. And when Murphy revealed that he was planning to knock down the Gaiety and replace it with an exciting cinema-theatre complex to seat 2,000 people, the company saw the sense in renting it. They agreed to a £4,500-a-year rent. Two and a half years later, however, Murphy's plans were no further advanced, and when the rent was due, he sought an increase. When that lease ran out another couple of years later, Murphy doubled the rent – and Eamonn and his partners saw red.

Fred O'Donovan exposed Murphy to the papers, over his future plans for the Gaiety. Murphy countered by issuing a High Court writ for libel against Mr O'Donovan, but made the silly mistake of denying that he ever intended pulling down the theatre. This gave Eamonn Andrews Productions a chance to go for a twenty-one-year lease by bringing a court action under the Landlord and Tenant Act, which states that if someone has occupied premises for a certain length of time they are entitled to a twenty-one-year lease. It was a bitter battle that went all the way to the Supreme Court. Murphy, who had dropped his libel action, fought like a tiger, but lost in the end. He tried to get his own back when the new twenty-one-year lease came up for a seven-year review by increasing the £15,000 rent to £60,000. Eamonn's company got it down by half, but the years of bitter haggling with the landlord were to come home to roost very soon. Mr Joseph Murphy was to have his revenge, all right.

By now, the late seventies, Eamonn's little empire was looking healthy. Eamonn Andrews Studios was a million-pound company. The Gaiety was staging a pantomime and summer show for twenty weeks of the year and being hired out the rest of the time. And the Dolphin Hotel and Portmarnock Country Club, which had developed management problems, had been sold off at a good profit. Eamonn was still riding high and Dermod's advertising agency was now the third largest in Ireland.

But within a couple of years, the two main sources of the company's income – the Gaiety and the Television Club – were in trouble, due to a rise in VAT to twenty-five per cent and the decline of ballroom dancing in favour of discos with liquor licences. Little could be done about either, but what brought matters to an ugly head was Joseph Murphy's claim that the company directors were breaking the terms of the lease by not keeping the Gaiety in a 'proper manner'. He said £350,000 at least was needed to put the building into a 'proper condition'. The company had spent some £250,000 on refurbishment and was keeping its head above water, but not doing enough business to find *that sort of money. Dermod, who was now involved in the day-to-day running of the businesses, approached the government and Dublin Corporation for funding, but Murphy heard about this and announced to the newspapers: 'There's no need for state help – I'll do the renovation myself.'*

Eamonn and co. thought that was the end of their financial nightmare. But it was only the beginning. No sooner had the government backed off than Murphy – who, no doubt, had been given excellent legal advice –slapped a claim on Eamonn Andrews Productions Ltd for £350,000. The company was technically insolvent. The directors had no alternative but to put it into liquidation.

At the same time, the rent for the Television Club went up from £7,000 to £50,000 a year. Dermod successfully negotiated for the increase to be spread over seven years, but the discos' stranglehold was squeezing the life out of dancehalls. The Television Club had, quite simply, had its last waltz.

That year, 1983, was a bad year. Eamonn would attend one meeting after another, then fly off to London and appear in front of millions of This is Your Life *viewers as though nothing was wrong in his life. He didn't tell me all that was going on – or going wrong! – but I knew, from the nature of the meetings in our home, that the businesses were in trouble; and it didn't help when, the week after the company closed the Gaiety doors for the last time, the Government reduced VAT from twenty-five to ten per cent. Whether the cut would have been the difference between profit and loss, success or failure, is immaterial. It was too late for the Gaiety, and too late for Eamonn Andrews Productions Ltd.*

And then, in the middle of all the financial crisis, a charming man in his mid-forties came into our lives. He was tall and bearded and handsome and he had an idea.

He had, he told Dermod Cafferky, come from Canada, where he'd worked on a boat that had been converted into a floating restaurant and disco. The business had been successful; there seemed no reason why it couldn't work in the basin of the Liffey. The man was named Brian O'Farrell. He was an ideas man – someone who could put such a project together, make it happen. All he needed was financial backing.

Dermod told Eamonn and my father, Lorcan. The idea appealed to them. It was fresh and original, and the location O'Farrell suggested was ideal. The waterfront had always been a rough area, attracting rough people, but, like the

East End of London, offered marvellous business opportunities. And, anyway, the boat could be launched as an up-market venue, which could discourage the wrong sort of clientele.

By now, O'Donovan had walked out of the business with a six-figure sum for his twenty-two per cent share holding. For months he had been saying he had heart problems and the company should take on a younger man as managing director. Eamonn and his partners tried to persuade him to stay, but finally they believed him when he said he needed to sell his shareholdings and go and live in Florida for health reasons. In the event, O'Donovan did not go to Florida. He stayed in Dublin and took up the chairmanship of the National Concert Hall and RTE.

I never saw Eamonn more angry than he was when he heard that O'Donovan was claiming Eamonn offered his job to someone else while O'Donovan was on his 'death-bed'. It simply was not true and Eamonn was shattered that someone who had been a friend as well as a business partner could say that about him. He hated legal action, but when he heard the story again, he fumed, 'I'm going to sue the next time I hear that.'

Soon, however, he had other problems on his mind.

The money put up by Eamonn Andrews Studios Ltd and a long list of investors was not enough; in fact, it was all gone before the launch date. Shareholders refused to invest more, so the company decided to open just half the boat. It was not ideal because it meant catering for less than half the number the boat was licensed for – but there was no option. If the writing was on the wall then, no one was admitting it: certainly Eamonn felt confident the enterprise was so good that enough business would be generated to fund the opening of the second half of the boat very quickly.

So we didn't dwell on the newspapers' prophecies of doom after that embarrassing quayside ceremony. We enjoyed the opening night party and, next morning, left for a two-week sailing holiday in Italy with Eamonn's accountant, Conor Crowley, and his wife Pat. We were confident that we would return to discover that, despite the financial headaches, everyone's faith was justified; that the idea of drinking and dining on the river under the stars had caught the public's imagination and business was booming.

But when we got back we found that the police had closed the boat. While attracting an up-market clientele, it had also drawn an undesirable element more interested in drinking and fighting than eating in the restaurant or *dancing in the disco. And some customers had been seen selling drugs, so the police had moved in.*

Suddenly, for Eamonn and for all of us, the floating dream had become a nightmare. It closed and did re-open, two weeks later, but the publicity had given the boat a bad name and the restaurant never had a chance. As summer moved into autumn, business simply got worse and worse and Eamonn, Dermod and Lorcan, the principal shareholders, came under pressure from creditors.

Eamonn would worry about the little things in life, but with major problems he was strong and brave and just got on with what had to be done to solve them. As the pressure mounted, he called meetings at our house and he and Dermod and Lorcan would tuck themselves away in Eamonn's study upstairs, trying to work out ways to come out of the disaster, losing as little face, and money, as possible.

Eamonn was never nervous or indecisive at these meetings. He was totally in control and could always come to the kernel of a problem, rather than get caught up in the woolly stuff around the edges. He would be tolerant of irrelevancies – chit-chat and jovial banter – but always knew the bottom line which was: Let's not have any doubts about what we're here to discuss and decide.

More tense meetings were held at The Quarry. Christmas 1983 was a very sombre affair, with Eamonn's mind on the imminent collapse of the company that bore his name and its subsidiary, Customs Line Ltd, which ran the Arran ship. The Official Receiver finally moved into the offices of Eamonn Andrews Studios on 13 January 1985.

It took some time to get used to it, but, finally, I saw the end of everything as good. The terrible strain of all those meetings on Eamonn was distressing for all of us. The publicity was worst: Eamonn felt so embarrassed, not only for himself, but for others. If no one had been well-known, newsworthy, the business collapses would have attracted minimal publicity; but because Eamonn was who he was, the whole affair made the headlines and threw the spotlight on to others.

Eamonn felt sad for Dermod when Arrow Advertising had collapsed; they had known each other for more than forty years and were very close. Eamonn felt fortunate in that he, himself, had a business life outside Ireland, but Arrow and the businesses with Eamonn were all that Dermod had, and with everything gone, the big man worried what Dermod would do. It is pleasing that, despite the agony of it all, they didn't fall out. In fact, Eamonn did not fall out with anyone. It was important to him that no one who had put their faith in the ship project would lose their money, and he picked up a certain amount of liabilities to make sure this didn't happen.

I was desperately worried for him when he went to London for a This is Your Life *programme; the thought of him being exposed to all the curiosity of executives and researchers and secretaries made me feel quite ill. But when he came home and told me what had happened I felt very proud of him.*

When he'd walked in, there was a deathly hush. Usually, there was a lot of laughter and joking, but this time no one knew what to say. Eamonn faced them all and said, with the twinkle they all knew so well: 'Rumours of my debts are greatly exaggerated.'

The play on the words of the legendary Mark Twain went down well and everybody laughed, no one, I'm sure, heartier than Eamonn. Tom Brennand asked if it was all right to make jokes about it and Eamonn said yes, but after that, no one did, no one even mentioned it. Not in front of Eamonn, at least.

I admired his courage so much. In the midst of financial catastrophe, he had to pick himself up and face his colleagues and get on with his work. It took a big, brave man to do that.

Friends were very kind, none more so than dear Spike Milligan. When he heard everything had gone under, he rang Eamonn and insisted on us going to dinner at his home. He was upset, he said, but wanted us to know he was flying the flag for Eamonn. A few days later, we drove through the snow and had a wonderfully comforting evening in the warmth of Spike's hospitality.

There were no post-mortems. It was done, over, finished. Eamonn, Dermod and Lorcan had taken a gamble, a carefully considered one, but a gamble, nevertheless, and they had coped with the failures as best they could. There was no point in apportioning blame to anyone. They just had to get on with their lives as best they could and put the disaster behind them.

At home, Eamonn did not have black moods. He was furious that it had turned out so badly, of course, but he never once screamed or ranted and raved and he made sure it never put a strain on our marriage. I kept as calm as I could; there was nothing I could do, so there was no point in getting upset.

But the trauma of those agonizing months bit deep into all our lives and, I'm sure, played a part in taking the two men closest to me and my family.

My father, Lorcan, was a night person: as managing director of the Gaiety, he was always around in his tuxedo; always in good spirits, infecting everyone he met with his good humour and joie de vivre. The theatre was his life, and when that was taken away, he had to readjust. He never did. For the first time in his adult life, he had nowhere to go at night, nothing to dress up for, and he never came to terms with it. He was seventy-five years young with so much still to offer, but he was never the person he had been before. He finally died of cancer. But it was what went before that broke his spirit and started his decline.

Many people said they thought we caught certain *This is Your Life* subjects too young – Tommy Steele, Barry Sheene, Bonnie Langford, for example. But there were moments when we arrived too late, when the proposed subject had outlived contemporaries who could have illuminated the achievements of his or her life and been happy surprises to boot.

On the other hand, some of our younger researchers came bubbling to the conference table with a great idea only to be told: 'We've done that story already.' It was always sad to see the faces fall. The resilient ones – and most of them are just that and more – often come back and say: 'Well, it's worth doing again.' One such case was Sir Matt Busby, the legendary soccer boss. We were happy to 'do' him again because he had, almost literally, had a second life. The Munich aircrash had destroyed his beloved Manchester United team and he, himself, had barely survived.

As the world of football and beyond knows, Matt not only picked up the threads of his own life courageously and doggedly, but rebuilt United to another world force. Obviously, it was a delicate area, but well worth trying. And after months of careful investigation and personal soul-searching – he was a dear friend – we decided to go ahead. It was a warm and wonderful show, but at almost the last moment we almost failed to pull it off. We had planned to spring the surprise on Manchester City's Maine Road pitch immediately after a game against United. City boss Joe Mercer arranged for Matt to make some presentations from the centre circle, after the final whistle. The plan was for a small table to be set up, a microphone placed in position and Matt come on to the cheers of the crowd.

I was to sprint – well, canter – from the tunnel, flanked by covering officials and players, and get to Matt before he knew what was happening. You can imagine the reaction we expected from the crowd.

Minutes before the final whistle, I was outside in the scanner van, watching the game on monitors and checking all those potential last-minute frighteners that lurk around before every programme – when, suddenly, the really big one hit us: the police superintendent in charge of operations decided it was too risky; he could not guarantee the safety of all concerned if the crowd erupted on to the pitch and, reluctantly, he was not going to let our programme go ahead. We were all shell-shocked. Maybe someone had slipped up and he hadn't been briefed properly. Maybe we had stood on his dignified toes. Maybe, for that matter, he felt the fans had become so excited that it was now a danger he hadn't envisaged earlier. One way or another, we were in trouble.

We tried to locate the Chief Constable of Manchester. But it was impossible, given the time available and the conditions we were working under.

Once again, it was that lovable lion-heart Joe Mercer who came to the rescue. He told the superintendent he would take full responsibility – and we got the go-ahead.

I made it down to the touchline just in time and started heading for Matt. The crowd *did* erupt, but, thankfully, Matt was cheered to the echo – by United *and* City fans. When it comes to someone like Matt, rivalries didn't count.

In my case, it was quite different, of course. Apparently, producer Malcolm Morris and the boys had been toying with the idea for some time and finally they got the nod from Grainne. We were coming towards the end of the series. The second-last programme had already been recorded for reasons that escape me now and we wanted a big finish for the last show. We found exactly what we wanted – a wonderful, heroic, colourful story of an English missionary, who was coming home after a lifetime spent in the field. It was full of surprises, humour, pathos. It had everything. I couldn't believe we should be so lucky for the last programme. I wasn't to know there was no such person! We had arguments about how and where he should be surprised and, looking back on it now, I realize that I won a lot of these arguments that might otherwise have given me a hard time. One thing we don't have is a team of yes-men or yes-women.

I must explain that, at this time, I was hosting the *Today* show every day except Wednesday, when *This is Your Life* would go out. My second home – or, more accurately my third home – was Euston Studios and I felt as if I spent as much time in my little dressing-room there as I did anywhere else. It's a routine you quickly get into and I was enjoying every moment of it. Current Affairs, Politics, Religion, Sport, Theatre. It was all there, live, exciting, unpredictable. I was as likely to be interviewing the Prime Minister one day as I was the newsvendor from Piccadilly the next. I tell you this to help you understand how the most meticulously laid plot almost went wrong. No predictable detail had been overlooked. I was expecting to do the missionary programme on the Wednesday, live, but, meanwhile, David Nixon had asked me if I would be kind enough to do a guest spot on his programme. He knew I very seldom did these if I could avoid them and he was his own hesitating, diffident self asking me. He knew too, of course, that I owed him a favour or two and that we were very, very old friends. Of course, I said yes. This was to take place on the Monday.

The week before, because of the recording, I had a free Wednesday and that's how everything almost went crucially wrong. I was in town visiting a friend in hospital – one of my colleagues in Butlins, of which I was at that time a director. The hospital wasn't far from the studios and, when I came out, seeing that it was a bright, sunny day, I decided to walk over to them and see how next week's programme was getting on. The *This is Your Life* offices were in the same building, of course, as the *Today* programme. I had, in fact, received an outline draft script from that great reporter-turned-researcher-writer, Jack Crawshaw, and I wasn't totally happy with it. I strolled into the Euston Studios, was about to get into the lift to go up to the *This is Your Life* offices when something made me change my mind and carry on to my dressing-room on the ground floor to check if there was any urgent mail or messages there. Had I gone upstairs at that moment, Malcolm and Jack and the others working with me on the programme had a number of giveaway things spread over the desks, notably old family photographs and memorabilia that might be of use on the programme. There would have been no way of hiding them, had I walked in unexpectedly. The second stroke of luck was that laziness overcame my bones and, instead of going up, I telephoned Jack, who, at that moment, had sat down behind his typewriter to hammer out a few glowing words about me for the next week's programme – the real programme. I gave him an earful about the draft script of the fictitious programme that I had before me. Obviously he hadn't put his heart into it, but there was no way I could have guessed why. When he heard where I was, he said he'd be down to see me right away. The scene now shifts back to Jack. Having given him what-for (he tends to exaggerate this part of the story) he slammed down the phone, banged the typewriter, and muttered: 'I can't write glowing words about that bastard!' Anyway, we sorted it all out a few minutes later without me even guessing that poor old Jack was trying to summon up enthusiasm for a non-existent missionary.

Monday rolled on and I was back in my dressing-room going through the research needed for the evening programme when Malcolm put his head around the door.

'Hey,' he said. 'They tell me you're going on David Nixon's show tonight. What's that all about? I thought you didn't like doing those things.' I explained and he said, 'Fair enough. Tell you what, I'm driving out there this evening and I'll give you a lift after your programme. What time are you expected?'

I told him about 7.30, thanked him and said: 'Fine, that would suit me down to the ground.' I got on with my work and, when I tried to make a telephone call, I was unable to do so and called the operator. She apologized. She said there was some fault on my line and that I'd have to ring her to get a line out. They'd have it fixed by tomorrow. I thought nothing more of it. Immediately after the programme, Malcolm popped in and I was starting to get nervous about the next show, as I always do, even though, in this case, I had been assured by David all I had to do was help him saw a lady in half! Malcolm now said, very casually: 'Oh, by the way, there was a message for you to phone Grainne at home in Dublin.'

'Hell, I can't phone her now. Besides which, the phone is out of order.' He told me to relax, as he often does, and said there was plenty of time before we need dream of being at Teddington, where the

Nixon show was taking place. I said OK and called the operator and gave her the Dublin number, saying that, if there was any problem about getting it quickly, to cancel it as I had to move out of the studios fairly soon. Within seconds, she had Grainne on the line.

'I know you're in a hurry, darling,' she said. 'But Conor was on the phone and said he has to go to Geneva tomorrow and won't be able to meet you as arranged. I thought you'd better know in case you didn't ring me later tonight.'

'Fine. Fine. How's everyone? Talk to you tomorrow. Bye.'

It was a brilliant, additional brush-stroke. It placed Grainne clearly in my mind's eye across the sea in Dublin, although she was, of course, already sitting nervously in Teddington Studios, from where she'd spoken to me. It's the sort of additional precaution that's well worth taking just in case, in the million-to-one off-chance the person in question has vaguely suspected something. Belt and braces.

Off we sailed to Teddington. *The David Nixon Show* had already started when they brought me down to the wings in the studio. David dashed out and apologized for not having had time to talk to me beforehand and, although I knew him as a nervous performer, I'd never seen him shake like this before, so I told *him* not to worry.

'All you have to do is what I tell you,' he said, and was gone. Next thing, he had the lady in the box, told the audience he was introducing a new assistant and called me on. I was starting to use the saw when David produced the most enormous *This is Your Life* book I'd ever seen. I thought it was another joke. I only began to realize it was for real when I spotted our resident *This is Your Life* photographer, Stan, in the audience. He's always there to take special shots for the final presentation version of the Big Red Book.

No time to think. The show was on its way. My bewilderment was soon overcome by emotion but I couldn't help be aware, even then, of the brilliance of the deception. The coolness of it. Sheer audacity. The Raffles technique. I had taken my children to school that morning in Dublin (one of the reasons I finally dropped the Friday *Today* show was to have a second bite at the school run and feel that I wasn't a total absentee father). What, of course, I didn't know was that Michael, who then drove me to the airport, had to double-back, re-collect the children from school, pick up Grainne and head for the next plane out. They couldn't have picked a better bunch of my pals and, of course, my ego was nicely buzzed by having Muhammad Ali bounce in by satellite, and the ever-youthful Joe Loss bounce in by legs. Most of all, of course, it was memorable because our three children were on this programme and I suppose I could truthfully say that's where *my* second life began. The moment that touched me most of all was when Grainne came on, kissed me and I could see, through the affection that I so happily take for granted, a flicker of anxiety, trying to assess whether I was pleased or not that she had decided to go with it. I told her then and I tell her now that I was most mightily pleased.

'Never again, though,' she said most firmly. 'Never again. I wouldn't go through that again for anything, not if you live to be a hundred!'

We came to realize over the years that the toughest part of the whole programme belongs to the subject's closest partner and we always tried to make that space of time as short as possible. Incidentally, an additional precaution on the grounds of secrecy was that we never told very young children until the day of the programme. Sometimes we also applied the same rule to beloved grandmothers, who couldn't, in all truth, be expected to keep a secret from favourite apple-of-the-eye grandchildren.

My mother revelled in my notoriety and could find no fault in anything I did, which must have been a great cross for my sisters and brother to bear. I was very conscious of this at times, but could think of no way to prevent it. She survived Dad by more than thirty years and I know how much she would have loved him to have been around to share the spotlight and nod proudly, but, hopefully, humbly, to the neighbours in those evening perambulations that used to be so much part of Dublin life. She tried not to miss any of my broadcasts or television appearances and woe betide me if I forgot to tell her about one in advance.

There *was* one I did forget to tell her about, mainly because I didn't know about it myself until the last minute. It was in December 1981 and I had just sprung a *This is Your Life* surprise on Russell Harty while he was togged up as Father Christmas at Selfridges. He was doing two BBC shows a week at the time and his producer asked me if I would pop in and surprise him on one of them the following Thursday.

Of course I said yes, but then discovered that Russell's programme was coming from Manchester and I had to be in Dublin the next day, the nineteenth, for my birthday: I definitely wanted to be home, because my mother had been confined to bed for several weeks, and would be looking forward to seeing me.

There was consternation all round when we discovered that the last flight left Manchester too early to accommodate Russell's show, but the TV company generously offered to hire a plane and fly me to Dublin themselves.

It was a ghastly night: cold, raw, windy and wet. I didn't want to look a gift horse in the mouth, but the little plane looked very, very shaky. The windscreen wipers didn't seem to be working properly and it was the last tightening of my nerves when we taxied in the dark and the pilot said: 'Keep your overcoat on – the heating isn't working' . . . and then proceeded to wipe the screen with his sleeve!

The bar was open, judging by some miniature bottles in a cardboard box besides me, and I was determined to swallow one as quickly as I could as soon as we were airborne. I did and I did. When the pilot pointed out the lights in the Isle of Man, I was convinced we were flying in the wrong direction; but we made it.

I was like a piece of ice when I got home. Grainne met me and I knew at once something was wrong: my mother was dead.

My sister, Treasa, who was living with her, told me my mother had caught a trailer saying there would be an extract from the *This is Your Life* programme of that week showing how we caught Russell with his beard down, so to speak. So she tuned in and it was a great consolation to me to realize that despite everything she hadn't missed my appearance.

She told Treasa it was very good, closed her eyes and went to sleep. And that was that.

I never liked funerals, although in Ireland they are very important and some people would sooner be dead themselves than miss the funeral of a friend. I preferred to go to church and say a prayer or two for the deceased and his family to the shaking of hands, the condolences, the carrying of the coffin, the graveside, the awful final clump of clay torturing those who survive.

I knew it was a mark of respect, a sign of faith even, but my heart broke for the widows and children, solitary survivors of any partnership. I was ashamed and annoyed when tears came to my eyes: I wanted it all over quickly. I prayed for my friends but I never visited their graves.

My mother had many friends and, it seemed, they all turned up to see her off. Many, I knew; some were just names, and, from some of the words whispered to me, there were faint echoes of her own separate life: the girl I never knew, the might-have-beens I could only have guessed at in the long years of widowhood.

There were some grand names, too, at the church: she would have been chuffed by that, but would have pretended not to notice.

With hindsight now, I could see the struggle she had had, trying to push me out in life, not wanting me to go too far, but anxious that I would shake off the shyness, the desire to hide, to be invisible; and the fear of stepping too far away from her apron strings.

How *This is Your Life* – or the 'Life' as the team called it – survived in Britain to be the institution it was always remained a mystery. Small boys would shout the title at me across the street. Waiters murmured it as they pushed menus under my nose. Total strangers took dares for rushing up to me in pubs, airports, theatres, with anything from a red telephone book to a red handbag, and stumble out the magic words.

Often, people wanted to know where I had the book hidden. And, just as frequently, well-known people, in the most unlikely situations, glanced over their shoulders, a trifle nervously. Once, I was in an ante-room in the Grosvenor Hotel, waiting to interview the actors and actresses in line for the London *Evening Standard* Awards for the Thames current affairs programme, *Today*. I was standing by myself, my hands behind my back, in one of which I held my radio microphone. To my pleasure and surprise, Sir Lew Grade strolled over and started chatting to me. As we spoke, I brought my hands in front of me and Lew spotted the microphone. He took a couple of steps backwards, seemed to pirouette on one toe, and glide back into the group he had just left. No wonder he had been World Champion Charleston Dancer! Anyone watching must have thought I'd eaten a lorry-load of garlic, but I knew the real reason for Lew's vanishing act.

The 'Life' gave me some of the most wonderful, touching, and exhilarating moments I ever had on television. It made life-long friends for myself and the team because, when the show is taken in the spirit it is meant, it is a unique and touching experience for the recipient.

For the most part, the press gave the progamme a helluva time at the beginning. Only one – dear old Peter Black of the *Daily Mail* – had the grace to admit, years later, that he might have gone too far. Critics come and go and new ones, from time to time, sharpen their teeth on the 'Life'. They attack its sentimentality, its alleged predictability, my own ambling idiosyncracies. And, of course, the really intellectual ones pounce on the discovery that it is only subjects of praise who were promoted, ignoring the fact that the programme is a tribute, a salute, a happy party surprise, a nod of gratitude from a community well-served.

One can imagine these critical characters organizing a wedding feast and announcing that the bride's mother is in gaol, and that the groom will have a lot of catching up to do on his father who's been married ten times!

From the very start, the programme was handled with the gentlest care. Our researchers are as delicate as surgeons, as caring as mothers. The guest of honour was always first, the viewer second. If the guest fails to enjoy himself, the team, too, has failed. It does not follow that because a guest has a wonderful time the viewers are bound to feel the same, but we always felt we were more than half-way there. I lost count of the times I heard a guest tell the audience at the end of the show: 'I didn't think it could happen to me . . . I never knew a thing about it.' Even the most cynical of critics must realize now that the programme really is secret. I always regarded this as one of the essential items to the guest's enjoyment, not only because a surprise package is something everyone loves, but because, for instance, it removes any possible accusation of ego and any responsibility for the choice of guests! Apart from the programmes we have cancelled, has anyone known beforehand? Someone somewhere must have had a tip-off, but I certainly never knew of such a situation. All very well, many people said – but how did you guarantee the secret was kept? Simple. First of all, we did not make any major move until we had the permission and blessing of the nearest and dearest, the closest and strongest: wife, husband, mother, daughter, son, partner. It was never difficult to explain that the subject would enjoy the night all the more if it was a surprise. And we made no bones about saying that we would cancel the programme if the secret was blown – though it may break our hearts to do so.

As the research moved outwards, each person was warned that if they told anyone, all they had succeeded in doing was depriving *their* friends of a wonderful evening, and how would they feel about that? We did not have to cancel that many programmes, but one, just before the 1986 season, was a shocking blow and we were almost in tears over it . . .

Sadly, Eamonn never completed this section. But I can tell you that the subject was Barry McGuigan. I can also tell you that I hated the disguises Eamonn wore to surprise the subjects; I was embarrassed by them. Although the opening sequence – the 'pick-up', the team called it – was the best part for many people, I cringed because I felt Eamonn always looked ridiculous. If he was going to be dolled up in something particularly bizarre, he would call me and say: 'Don't look – you're going to hate it.'

Guessing the 'Life' subject became a game between us. He liked to think I would try to find out who it was, but nearly always I didn't bother, which bothered him. If I did try, he never ever told me. The secrecy was everything to him – and I do mean everything.

The return of *What's My Line* to British television after ten – or was it a thousand! – years looked simple enough. In fact, it had taken years to come to the decision, and months of meticulous preparation, before we hit the air.

I had been pressed hard many times to bring back what had, in fact, been the first and probably the most successful panel show. Much as I had enjoyed it first time round, I was reluctant to forsake the new for the old. When Jeremy Isaacs, in his restless wisdom – before being corralled in Channel Four – decided to replace the very successful *Today* show with *Thames at Six*, and cuddly-bear newscaster Andrew Gardner, the pattern of my television appearance suffered dramatic change.

Life was easier, of course. Instead of five shows a week, I could do two, or even one, and still fulfil my contract. But I worked better under a head of steam, so I kept looking for at least a second programme. I had a happy, but most undemanding, season on *Time for Business*, under the production hand of Rab Butler's genial, bearded, civilized son James.

Then we had another stab at the *Eamonn Andrews Show*. Whatever it was on-screen, it was horrendous behind. It was bizarre from the beginning. Production was given to a woman of great charm and force, who had made a name for herself as a steely executive, concerned with million-dollar deals in drama and film, and employed originally by Lew Grade. Her name was Stella Richman. She had inherited from her late husband the well-known White Elephant Club in Curzon Street.

A measure of the improbable success of this short-lived series is that our early official programme meetings took place in a fairly tatty, unheated room somewhere at the top of the club, since facilities were not available at Thames Television itself.

I had Tom and Roy with me, but, otherwise, the team was new: charming but new; young and new.

We were never really clear about what kind of show we wanted – or what calibre of guests. Stella, it appeared, wanted to catch nothing but Big Fry, but we knew from experience it wasn't possible to sustain a flow of four or five guests a week at that level. There were other differences, and I found myself, very, very unhappily, in the middle of many an argument.

An experienced, but moody, scriptwriter was imported to write, among other things, funny lines for me. I had never felt very easy about this. David Frost goes out in front of a tele-prompter and delivers a clatter of gags with the panache that has helped make him the success he is. But I tended to want to stammer and apologize, and explain that I am reading off a tele-prompter. I wanted to disclaim the jokes I had no faith in; and admit I didn't deserve applause for the ones that weren't mine. No wonder the poor scriptwriter threatened to jump off the roof more than once and finally resigned.

Paul Stewart Laing, our director, arrived at the White Elephant on his bicycle. He was a delightful and dedicated character, but within minutes would be having shouting matches with Tom and Roy. Somehow we got on the air despite technical catastrophes and a set in the New London Theatre that, for my money, was never meant to be used in this way and destroyed any hope of cosiness or intimacy necessary for success.

I got the feeling we were beginning to pull it around towards the end of its run and I had a stack of supportive letters when it was decided not to resume it the following season.

Meanwhile, Bryan Cowgill had joined Thames Television as managing director, and I couldn't really blame him for being less than enthusiastic for a talk show that was so torn asunder inside the organization, quite apart from its lack of spectacular success outside.

Next, I was to try *Top of the World*, a courageous technical effort to launch a satellite quiz, linking London, New York and Sydney. In the event, New York became too expensive and we settled for Miami. The show was a kind of *Mastermind* with wings, but it became top-heavy with technicality, short of cash and slow to catch the public attention. On top of that, it was a high-brow quiz and would have needed two or three seasons to mature and grow. But it wasn't to be and, coming up to 1983, I was again looking for a show.

Was it time, I wondered, for *What's My Line?* One of the proposi-
tions put to me outside TV was to try to emulate the daytime version
of the programme they had done in the States. The last time I had
appeared on that, they were recording five shows in one day and the
prospect appalled me on several grounds, not the least of which was
that I was a total, if sometimes irrational, devotee of live television.

I also happened to think that part of the original success of *What's
My Line?* in Britain had been its identification as part of the current
scene; something growing there like a tree, or flowing there like a
waterfall. It wasn't a game where the scoring mattered, although it
was fun to win, no matter which side you were on.

I felt the time was right to bring it back. There is no slide rule for this
kind of thing. You rely on instinct, which is one way of hoping for
some credit if the decision turns out to be the right one.

Thames Light Entertainment boss Philip Jones agreed to have a go.
But he was not convinced that the public cared if a programme was
live or taped. I fought as hard as I could for live shows and, in the end,
Philip came up with what I thought was a very generous compromise,
bearing in mind we could have taped the first series of fourteen
programmes in a couple of weeks at probably a tenth of the cost. The
compromise was that we could present the first programme live and
record a second one immediately afterwards, which would go out the
following week. It meant every second programme was live and the
recorded ones dated by no more than a week.

We were away. My old friend Gil Fates from New York, who had
spent a lifetime producing *What's My Line?* with Franklin Heller, was
brought over to look at the pilot programmes. Leslie Jackson, the
original BBC producer, who had retired, and his successor, Dicky
Leeman, were consulted for their advice. We got two bright, up-and-
coming researchers, Caroline Blackadder and Brian Klein, Maurice
Leonard, who had worked for years on the production team of *This is
Your Life*, as producer, and my old sparring partner from the *Eamonn
Andrews Show* and *This Is Your* Life, Malcolm Morris.

We spent months poring over names and possible panellists. We
agreed we wanted very special people and – no reflection – not
established panellists, no matter how good they were.

Admittedly, there was – in my mind at any rate – temptation to look back at the old *What's My Line?* and try to replace Gilbert Harding and Isobel Barnett and Barbara Kelly. Hold it. Why should we have to replace Barbara Kelly? Barbara Kelly was here. Let's ask her. To my delight, she was all for it and, as millions of viewers were to see, looked as if the years had passed her by, leaving her as we remembered her when she dangled her famous earrings way back in the fifties.

That was that, then: let's build from there. We wanted a blend of youth and maturity, but I was certainly keen to have a heavy philosopher: not necessarily as acerbic as Harding, but someone dependable and real and witty, and not afraid of anyone. John Mortimer came into my head, but he was busy writing. We argued fearfully about people who might not have wanted to take on the task anyway; when you run a television show, it's vital to be arrogant enough to assume that everyone else wants to get on to it.

J. B. Priestley came to mind, but it was a shade too late for that. What about George Gale, the fairly testy newspaper columnist? I'd worked with him on *Today* and had listened to him on Capital Radio's phone-in where he suffered fools with sufficient impatience to make him a most interesting thought.

Someone pressed for Derek Jameson, the ex-Fleet Street editor with the Cockney accent you could cut with a knife, who was in the incomprehensible course of suing the BBC for what seemed to me to be precisely the sort of thing he had himself been sued for.

He was worth trying. He was different. He was earthy. He was fearless. And, behind those Miss Piggy eyes, there was really a twinkle.

Now (sorry Derek), for a bit of sex appeal. Maurice suggested Sacha Distel and we applauded the fine idea until cooler consideration reminded us that Sacha, for all his excellent English, would be out of touch, not only with some of the vernacular, but current and localized information, that would be needed to keep the game itself going.

Someone came up with Patrick Mower – cocky, reasonably irreverent, handsome. He would be appearing in a West End play and would be able to do the first live show at 7.30, but not the second, recorded one. Who would alternate with him? We didn't want another actor, so we rummaged around sportsmen, writers, musicians and came up with that ebullient ex-MP and bestseller author, Jeffery Archer. He, too, was prepared to take part in a pilot; a polite way, if you think about it, of disguising an audition.

The second girl was the problem. The first temptation was to look for someone much younger than Barbara (not younger-looking, Barbara, just younger), and we started considering pop and film stars. I allowed myself the odd reverie that I was Hitchcock, a Cubby Broccoli, rolling my eyes over acres of pulchritude. The names spun around and two contrasting creatures emerged: the glamorous Rula Lenska and the equally glamorous, but oh-so-different, Jilly Cooper. Actress versus writer.

Meanwhile, Grainne came up with an idea: how about our friend, Lady Miranda Iveagh? Brilliant: not only a beautiful, intelligent lady, but a title, to boot. No matter what they tell you, people love a title. I had seen Miranda on Irish TV talking about fashion and knew she had a presence to go with that beauty.

I phoned her, breaking the rule of a lifetime not to get personally involved in the choice of, or invitations to, people on my shows.

Miranda, who was living in London, made all the right noises. She was interested, flattered, but . . . I invited her to lunch. We had a delightful time. And I got so carried away I forgot to submit a claim for expenses. There were problems, but Miranda said she would do a pilot.

Carried away with my head-hunting, title-chasing, I suggested another Irish friend of ours – the suave, just short of arrogant, Lord Henry Mountcharles, who had already dipped his aristocratic toe into the pop world by helping promote open-air concerts at Slane Castle, notably one with the Rolling Stones. Henry also agreed to do a pilot.

The pilots were an almost embarrassing success: everyone was good. Miranda opted out with genuine regret because of family problems. Rula being an actress, as Barbara basically was, we plumped for Jilly.

Patrick Mower had gone a little overboard on the pilot and had almost taken Jilly with him. But, nevertheless, he was very good, very sharp and very with it. As long as we could protect Jilly from actually being seduced on air, he was our man, alternating with Jeffery Archer, who played the game with deadly charm and a kind of Kung Fu logic.

We were all set to go when Philip Jones told us that Eric Morecambe and Ernie Wise were interested. Naturally, that meant we were interested, too. Even though we were interested in having four panellists, there was nothing stopping us having five for the pilot shows. Eric, in particular, was anxious to do a pilot to see if he could play the game and enjoy it. He did both.

We decided that George Gale's, throwaway, friendly, head-scratching, but pretty deadly, style of questioning was somehow right for that end of that panel, so, if we wanted the two top comedians, we had to drop Patrick and Jeffery.

Malcolm suggested having five on the panel, but rejected the idea when his directorial eye started thinking about cameras, camera angles, anticipation shots and the time it would take to get from one questioner and back again. Every panel game in the world, it seemed, had no more than four panellists, so, in the end, we rejected five.

During the night, I started thinking about Mark Goodson and Bill Todman. While trying to coax me to host the game in America, Mark had reminded me of how the simplest solutions were always best. Serenading me in the lush surroundings of New York's 21 Club, he told me how he and Bill thought of enlivening the game by introducing a mystery guest. They were able to entice some of the biggest show-business personalities to wear a hood while the panel tried to guess which famous face was underneath. Mark and Bill would agonize over breakfast about the waste of precious minutes when the viewer could not share the joy of watching the famous face.

Then, one morning over their bagels – hey presto! – they decided to mask the panel instead: put pretty masks over them and let the viewers see the famous guest. Remembering this, I said to Malcolm the next morning: 'What's so sacred about four on the panel? Why don't we have five?' To hell with the camera angles, I said – let's try it: it had to be better value, seeing five faces instead of four. So long as we could keep the pace up, all would be well.

Keeping the pace up, of course, largely fell to me and, in the process, I was bound to be accused of treading on corns and pauses and thoughts. I was used to that. I remembered many years before, dear Isobel Barnett asked to see me privately and, over a cup of tea at my home, complained, more or less on behalf of the panel, that I was interpreting the rules too harshly and, at times, unfairly.

I explained that there had to be a certain amount of head-on collision between the panel and myself; and that one of the essentials of the programme was that I would have to be on the challenger's side, not the panel's. The sagger-maker's bottom knocker, or the plumber's mate, or the chicken sexer may have exotic job descriptions, but, beneath it all, they were nervous people tilting at the windmill.

Isobel took my point and we had a good laugh over it. It was so sad she was not around to see the show return.

The pilots were most encouraging; it was a bit like diving in a pool for the first time in years and discovering you could still swim. Nevertheless, when the clock started creeping past six o'clock at Teddington Studios on Monday, 26 March, the nervous tensions were positively palpable.

I looked at the weir, sparkling in the spring sunshine and could feel again that empty tumble inside my chest. We would have just twenty-six or twenty-seven minutes to try to persuade most of our viewers to switch off the day's cares and have a chuckle and a challenge. If we didn't, we would have failed.

We had spent hours analysing the pilot tapes; let's hope we'd got those simple things right: the set, the light, pens that would flow, numbers that would turn over, to stand up or sit down, to shake hands or not to shake hands, a little bit of music there or not, to discover the panel seated, or have them walk in and lose maybe a precious minute in the process, to dress formally or informally, to persuade the panel and the public that it was not a guessing game, but a game to play . . . and so on and so on.

Security was paramount. Maurice Leonard and myself, nurtured on the cloak-and-dagger secrecy of *This is Your Life*, felt it as natural as breathing. We had to impress it on the rest of the team.

We had a separate secret door for the mystery guests, so that the panel could not spot them through a window or in a corridor. Challengers segregated, as if they had some virulent disease, came to my dressing-room one by one, via a back stair; we had whispered, giggling confabs, to be sure we were talking along the same lines. All had caught the spirit of the show and were determined to win one of those prized certificates for beating the panel. I could feel it was going to be fun.

We had some ticklish occupations for the first show: Mitzi, a glamorous wrestler, the gas lamp lighter, the bird scarers from London Airport, the bee-keeper who, sadly, didn't make it because we ran out of time; and our stand-bys, the telescope-maker and the dog beautician.

Fifteen minutes to go. At the end of the corridor, the panel were being offered a sandwich and a drink and I popped in to wish them luck. There was Barbara, looking cool and pert; Eric Morecambe, with wife Joan, was cracking jokes to keep tension at bay. Snappily dressed Patrick Mower was cooler than he had any right to be: not only was he going to go live on TV, but he was due on stage in the West End by 8.30. Jilly Cooper was talking nineteen to the dozen and telling everyone – well, nearly everyone – that they looked fabulous; and in one heady sentence elevated me to Divinity. George Gale, clutching a glass of beer in one hand, looked as if he was about to burst into tears. Too nervous to say much more than 'Good luck', I waved goodbye and whisked down to the floor below and the heavily-guarded mystery guest – Steve Davis, the world snooker champion.

We had been trying for people such as Ronald Reagan, Frank Sinatra, the Queen Mother, the Duke of Edinburgh and Lord Olivier and, quite frankly, I wondered how this cocky young man would go down with our audience. Would they all know who he was? I needed my head examined. The audience went wild when he appeared, and he dealt with the whole proceedings as if he had been a matinée idol for twice his years. In our brief chat beforehand, he was so cool, and urged me not to mention the music concert he was going to afterwards in case his fans headed there and caused disruption. He was probably right about that, too.

Five minutes to go. Time to get to Studio 2, at the other end of the building. The lift, sir? No thank you, too risky – let's walk. The challengers were all assembled in an ante-room, chattering away like birds in a cage. The panel was already being introduced by warm-up comedian George Martin. I could feel my throat drying up. The make-up girl tapped away a hint of perspiration on my forehead. The felt pens for signing-in were stacked neatly beside me; the first one was being tested. And then I heard the golden voice of that ace of announcers, John Benson, sing out three of my favourite words, *live from London* . . . followed by: *What's My Line?* . . . with Eamonn Andrews. We were on.

Afterwards, everyone was babbling with delight. Or was it relief? Most people kept saying it had been a great show, but I'd learned long before to distrust the well-meaning backstage euphoria that follows almost every performance. I need not have been so cautious: next day the overnight ratings were good – and then, to my joy and relief, we went straight into the Top Ten.

It was a great start. Now we had to sustain it for thirteen or fourteen shows.

Having got the first 'Line' away live, we picked up the following Monday with two shows – one live and one taped. Jeffery Archer, who alternated with Patrick Mower, from the third show, took the game very, very seriously. He learned the trick of dividing the field, of not wasting questions, and was quick to spot my hints that were not readily recognizable unless you knew the answer. He appeared to be so precise, so methodical, approaching meticulous dedication; I suppose that's why he's sometimes accused of being a computer novelist.

At the time, his political novel, *First Among Equals*, was about to be published, and he'd promised to get me a proof copy to read in Crete, where Grainne and I were going on holiday the day after the show. Moments before I was about to go on stage that Monday night, Jeffery pushed a copy of his book into my hand. It just didn't occur to him that I could not walk on clutching an unexplained book. Or, as I pondered afterwards having got to know him better, did it? Anyhow I did read it in Crete and I must say he's quite a storyteller, whatever you may think about his style.

Everyone who remembers the original *What's My Line?* remembers the sagger-makers's bottom knocker, and we were under a lot of pressure to find bizarre occupations; we had fun with jobs such as bottle washer, fishcake maker, pyjama corder, pheasant plucker, sporran maker, carrot grader, fish skinner, turkey stuffer and a young lady named Rosanna, who proudly announced herself as dangle designer.

Finding mystery guests was no problem, since we were in the Top Ten. Denis Healey was caught too quickly, but hilarious in the process; people have said this tough, almost brutal, politician would have made a great comedian and I agree. Peter Ustinov popped in on his one day off from a Broadway play, would you believe? The astonishing Barbara Cartland sailed in, with every second of her arrival time and departure plotted more precisely than had she been royalty. Ringo Starr came along, provided we arranged for him to see *Coronation Street* afterwards. My old boss, Joe Loss, bounced on with the same spring in his step, it seemed, as when I'd first met him at Dublin's Theatre Royal. And, if you're looking for contrasts, we had petite and pretty Petula Clark one week and Big Daddy the wrestler, the next.

We finished the series in July with a mystery guest known the world over – Douglas Fairbanks Junior: mellow, elegant, every inch the courtier. What a pity he's a Yank. Somehow Lord Douglas Fairbanks, or, perhaps, Count Douglas Fairbanks or even King Douglas Fairbanks sounds just right.

The fact that his father is the only actor to have had a stamp issued in his honour is fine, but somehow not quite as good as a title.

Part III

If I needed proof that Eamonn loved me, he provided it when we learned my father had cancer. Daddy couldn't bear the thought of dying in hospital and Eamonn agreed he and Mummy should move in with us at The Quarry. It was an unbearably terrible time: Mummy was diabetic and arthritic, and unable to do even the simplest thing for herself; and my poor Daddy was simply ebbing away. All Eamonn and I could do was try to make everything as peaceful and uncomplicated as possible for them: to ease the suffering as much as we could. Neither of us had any experience of such a harrowing task, and at times I would want to retreat to the privacy of the bedroom and weep at the sadness of it all. But Eamonn was a towering fortress of strength and he helped me through; helped us all through.

He worried about Daddy's dignity in death, and would go to his room and sit at his bedside, holding his hand, and talk to him; putting into words a lifetime of love and respect. When Daddy needed to eat, but didn't want to, Eamonn would gently force the food down him; and when Daddy needed to go to the loo, but was too weak, Eamonn would deal with that, too, with all the caring and patience and discretion of a trained nurse.

I was proud of Eamonn for the manner in which he coped during those final drastic weeks and I was proud, too, of the way my Daddy faced the inevitable. He had always been a chirpy, effervescent personality and he battled hard to retain his lively outlook to the end. He had always loved women; and once, when Mairead, our housekeeper, who is a trained nurse, was giving him a bedbath, he laughed when she reached for a towel to spare his blushes. 'What the hell are you doing that for?' he said. 'You're quite safe. You'll find nothing down there.' It was a characteristic quip that gave us all a welcome smile amid the awfulness of it all.

And then, near the end, when Eamonn was scurrying around, doing this and getting that for him, Daddy's impishness was there again. Looking up at me from his bed, he said: 'Grainne, how did Eamonn Andrews become my waiter?'

Daddy was dead a few days later, but I shall never forget his brave humour as he prepared himself to die.

Mummy went to her beloved Lorcan one year, almost to the day, later. We buried her next to him in Balgariffen cemetery.

Eamonn was to join them there, making me an orphan and a widow, in just four years.

Suddenly, towards the end of 1984, Eamonn developed high blood pressure. He was given pills which, much to his annoyance, slowed him down. Then a rash came out on his face and spread to his neck. We went to a dermatologist, but the rash wouldn't go away. Gradually, it spread to other parts of the body and he started getting styes. We went to other skin specialists, but no one, it seemed, knew what it was. No one knew it was the start of Eamonn's circulation breaking down.

What Eamonn did know was that he had a bad chest; the same bronchial problems that had killed his father. Throughout his life, Willie Andrews had not drunk alcohol, but had smoked heavily. Eamonn saw the danger signs and cut out cigarettes in favour of Havana cigars. Sometimes he had trouble with his breathing, but the good days heavily outnumbered the bad and he put it down to a hereditary weakness he would have to live with.

We had always been considered a high-profile social couple, going to film premières, theatre first nights, star-studded lunches and dinners. Always, the next day, Eamonn would be up early, eager to go jogging or work out before throwing himself into work. But I started to notice a change: he would not have the same enthusiasm for show-business gatherings; nor for working out the next morning. At first, I put it down to him having had a whisky too many the previous night. But the more he complained of feeling tired, the less I thought he was merely suffering from a hangover. We started going to fewer and fewer functions. And, finally, when Eamonn always felt bad the next day, he would say: 'Not another bloody lunch,' and I said no to almost everything; the previously sociable Mr and Mrs Andrews were now only available for the odd dinner party. From now on, Eamonn was conserving all his energy for his work.

He was having regular medical check-ups. And shortly before we went on holiday in the early summer of 1985, he had three days of intensive tests for insurance purposes. We went to the hospital to get the results the day we were due to fly off and Eamonn came out of the doctor's office grinning broadly. He had been declared A1.

Oh, there was one thing, he said: the tests had revealed his colour blindness. It gave us something to smile about as we left for Portugal.

The weather was perfect throughout our two weeks and Eamonn returned, tanned and relaxed, and looking forward as usual to another series of What's My Line? *and* This is Your Life. *It was the last time I was to see him looking so fit.*

The following March, he had to be taken from The Quarry in the middle of the night, fighting for breath.

I woke up hearing Eamonn panting: 'I can't breathe. You'd better get a doctor.' I was up in an instant; I put on the light and saw Eamonn standing by the bed, looking as white as his towelling dressing-gown. Frightened, I dashed through to the other end of the house and woke Mairead. I asked her to stay with Eamonn while I phoned the doctor. Then I dashed up to Eamonn's study and dialled. In my panic, however, I was phoning a personal friend who practised a hundred miles away! He told me to phone our local GP Dr John McCurdy. Furious with myself for being so stupid, I phoned him and he said he would be there as soon as possible.

When I got back to the bedroom, Eamonn was sitting on the bed, still fighting to breathe properly. I tried to find some comforting words, but my anxiety had numbed my brain. I looked at Mairead; she was trying to hide her tears at the sight of him. I prayed Dr McCurdy would not be long.

I did not want to wake the children because I didn't know what was wrong; but Emma had heard me wake Mairead and had got up, wanting to know what was happening. Dr McCurdy arrived ten minutes later. He examined Eamonn, then said he was going to ring for an ambulance; Eamonn must get to hospital at once. I quickly dressed and started to pack his things, my mind in turmoil; Eamonn was sitting on the bed, white as a ghost, his heart pounding. By now, Niamh and Fergal had woken up, and Fergal went down to the front gates in Carrick Hill to direct the ambulancemen to the house. Niamh was slightly hysterical; Fergal was just himself: quiet and watchful.

Eamonn was taken out in a wheelchair, a heavy overcoat over his dressing-gown. Emma insisted on coming with me and we sat in the back of the ambulance, worriedly watching as Eamonn was given oxygen. His heart was still pounding.

As he was taken into intensive care, Eamonn, predictably, started thinking of work: he asked me to ring Malcolm Morris, the This is Your Life *producer,* to tell him he would not be in London the next day; that the planned show would have to be cancelled. I was not to say what had happened, however; the fewer people knew he had been taken to hospital, the more chance we had of keeping it out of the papers. I told no one, in fact, and we got away with it for months.

When I went back to see him later that day, Eamonn seemed to have made a remarkable recovery. The doctors told me the breathing difficulty was caused by problems in Eamonn's chest and lungs, but his heart had been affected, too. When Eamonn heard this, he admitted he'd been frightened. 'I thought I was going to die,' he told me in a quiet moment. I didn't tell him that was what we had all feared.

Eamonn thought he was in that hospital for just a week, but he was there for three. When he came out – in time for Niamh's eighteenth birthday – he had lost two stones. His face looked as if it had caved in and clothes, which had fitted his huge frame snugly before, now hung pathetically loose. Eamonn had no vanity about his appearance. But he did care how he came over on television, and, in the weeks following that first attack, he would stare at himself in the mirror and sigh sadly: 'I hate the way I look.'

I set about putting the weight back on: I asked Mairead to give him lots of rice puddings and apple pie and cream, and any other fattening products she knew he liked. And, although he had never been one for popping into a pub for a pint, I coaxed him to go with me or Emma to watering holes in the villages near our home, because I felt that a couple of pints of Guinness would be good for him. But, although no one knew it then, he was getting weaker and could usually manage only one pint; also, his circulation was so bad he felt the cold, and no sooner were we out than he was wanting to go back. He had become an old man overnight.

Amazingly, he went back to do the last few This is Your Life programmes and to record a new What's My Line? series. I didn't think he was well enough, but there was no stopping him; he could not wait to get back to work. I consoled myself that we were flying off to Portugal again the following month. It was obvious, to me at least, that he should not have rushed back into the hurly-burly of London TV life after such a frightening attack; the tranquillity of the villa would be just the convalescence he needed. I wished the days away. I longed for the warmth of that Algarve sun and the fresh sea air that would breathe new life into the pale, gaunt shadow that was my husband.

We had become very fond of the villa in Vale de Lobo. In the past, Eamonn had never really enjoyed holidays abroad; he found them a bit of a hassle and would come home, saying: 'Why did we bother to go away?' He always said he felt that returning to Dublin was a holiday. But the villa was different. It was quiet and he loved the privacy. Neither of us wanted to do much on holiday, except explore the beach restaurants or maybe take a slow drive somewhere, or simply lie around reading or chatting, and that April, I was sure it would be like it had always been: he would soak up the sun and swim and we'd have romantic candlelit dinners under the stars, and he would get back to how he was and put that worrying attack behind him.

But, sadly, those two weeks were proof, if I really needed it, that Eamonn was never going to be the same again. He didn't sunbathe. He didn't swim. And he preferred to cook dinner at the villa at night because he couldn't face driving to the village restaurants.

He would lie awake most of the night. He was inclined to sweat anyway, but throughout those two weeks he sweated dreadfully, and in the mornings the bed and his pyjamas would be soaked.

During the day I would lie in the warm April sun by the pool, but Eamonn would sit in the shade, wearing a woollen cardigan. He had loved the sun all his life and now he was so ill he couldn't face it. He sat there, those mornings, reading or working on his autobiography, and I watched him, fearfully worried about his condition, but not wanting to draw attention to it in case it upset him.

It was to have been the holiday that brought him back to me, but there he was, frail and weak, slipping away before my eyes.

Over the next eight months, Eamonn put on some weight, but it was clear to me that he would never be the same burly giant, the big fellow, again. It didn't matter, I told myself; it didn't matter a damn, so long as there was nothing seriously wrong with him that would affect his life and his work. But then, towards the end of 1986, he started getting styes again; and his teeth began giving him trouble. We went to doctors and specialists, but no one could tell us what was the matter. Eamonn, it seemed, was a medical mystery.

For the first time in our marriage, I talked to him about his workload. I'd never dreamed of questioning it before, because it was his way of life; it was what I'd always known and I took it for granted. All the time he was healthy and functioning well, and enjoying himself, I was happy for him to work at his non-stop pace, be the workaholic. But now, looking at his gaunt face, and seeing him struggling, I wasn't so sure. I tried to put my foot down, to persuade him to ease off, even a little; but he wouldn't hear of it. I pleaded with him to at least stop putting himself under pressure to write articles for the Catholic Herald. *But he pooh-poohed this as well: he had been writing every week for thirty years, he said, and it was a joy, not a pressure.*

Then, just before Christmas, an eminent doctor in Dublin, Professor Counihan, told him, quite bluntly, that he should consider retiring; if he didn't retire, but kept pushing himself, his condition would get worse, perhaps fatally so. Eamonn looked at him and said, quite seriously: 'I would die if I retired.' The professor laughed at that and we left his office to go to the airport and London and more work. We sat in virtual silence, neither of us wanting to talk about what we had just heard.

And then, in January, we drove down to a rented cottage in Dingle on the west coast. And in the middle of nowhere, Eamonn had another attack.

He woke up at around 2 A.M., fighting for breath. Between gasps, he asked me to get a doctor – but there was no phone, and the nearest house was nearly a mile away across a field. I threw some clothes on; I told Eamonn to take his emergency pill and ran out into the cold January night. I had no idea where I was going. I dashed across that field as fast as my legs would carry me. I crawled under a fence, and ran to the house, now fighting for breath myself and thinking all the time that I was going to be too late; that my poor darling was going to be dead by the time we got back.

Someone in the house rang for a doctor, then somebody else drove me back to the cottage. Dreading what I would find, I let myself in, then I heard Eamonn's voice from upstairs: 'I'm out of it . . . I'm out of it.'

I rushed up. He was back in bed. I held him in my arms and told him a doctor was on his way, and it was only later I realized that, even in his darkest, most terrifying moments, my caring husband was trying to protect me. He, like me, believed he was dying that night, and he was arranging his body in the bed as though he were sleeping, so that I would not have the shock of seeing him dead on the floor.

The next morning, he'd recovered and I wanted him to take it easy; I had provisions and wanted to stay in and cook lunch and relax in front of the fire. But Eamonn would have none of it. The attack had passed and now he was thinking of work again – an article he was writing for High Life, *the British Airways in-flight magazine. He was going to write it that morning, then he wanted to drive to a local wildlife reserve and have his photograph taken; it would fit the article perfectly, he insisted.*

I tried to talk him out of it, but there was never any point arguing with Eamonn if his mind was made up, and that afternoon I found myself taking the picture he wanted. He was so thin and white, but the magazine used the picture because it did fit the article.

Even Eamonn was shocked when he saw himself. 'I look ghastly,' he said. 'You did *look ghastly,' I told him. 'You almost died the night before.'*

Deep down, Eamonn knew that he was crazy not to heed the advice Professor Counihan had given him. But work was all-important to him. He loved it and he lived for it. Naturally, he did not want it to kill him, but he did tell people he hated the thought of retiring and would prefer to die working.

This will explain why, just a month after nearly dying in Dingle, we were getting on a plane to Los Angeles to record not one, but two, This is Your Life programmes – on Dudley Moore and Christopher Cazenove. It was quite the most stupid thing for Eamonn to do; and, looking back, I wish – oh, how I wish! – I'd been able to do something, say something, to persuade him to call the trip off. But the two shows meant so much to Eamonn, and when he was determined to do something there was never anything anybody could do to deter him. Anyway, despite the scares I'd had, I honestly had no idea just how ill he was; nobody had. As a cover-up Eamonn's performance matched Watergate.

But, quite frankly, the trip was a nightmare from start to finish. Eamonn's breathing problems started again before we were even at Heathrow. And several times during the twelve-hour flight, he was heaving so violently, I thought he was going to die. I sat there, looking at him, trying to comfort him, all the time wondering what the hell was he doing here, going through hell for a TV programme, when he should be at home, taking care of himself.

Somehow, he got through that flight. And the next day, in Beverly Hills, we decided to go to 11 A.M. Mass at the famous Church of the Good Shepherd, about half an hour's stroll from our hotel. We were tired and disorientated from jet lag and I felt sure we would take a taxi. But Eamonn wanted to walk; he said the exercise would be good for him. I agreed. I was not that keen, but it was *a bright, sunny February morning and if a walk would help Eamonn feel better, then who was I to argue? And, anyway, we had to go past the fashionable, highly expensive shops in Rodeo Drive, which would be interesting. I sound like a yes-woman; but I'm not. I just loved Eamonn so much, I always wanted what was best for him; or what I thought was best for him.*

Well, that morning, I should have stuck out for a taxi. The walk was uphill most of the way and after just three blocks, about 300 yards, Eamonn was gasping. He didn't say anything, just struggled on; but I wondered whether we would make it. Somehow we did, and it was with some relief that Eamonn sat down in a pew. But he was heaving during the service and I feared he was going to pass out.

In the street afterwards, he said, with characteristic understatement: 'I had a hard time.'

I said: 'I know. We should have taken a taxi.'

We took one back to the hotel.

Eamonn was convinced his breathing trouble was caused by a virus and he wrote about it a couple of months later.

We had to pack a lot of work in before we could even contemplate folding our tents and heading west. It meant doing extra shows to cover the gap and being ready to crash straight into action on our return. Some sort of bug began to hit our team around now and, it being the depth of winter, I suppose we were more susceptible than at any other time.

I knew the first day I arrived and met Brian Klein. He could hardly talk and was snorting and sniffing like a faulty cistern on its last legs. How he survived to the end of the trip I'll never know. It hit different people in different ways over the ensuing weeks. Malcolm, for the first time since we'd worked together in the fifties, fell into bed and missed a show on our return.

I didn't know what was the matter, but I knew it was playing hell with me. I had, as my wife would say, about as much energy as a cat, which for her, for some strange reason, means no energy at all.

It was clear that the bug was hitting my chest, affecting my breathing and, in the process, my energy. This was to be the pattern until the end of the season, which included *What's My Line?* and I was, of course, crazy not to heed my doctor.

As a result, I was, I imagine, working on reserves that should have been left untapped. I was taking antibiotics and not giving them a chance to work. I was getting weaker by the day without really noticing it, because I'd be up as well as down. But I was going to pay for it later back in England.

If Eamonn had finished his book, he would, I'm sure, have recounted our visit, the following Sunday, to the Hollywood home of one of our dear friends, Michael O'Herlily, whose brother, Dan, was director of Hawaii Five-O. *The sight of the house made Eamonn and me feel weak just looking at it – and not because of its palatial splendour. It was built on a cliff . . . and there were, without exaggeration, more than 100 steps up to the front door.*

We stared up at it in disbelief. I thought to myself: I don't know about you, darling, but I'm not sure I can make it myself.

I did, though. And so did Eamonn. I can picture those damned steps now: even a perfectly fit person would have found it hard climbing them without being out of breath. And although Eamonn was joking when he said afterwards, 'I thought I was going to die,' it was ordeals like that which speeded his decline.

As far as This is Your Life *was concerned, the trip was successful: Dudley Moore and Christopher Cazenove were 'picked-up' without being tipped off in advance and the shows went down well when they were shown in Britain. But, knowing now how unwell he had been, I feel they were a personal triumph for Eamonn and marvellous testimony to his professionalism, dedication and ability.*

I wish he had finished writing the Los Angeles Adventure; it would have been interesting hearing him describe what it was like working in strange studios with technicians he had never met; and of 'picking up' Moore and Cazenove in obscure desert locations. As it was, apart from the virus worries, he got only as far as the initial problems of the programme.

The case was made again and again at our meetings that Dudley Moore, who had been a subject for the programme fifteen years before, had had a 'second' life – the life of a Hollywood star, too big to be even bothered by the 'Sex Thimble' epithet.

It was all very convincing, but it was also all very expensive. So we had to find a second target that would tickle the British fancy. It was a godsend to us now that Christopher Cazenove had made it big in one of the biggest soaps, *Dynasty*; and, on top of that, had a fascinating, up-beat, up-market background not given to many actors.

We decided to go for broke. Indeed, at one stage, Thames Television, when they saw the bills coming in, reckoned they were the ones that were going for broke. However, they were very understanding and gave us the kind of support without which you cannot undertake shows like this. You've got to get in there confidently, particularly in America.

Preliminary research was vital, tough and difficult. It included Malcolm, our producer, bargaining with American studios and hotels – and a hundred and one other facilities needed to take care of the high-powered technicians, production staff, messengers, writers, fixers, leg-men and, of course, guests. On-the-spot work was chased in the early stages by Brian Klein and Caroline Blackadder, where I guess some of the hardest tasks were to persuade some of those gum-chewing Hollywood cynics that secrecy was top priority; that if either of our two target names discovered we were after them, we would cancel the show whatever the cost. Fortunately, by now, we had so many American stars coming on the shows that our integrity was now being accepted by most.

'Crazy, but OK, if that's the way you want it,' was not an uncommon reaction.

When the This is Your Life *programmes were in the can, the London production team flew home and Eamonn and I went down to Bermuda for a holiday. It was supposed to be a quiet break during which Eamonn could relax and forget the pressures he'd been under in California. But no sooner had we arrived than the pressure was on again: a* This is Your Life *researcher who had been entrusted to deliver an article Eamonn had written for the* Catholic Herald *had lost it. The* Herald *needed the copy urgently. And Eamonn, who had written it in longhand in the hotel between programmes, did not have a copy. I heard him tell his secretary in London that he was going to sit down there and then and rewrite the whole piece. He'd ring her back in half an hour. I winced. I felt it was all unnecessary. And that he was putting himself under too much pressure.*

But Eamonn liked working under pressure, always had. He always met his deadlines. And, although he was angry and frustrated that his article had been lost, he wasn't going to miss this one. I went into another room to let him get on with it, marvelling not only that he thought the problem was so important, but also at the professional way he solved it.

At Easter, a few weeks later, however, my marvelling was to turn to misery and I would wonder, with some anger, at the price Eamonn was paying for this obsessional dedication to his work.

His breathing troubles started again at our flat in Chiswick, just before the Easter weekend. I immediately arranged for us to fly home so that Eamonn could see his doctor in Dublin. Eamonn was very weak and heaving, and the doctor ordered him to go in for tests the following Monday. Eamonn looked awful and could barely walk; Mairead and I felt he should go to hospital there and then, but consoled ourselves that there was probably no point, since nothing would be done until the Monday. At 11 P.M. on Sunday night, however, Eamonn started fighting for breath and gasping, even worse, if that's possible, than during the previous attacks. Convinced he was not going to make it this time, I called Emma and asked her to get the doctor. I can't remember why, but he was not available and we had to wait for a locum to come from a long way away. It was agonizing waiting for him, but, amazingly, Eamonn came out of it yet again, and by the time the locum arrived he was breathing and talking fairly normally.

But the experience left Emma in a state of shock. She was aware he'd had some form of heart failure in January and the previous March, but she had no idea how sick he really was. Eamonn always put on a good act of being well, even if he was feeling like hell, and Emma and the others were fooled by him. Now, Emma had seen the truth for herself; she broke down and sobbed later, and told me she believed her Daddy was dying. Of course, I tried to console her; told her that it was only chronic bronchitis. But I could see it didn't wash. I wasn't such a good actor as Eamonn.

The next morning, Mairead drove Eamonn, Emma, Fergal and myself to the hospital. He was nervous and worried, but he was concerned for us all, too, and apologized for not talking much on the journey. It was typical of him to be so thoughtful.

The hospital kept him in for two weeks, and when he came out he looked better than he had since Dingle, although he had lost what little weight he had regained, and his face was as gaunt as ever. Once again, I seized on our customary holiday in Portugal as the answer to Eamonn's problems. He had to do a few more What's My Line? and This is Your Life programmes before we flew out in May, but it wasn't long to wait; it wasn't long before he would be able to switch off and think less about work and more about himself. Hopefully, he would feel able to enjoy the sun more than he had the previous year. I counted the days to that holiday; it was like a lifeline.

Before we were able to escape to our little haven, however, we had to deal with an embarrassing rumour that put Eamonn in the headlines again for the wrong reasons. It started with a phone call to the flat in Chiswick while Eamonn was on his way home from work.

The caller announced himself as a British national newspaper journalist and calmly asked me if it was true that Eamonn had Aids. I was embarrassed and furious, and slammed the phone down. Eamonn, as a journalist himself, had instilled in me the need to be courteous and friendly to the press, but I found it impossible this time. Here was I, worried sick about my husband, being asked something like that. The question itself was bad enough, but what an impertinence asking the wife. I was appalled, but I didn't tell Eamonn.

That journalist did not call back, but later a reporter from the News of the World turned up at the door in Dublin – knocking half a dozen times in one afternoon. When I explained that Eamonn wasn't at home, the reporter tried to question me about a supposed mystery illness. I refused to be drawn and the newsman left. I thought that was the end of it, but he must have hung around, because when Eamonn finally arrived home, he knocked again. Typically, Eamonn invited him in and offered him a drink.

The reporter, Stuart White, said the paper had received phone calls from worried viewers, shocked by Eamonn's appearance on What's My Line? the previous Monday. Did he have cancer? they wanted to know. Anxious, as always, to be candid and open, Eamonn admitted he had lost more than a stone in the past six weeks, but stressed that he didn't have cancer. And he added, in all innocence: 'I suppose I'm lucky that people aren't saying I've got Aids.'

He blamed his weight loss and haggard appearance on a virus infection which had affected several of the This is Your Life production team. And then he pinched what appeared to be an ample amount of stomach and said: 'I'm putting weight back on now. Do you want to feel the evidence for yourself?'

It was a good piece of acting that fooled Mr White. The following Sunday he wrote a story around his exclusive interview with Eamonn under the headline: I'M FIGHTING BACK TO LIFE, SAYS EAMONN.

But Eamonn's performance didn't fool me. I still counted the days to our holiday when, hopefully, the Mediterranean sun would work a miracle.

He didn't want to worry me, but I only had to look at Eamonn or listen to him talk to know how bothered he was by his condition. He knew he wasn't well, and from the moment we arrived at the villa, he rang Dublin to tell his doctor how he felt; and to ask advice on what he should be doing.

He seemed in much better shape than on the last trip. He felt exercise was good for him and even when he didn't feel like it, he forced himself to swim every day. He never moaned to me about feeling unwell, but he would say he looked like a refugee from Belsen and he never stopped trying to put on weight. After the second attack, however, it was a losing battle, because he found it such an ordeal to eat. He started getting a sun tan, which helped him look better than he had before. But he was still so skinny it worried both of us.

It was a holiday for peace and quiet and not getting steamed up, but one day a taxi-driver got Eamonn in such a state I thought there might be a punch-up. Eamonn would always lose his patience if things weren't done properly and he felt this particular driver had let him down.

We had asked him to take us to a supermarket some distance from the villa, assuming he would bring us back with what we bought. When we arrived at the supermarket, he demanded the fare and said he couldn't wait. Eamonn refused to pay him the money, saying he would pay at the end of the return trip. The driver started waving his arms about and yelling in broken English that he *would report Eamonn to the police for not paying the fare. The row went on and on, and, eventually, Eamonn lost his cool and started shouting back. I was worried for him; in his condition, he didn't need that sort of aggravation. 'Let him go, darling,' I said. 'It's not worth it. We'll find another way to get back.'*

Suddenly the driver said: 'That's it. I'm calling the police.' And he started to pull away, with Eamonn hanging on to a door. I shouted to the driver to stop, and persuaded Eamonn to pay the man off. Eamonn was still shaking with anger as we walked round the supermarket looking for something tasty for dinner. In the event, the manager called a cab to take us back to the villa.

Thankfully, that was the first and last bit of aggravation that holiday. The rest of the time we spent lazing in the sun by day and eating Eamonn's evening meals by candlelight at night as we played our favourite cassettes: Rachmaninov, Chopin – and Acker Bilk.

The villa's letting agency thought we were out of our minds that trip. Not in our choice of music, I hasten to add, but in our request for fuel for a fire every night. The temperature was in the sixties but Eamonn always felt chilly.

Life was going out of him that last summer.

He had always been an early riser, getting up at 6 or 6.30 to go jogging or to Mass, but now he would stay in bed until midday. And where, before, he was keen to get busy, he now stood around in the kitchen, idly chatting to whoever was there. On Sundays, when we all went to Mass, he had always been the first one up, nagging the rest of us to get a move on; he was uptight about being late and would shout to the last one of us: 'Come on, we're leaving.' But now, everything in him was slowing down, and he was the one we would have to hurry. He always made it, though. It was a supreme effort for him, but he never missed Sunday Mass in those last terrible months.

He had always loved entertaining, particularly summer barbecues in the garden. He loved all the palaver, the ritual of cooking steaks and chops and chicken, and he'd often force it on us, even if we didn't feel in the mood. Trying to bring some normality back into our lives that summer, I would say: 'Let's have a barbecue – chicken wings.' But he'd just look at me, his eyes dull and uninterested, and shake his head: 'No, darling. I really don't feel like it.' So I would organize something else, keeping my fingers crossed he would enjoy it.

He had his greenhouse where he grew marrows and tomatoes and parsley, and he'd loved going down to it every day just to potter around: I always knew where to find him if he was wanted on the phone, or his lunch was ready. That last summer he didn't go down to his greenhouse once.

As the Dublin summer made way for autumn, the sad reality of what the future held, contrasting with my memories of healthy, fun-filled romantic yesterdays, was horrific to contemplate.

Eamonn treasured what he called his 'Gladstone' bag. It was a huge, triangular black bag with high sides, the biggest bag allowed as hand-luggage, and he took it on every flight to London. That bag became part of him. When he left the house on Monday morning, it would be filled with a This is Your Life *script, business letters and notes of ideas he was working on. When he returned on Thursday afternoon it would still have business papers, but it would have two bottles of duty-free champagne, too, and gifts for me and the children. That heavy bag was strong and dependable – a sort of symbol of Eamonn himself. It was so much part of him and he had a thing about carrying it. When I bought the bag, in Harrods, I loved it, too. But, in the last months of Eamonn's life, I came to detest it. For as he grew weaker and weaker, so weak he could barely walk, the bag tormented him because he didn't have the strength to carry it.*

One Thursday in September, Eamonn arrived home, looking deathly pale and drained. He put the heavy black bag on the floor and sat in his chair wearily. Emma went up to him to kiss him and I could see she was shocked at how ill he looked. Eamonn put on an act for her, trying to convince her all was well, but she left the room looking worried. As soon as she had gone, Eamonn dropped his defences. He looked at me and said: 'I'll have to get the doctor.'

We had been seeing doctors most of the year; a week hadn't gone by when we hadn't gone to one specialist or another for tests. I was fed up with them. And to hear Eamonn talk of doctors a minute after walking through the door made me see red.

'Oh, eff the doctor,' I said.

For a second, Eamonn looked shocked. Then he burst out laughing. I did, too. We laughed loudly for a long time and it took the sting out of what could have been a tense moment.

It also helped convince Emma that her Daddy could not be as sick as he looked if we had found something that funny.

That trip was the last one he made on his own. When he was getting ready to leave for London the following Monday, he said: 'I feel so weak I can hardly walk.' I knew then that I could not let him get on that plane alone. One only had to look at him to know that he could collapse at any moment. In the past, I'd gone to London only once a month, as a treat, but now I told Eamonn I was going with him every week.

Those flights became a major ordeal for us. Often, I thought he was going to collapse; sometimes, he would be gasping so badly, I felt he was dying right next to me. Many times he would say afterwards: 'I thought I'd had it.' And through it all, the black bag he loved so much gave him comfort: all the time he could carry it, he was all right, he seemed to be thinking.

He would stumble along those endless airport walkways, often hitting the walls because he didn't have the strength to keep his balance, and all the time clinging to that damned bag, insisting he carried it himself. I would hold his elbow to keep him steady, but he wouldn't let me take the bag.

As our wedding anniversary was coming up in November, I told Eamonn I was planning to buy him another bag – a lighter, Gucci one. But he told me he didn't want one; he liked his old black one.

In the final days, he did give in and ask me to carry the bag; he had lost so much strength, he couldn't lift it. I don't know how I managed. Even empty, it weighed a ton.

The last Tuesday in October, Eamonn pulled up outside the hairdressers in Malahide in the green Mercedes. He had been meeting me there for fifteen years, but the rendezvous had never lost its magic. It was a ritual: he would pick me up around midday and we'd go to lunch at King Sitrick. I always found it very romantic, like a first date; and I think Eamonn did, too, even though we talked about all the usual husband and wife things.

Only once was the romance missing and I have a power strike to blame for that. The driers in the hairdressers weren't working and when Eamonn arrived, I walked out to the car with a towel wrapped round the rollers in my hair. Eamonn was horrified; ever since his youth, he had thought it slovenly for a woman to be seen in public in rollers. He said we would have to have lunch at home that day. And he drove to Portmarnock the back way, so that no one would see him with this 'awful' woman in his car!

On this Tuesday, however, no rollers were in sight and we drove down to the harbour for our customary lunch. On the way, Eamonn held my hand and said: 'You know, darling, this is all I ever wanted in life – to be taking you out to lunch like this.' It was nothing for Eamonn to flatter me: he was always saying how lucky he was to have a good marriage in such a precarious business. But what he said that day struck me as strange, and I wondered afterwards whether there was more to it; whether he knew deep down, that soon he wouldn't be around to do the things we loved. And he did love that restaurant.

Once, Dermod Cafferky and I were having lunch there and he asked me: 'What's Eamonn's favourite restaurant?'

'Here,' I laughed immediately. 'He's never been anywhere else in Howth.'

That Tuesday, Eamonn had skate, which he had always enjoyed. But this time it was an effort for him, and I could not wait for lunch to be over; I couldn't bear to watch him struggling. Afterwards, Eamonn suggested we walked out to sea on one of the two piers. It was a bitterly cold day, with a biting wind, and I would have preferred to go home to the warmth of The Quarry; but I knew Eamonn felt the exercise would be good for him; and, although I didn't know he had such a short time left, I wouldn't have tried to stop him doing anything he wanted. And, anyway, it was one of his better days: he was weak, of course, but I wasn't aware so much of his breathlessness.

What I was painfully aware of, and hated, was his navy-blue anorak. He had the hood pulled up and the unflattering orange fur lining fringed his pale, gaunt face. He had bought the anorak for working in the garden and he'd worn it that day because it was warm for walking down the pier. I told him not to wear it again – it looked ghastly. But Eamonn just laughed; he had never been too concerned with what he looked like when he wasn't in front of the cameras.

I thought we had the pier to ourselves, which wasn't surprising, considering the biting October chill. But a couple of hundred yards along, we saw an old man in black sitting on a stone step, his hands resting on a walking stick.

'You won't believe it,' Eamonn said, as we got nearer. 'But that's Brother Carew.'

I looked at him blankly. 'Who?'

'Brother Carew. He was one of my teachers.'

We went up to him and said hello. The two men knew each other: Eamonn had kept in touch after leaving school and Brother Carew had turned up at The Quarry on his bicycle a year or so before, when he'd heard Eamonn was ill.

They talked for a while and then the three of us walked back to the harbour. Eamonn was so pleased we had bumped into Brother Carew and so was I: I honestly don't think Eamonn would have made it the whole length of the pier and back.

Fergal didn't say much about his Daddy's condition and Niamh saw only what she wanted to see. But Emma was totally aware of what was happening and I found comfort in confiding in her, although it was difficult to put my fears and worries into words. Emma talked openly to me, too, and told me she believed her Daddy was dying.

Eamonn and I left Portmarnock for London on the Wednesday: he had one This is Your Life *show to record that Friday, another the following Tuesday and then, on Thursday, we were going to Lanzarote in the Canary Islands for two weeks. Standing in the drive of The Quarry to see us off that Wednesday,*

Emma had a strange look about her and I learned later that she had this terribly strong feeling that this was the last time she would see her Daddy alive. Eamonn had told her always to expect the worst, then you will never be disappointed, and she was, she said, probably trying to come to terms with him dying before it actually happened. That night, after we had left, Emma heard Mary Black singing 'Till' on television and it made her think of her Daddy, and she couldn't stop crying

No sooner had we arrived in London than he was making arrangements to dictate letters to his secretary, Margaret. He was really hyperactive, as if he wanted to cram as much as possible into the trip because he was running out of time. He was still dictating letters at 5 P.M. the following evening.

This is Your Life that Friday was Jimmy Cricket. How Eamonn got through it, I don't know. He had a fever and couldn't breathe or talk properly, but he psyched himself up to go on stage and somehow dragged himself through.

On the Saturday he wanted to go to the theatre. We didn't, because he simply wasn't up to it, but it was typical of him in those final weeks. Suddenly he wanted to go places, do things, see people. Suddenly all those things he had found tiresome were important.

It was a complete reversal of how we had been living and, once again, I found myself thinking: Does he think he's dying?

He was in a bad way when we went to midday Mass at Brompton Oratory on Sunday. One of the exercises he was proud of was being able to get out of a chair without using his hands to lever himself up; he'd seen Joan Crawford do it and was impressed. But that Sunday, he was so weak that he had to grab the sides of the pew to drag himself to his feet. Then, as he walked to the altar, he swayed and his back heaved as he gulped great gasps of air. I'd held him up many times in those final desperate months, but not that day. I wanted him to make it on his own.

He had left me to choose the restaurant for lunch and I'd gone for one off the Fulham Road, which I'd seen advertised in a magazine. When we got there, I was horrified: there were seemingly endless steps from the street down to the restaurant. Had I known, I would not have gone near the place. Eamonn, bless him, saw the funny side: as we were waiting to order, he looked at me, deadpan, and said: 'Next time, I'll choose the restaurant.' After what I'd been going through in my mind in the past few days, I was so, so pleased to hear him talking about 'next time'.

He ordered a glass of champagne and was in good form, more like the Eamonn of old. He ordered saddle of lamb, quite enthusiastically, and I sat there hoping that for once, he would be able to wolf it down and enjoy it. But when the lamb arrived, he couldn't face it and it went back untouched.

Eamonn was unconcerned about the wasted meal and keen to talk about the big This is Your Life surprise he was going to spring the following Tuesday.

Normally, I would have been as much in the dark as usual about the subjects of the programme. But I knew it was Cliff Morgan, the former Welsh rugby international, now a top BBC executive. Eamonn hadn't told me; someone else had. But it didn't matter: at that stage Eamonn needed all my support, and the traditional secrecy of the programme took second place to our relationship.

He admitted he was worried. It was going to be a big show and a long night: he was going to an anniversary boxing dinner and the surprise on Morgan would be sprung immediately afterwards. It would have been a strain for a fully-fit Eamonn Andrews, let alone a weak one. We talked it through and Eamonn agreed he should pace himself. He would have a rest that Sunday afternoon, then cancel a meeting the next morning and save himself for the programme.

When we left the restaurant I began the long climb up the stairs first, so I don't know how bad Eamonn's breathing was. But he told me in the taxi home to Chiswick that he didn't think he was going to make it. It hit home just how unwell he felt when he asked me to go out for the Sunday papers – something he normally did himself. I said 'OK,' but, a few minutes later, he changed his mind and said he would go; the exercise would do him good, he said, and give him some strength for Tuesday's programme. I begged him to go to bed and rest. But he wouldn't hear of it: he had always believed that exercise was the best form of medicine.

As he closed the door to walk to the newsagent's, my heart was heavy with worry. Those steep steps in that damned restaurant . . .

On Monday he woke up in a panic. He felt he could not get out of bed. Somehow, he managed it. Without saying a word to me, he rang Professor Counihan and said: 'I think the fluid has come back on my lungs.' Professor Counihan said it was a possibility and advised Eamonn to ask his doctor to arrange for some X-rays. The doctor came and before we knew it we were in a taxi heading for Cromwell Road Hospital. Eamonn looked ghastly; his face was grey and it seemed to have shrunk overnight. He looked as though he was dying. The taxi-driver had seen some boxing on television and kept on and on about it, but Eamonn didn't say much; he could hardly speak.

At the hospital we got a shock. We thought Eamonn was simply going to have X-rays, but someone at reception said he was down for admission. Eamonn looked at me, fighting hard to conceal his anxiety, and asked me if I would mind going home to fetch his pyjamas and toilet things.

When I got back in the taxi and told the driver what had happened, he was very apologetic. 'I'm sorry,' he said. 'I shouldn't have talked so much.' I told him not to worry, but asked him not to say anything to anyone about Eamonn going into hospital. He was one of our regular mini-cab drivers, a good pal of Eamonn; he promised not to say a word.

I dropped Eamonn's things off, then went back to the flat to be alone with my thoughts; and the thought that was always there, fighting its way through all the worry and confusion and fear, was that this time my dear, brave, beloved Hymie just might not make it. I didn't know why I thought that, because no one, not one doctor or specialist, in all those twenty terrible months since his first attack, had been able to tell us precisely what was wrong. He had a weak chest, we knew that; that's why he had cut out cigarettes then cigars. We knew he had high blood pressure, too; that's why he had been taking drugs for four years. We knew his heart had been affected in some way in that first attack. But he hadn't had a heart attack. And, despite the horrendous breathing problems, nothing major had been found to be wrong with his lungs or kidneys. Even the appalling weight loss that had reduced him to a pathetic shadow of the man I'd known had been left unexplained. If it wasn't cancer – and certainly not Aids, for heaven's sake – what the hell was it that had struck him again and confined him once more to a hospital bed?

Alone in that flat, I thought back over the months he had been unwell; all those months he had put on the performance of a lifetime for the children he adored; the months when his bravery and strength of spirit had made even me think I was imagining or exaggerating it all, and that maybe it wasn't as bad as it appeared.

I thought and remembered and regretted and wished, and then, when it was time for me to go to the hospital again, I hoped.

I hoped I was wrong. I hoped that they would tell me they knew, at last, what was wrong. And that he was going to make it.

When I saw him that evening he was being drip-fed. There was a protective guard on one side of the bed, and when I walked into the room, he quickly covered it up and said something about it being there to support the drip. I wasn't fooled. He'd probably fallen out of bed and the guard was to stop him doing it again. I didn't say anything; I didn't want to upset him. But I was touched. It was typical of Eamonn to be thinking of me at such a time; to be taking care of me even in the middle of his personal crisis.

I was introduced to a chest specialist, Dr Empey, who immediately said: 'Your husband will not be making any television programme tomorrow night.' My heart sank; what on earth had they discovered? Then he said: 'I would forget about going on holiday to Lanzarote. Things would be difficult there in the event of an emergency.'

My hopes rose a little: by the sound of it, he wasn't ruling out a holiday to an appropriate place. So Eamonn might be coming out. The doctor told me he had called in a heart specialist, who would be seeing Eamonn the next day. Until then, there was nothing more he could say.

I then talked to Eamonn, who was still only concerned for me. 'It's a rotten time for you,' he said, tenderly. 'You're not going on holiday – you're going to spend the time sitting here.'

'Don't be silly, darling,' I said. 'I don't mind. The main thing is to get you better. Then we can go away somewhere nice for as long as we want.'

'I'm not doing the programme tomorrow because I'm too weak.'

'I know, darling,' I said. 'But now that they're taking you off all those drugs, you'll get your appetite back and put on weight and be strong again.'

I was trying to be positive, clinging to that hope. I'd seen him come through three worse attacks and I wanted to believe he could recover from a fourth. I feel it unlikely I convinced him: Eamonn had always had an uncanny knack of seeing through people, knowing when he was being spun a line. He probably knew how ill he was; probably knew that our time together was nearly over.

I left the hospital to spend the night alone. I didn't think I could ever feel so miserable.

I must have got off to sleep eventually, but in the morning my eyes were red and sore and my brain muzzy as though I'd been awake all night. I pottered around the flat, in a sort of trance, not really sure what to do with myself before I went to see Eamonn later that morning.

At about 11 A.M., Sheelagh O'Donovan, who had been Eamonn's agent for more than twenty years, phoned with some good news: Thames had signed Eamonn's contract for another three years of This is Your Life *and* What's My Line? *I was delighted; it would be a great psychological boost for Eamonn, and I told Sheelagh to take the contract to the lawyers so that they could prepare it for his signature. Now, I was looking forward to seeing Eamonn. Professionally, the worst that could have happened to him would have been not to have his contract taken up; and although he had known for some months that his Thames bosses were reviewing it, he would be pleased to know that all the contract needed was his signature, not theirs.*

He was pleased about the new contract, but, understandably, he was keen to talk about his health. And he wanted me to know that he felt I'd been right all along: he'd been wrong to put all that strain on his heart: how he wished he'd listened to me pleading with him to slow down.

I asked him if he would now consider retiring at the end of this new three-year contract. For the first time in our lives, he said he would seriously think about it. How lovely it would be, he said, with a faraway look, to build that high tower where he would be able to look out to sea, and write a novel without the phone disturbing his concentration.

We'd had similar conversations before, but the workaholic in Eamonn had always pushed the question of retirement aside as offers of more work came in. His poor health and the introduction of satellite TV, however, could be just the spur to make him do something positive about it. He had always striven hard to keep This is Your Life *at the top of the ratings – and succeeded. But with satellite TV, there would be so much competition, the ratings would not matter; no show could be number one. And live TV – something Eamonn had fought and fought for – would be a thing of the past. Already, they were talking of doing six* What's My Line? *shows in one day – and Eamonn could not bear it; he said it would reduce the quality of his work.*

Aware of his sadness at the changing picture of television, I felt some hope for our personal future. If it meant he would be happy to leave when his new contract ran out, and start on something less demanding on his physical resources, it would be wonderful.

Knowing Dr Empey was coming to do even more tests on Eamonn, I left the hospital for Chiswick, feeling a little brighter than when I went in.

I was hopping mad when I went to the hospital the following morning: the Sun had been pressurizing me the previous day for news of Eamonn's condition, and they had carried a piece that morning which I didn't much care for. My mood was not helped when I got to the hospital to learn that some administrative person had gone to Eamonn, asking for £1,000 deposit for the private room. Eamonn had obliged, courtesy of his Midland Bank Gold credit card; but that wasn't the point. Surely, whoever is responsible for the hospital's finances could have shown more discretion and diplomacy, if not compassion? Surely, someone could have asked me to pop into an office and sign a cheque? They knew I was there twice a day. Surely, it wasn't necessary for someone to go to the patient's bedside and talk about money when, clearly, his mind was on other things? I didn't let it get me too upright, however; Eamonn had taken it in his stride and sorted the matter out, so I let it drop.

I was meeting Sheelagh to pick up the contract for Eamonn's signature, so I left, promising to be back that evening when he would have the results of the tests on his heart.

I learned later that before the heart specialist came in to talk to him, Eamonn seemed to be in good spirits and, as usual, getting things done. He amazed Margaret by phoning her at home with some more requests for secretarial help. There were a couple of other things on his mind: one was an additional paragraph to his last Catholic Herald *article – there you are, still thinking of work even on his hospital bed! – the other was our anniversary the coming Saturday. He wanted Margaret to ring Roy Fewins, the* This is Your Life *stage manager, and ask him to arrange for thirty-six red roses to be delivered to me at Chiswick on Saturday morning. They were never sent. By then, Eamonn was dead, and I was at home in Dublin planning his funeral. But I would learn, that traumatic Tuesday, that my beloved Hymie had not forgotten our thirty-sixth year of married happiness. Our dear friend, Malcolm Morris, had arranged for those anniversary flowers to be the first to adorn his grave.*

The official cause of death was 'failure of the heart muscle'. No doubt, the years of Eamonn's slavish devotion to work did take its terrible toll, but nothing will convince me that my poor darling did not die from something that has no place in the uncompromising world of medicine . . . a broken heart.

EPILOGUE

I found it hard to write my contribution to this book. Eamonn's life was very public, but he insisted our family life remained private, and it has been a battle for me to decide what, or what not, to write. The loyalty he instilled in people, me particularly, was so great that it bothered me that I might betray him by, unwittingly, breaking a trust or revealing something personal he would have wished to have been left unsaid. This is not to say that there were any skeletons in either of our cupboards: scurrilous deeds or scandals that we would want to remain secret. Anyone who expected that sort of book has been disappointed. The truth, as I hope I've shown, is that, behind the television personality, was a warm, caring family man who, when the spotlight was off, loved to enjoy the simple pleasures of life. And our married life, was, quite frankly, very normal.

It was this loyalty to Eamonn that persuaded me to write this book. If I owed him anything for thirty-six wonderfully happy years, it was to finish what he had begun before his illness sapped him of the remarkable energy and perseverance that had been such a striking feature of his success. He was the writer in the family and, had he lived, he would have completed the definitive Eamonn Andrews Story in his own style. But even then it would not have been a name-dropping book, full of showbiz gossip, for, despite being voted TV Personality of the Year four times, Eamonn was not what you would call a show-business person. Throughout his career, he met hundreds, if not thousands, of celebrities, but he would never have presumed to call them friends; certainly he would never have written about them as such. Show business was his work and, when that work was over, he would wind down and return to Dublin to relax in the company of lifelong friends – such as Dickie Duggan and Az Guirey – who were not connected with TV, radio or the theatre. Eamonn was interested in, and liked, people; and if he had nothing kind to say about anyone, he would rather not say anything. His autobiography would not have been one to grab the tabloid headlines; rather a private memoir filled with personal reminiscences important and special to him. That's the responsibility I took on with the completion of Eamonn's own words. And that's why I have found it far from easy.

In life, I leaned on Eamonn. And in the harrowing months after his death I leaned on him still. My favourite photograph of him hangs in the bedroom, and I would look at his face and talk to it as if he was in the room with me. To many people, talking to someone who isn't there may sound a little strange, to say the least; but all those who have lost a dearly loved one will understand the comfort I got from talking out loud to that picture. When there were people around, I was able to hold myself together; I found an inner strength that helped me survive and not mope around with a tear-stained face, making everyone else miserable. But many times when I was on my own, the enormity of my loss would engulf me and I would rush down to the sanctuary of that bedroom and close the door and pour out all my heartache to the picture. And it always made me feel better; gave me some comfort. Gradually, I started talking to the picture more and more, not just in grief-stricken moments of loneliness, but sometimes when I just needed encouragement. Even writing this book I would gaze at that picture lovingly, imploring my poor darling to help me do it the way he would have wanted. It is only a picture, and the only words that ever come from it are in my imagination, but the solace it has given me has been quite astonishing. I'm not as religious now as I once was, but I do believe it is as if Eamonn is still watching over me.

Looking at that picture several times a day all those months after his death, I would fight to forget the awful sadness of his last days, and my bitterness at the heart specialist's deadly warning, by thinking about all the fun times Eamonn and I shared. And he was such a larger than life character that, even in death, just looking into those bright blue, all-knowing eyes brought magical memories flooding back.

The moment, for instance, when it hit Eamonn just how powerful television was. We were on our honeymoon, driving across the Kerry Mountains in our little Hillman, and Eamonn stopped to give two hikers a lift. One of them stared at Eamonn a long time, then said in a strong North Country accent: 'Hey, you're on television, aren't you?' Eamonn nodded, his smile betraying the pride he felt at being recognized so far from England. 'I don't know your name from Adam,' the hiker said, 'but you're the lad on that What's My Line?' Eamonn nodded again, and admitted later that his cup would have been full had the stranger known his name!

Four years later, two little boys were staring at him as we stood in a coach queue at London Airport. 'Hello, Andrews,' said the smaller one. His companion, showing a nice regard for etiquette, dug his pal in the ribs and said: 'Amos to you!' Eamonn loved that one.

They were wonderfully exciting years, the fifties, when the shy young lad who'd felt sick with panic at performing in front of a handful of relatives was being seen and heard by millions throughout the land, and travelling the world, doing the work he adored, at someone else's expense. I consider myself very lucky to have been part of that. Looking back, I suppose I played second fiddle in those early married years, but, as I've said, Eamonn was a great teacher and it wasn't long before I began to assert myself in the power stakes. And while it is true that I believed there should be only one celebrity in the family, I was, most certainly, no shrinking violet. I like to think that we grew together.

Even in the dark times, when I'm at a low ebb, looking at that picture can bring a smile . . . like remembering how Eamonn booked a dental appointment for a total stranger – via Telstar, the first satellite TV transmission from Europe to the United States. Eamonn introduced the British contribution to the programme standing in the sea in gumboots on the Cornish coast. Several days later, he received a long nostalgic letter from an exiled Irishman in Toronto, with the P.S.: 'I understand you know Vinny Ryan, the dentist, in Clontarf. Would you tell him I'll be home in March, and would he please make an appointment for me.' It was typical of Eamonn to do precisely what his faraway viewer requested. The programme was the greatest achievement in international TV communications, but Eamonn was delighted to bring the whole thing down to fundamentals.

Huge audiences are great for the ego, of course, but one of Eamonn's greatest thrills was broadcasting to what could well have been the world's smallest radio audience. The show was Calling the Antarctic – a programme of current affairs, sports results and record requests beamed to about seven research scientists scattered around the Weddell Sea. Eamonn took a double pride in doing those weekly broadcasts: he was excited at being part of something built in eights and tens, not millions, and thrilled at joining, even in a remote way, men he referred to as brave adventurers of the twentieth century.

Another little secret that makes me smile is the particularly cutting letter Eamonn received from the managing director of a large company after This is Your Life featured Tommy Steele. The businessman thought the tone of the *programme had been lowered by presenting a pop singer and said so in stringent terms. When Eamonn finished reading the letter, he turned it over and saw the most delightful message scribbled in ink. It said: 'I am this man's secretary. I have had to type this letter, but I must tell you what I think. I think if Tommy Steele was good enough for the Queen, he should be good enough for him!' That appealed to Eamonn's sense of humour and he wondered more than once whether the lady kept her job.*

Eamonn was a lovable romantic and he adored taking me to Paris to celebrate our anniversary. Normally, everything went wonderfully well – except for the odd hiccup, like the Last Tango in Paris *episode – but one year a clothing catastrophe left Eamonn red-faced. Like all good tourists, we decided to go to the legendary Lido, but decided to dress up so that we would not actually look like foreigners.*

I had packed Eamonn's dinner suit, but had forgotten the bow-tie. Eamonn said nothing to me, but, as I was getting ready, I could hear him getting more and more heated up as he searched our suitcases. Unknown to me, he spotted my black velvet dress and, with a pair of scissors, skilfully cut himself a narrow bow-tie, which was the height of fashion at the time.

It rather took him back when we arrived at the famous restaurant and discovered that, apart from the waiters, he was the only one in the place wearing a bow-tie! For some reason I cannot remember now, I said later: 'If we're going out tomorrow, darling, I must wear my black velvet dress.'

Eamonn gulped. 'You mean the one I'm wearing.'

Just when I was about to ask him what he meant, two elderly American women came over and greeted me, somewhat over-enthusiastically, as Elizabeth Taylor – an occurrence I'm flattered to say happened quite regularly! My embarrassed protests only convinced the ladies that I was, indeed, the famous actress. Just in case any newshounds were around hunting for gossip, Eamonn went on record that night as saying: 'That was no Taylor, that was my wife!' Come to think of it, I wonder what did become of that black velvet dress!

How can I look at that photograph without being amused at the memory of the stray dogs which came in right on cue as Eamonn read the Easter Sunday Lesson in church at Portmarnock. I forget which part of the Bible he was reading, but just as he said 'Many dogs have surrounded me . . .' two nosey mongrels who had wandered in at the rear of the congregation started barking loudly. Our three children, and I'm sure everyone else, thought it wildly funny, and Eamonn took pleasure in relating the story. He took his religion very seriously, but that didn't mean it was devoid of humour.

He was a great story-teller, and the children still delight in remembering how he would enthral them with magical stories, invented effortlessly, it seemed, out of a fertile imagination. He loved an audience for his jokes, too, although he was never one of those natural-born comedians who relate one joke after another. He would work in his jokes as part of the conversation, always bearing in mind that I'd probably heard the same joke a dozen times before. 'Grainne has heard this before,' he would say, quickly and politely, before I could accuse him of being a bore.

What a thought! How on earth could anyone – even a wife of so many years – be bored by such a lively mind and sharp wit. Although I do admit to finding some of the business functions we had to attend a little tedious, I never tired of listening to Eamonn's after-dinner speeches. I was weaned on them, of course, but sometimes he would even surprise me by picking up on something a previous speaker had said and referring to it in an amusing way that made his own speech special and not something he had prepared days before with no regard for spontaneity. He loved audience reaction and would be quick to know if something had not worked. But he was such a professional, even in this area, that he always asked my opinion, and took notice of it.

He was always aware of what was expected of him. At parties, for example, I would know immediately if he was 'on', singing for his supper, as it were. People would expect him to talk, to tell some funny anecdotes in that famous Irish brogue, and he never let them down. To me, it was part of his charm that he always did it so well.

This is not to say Eamonn was not capable of an acid tongue when the occasion warranted it. He could put someone down with a biting remark if they deserved it . . . which is why he got the nickname 'Fangs' from his close friends at Portmarnock Golf Club!

And he could be quite wicked after some of the huge parties we used to throw in the late fifties and early sixties in Chiswick. We enjoyed the actual 'do', of course, but both agreed that the best part, really, was talking about the guests afterwards: you know, how he or she or they had behaved. We'd spend hours discussing the good and bad sides of people and enjoy making each other laugh at our observations. For the most part, Eamonn would go out of his way to see *the good side of people, but in life that's not always possible, is it? And some of our guests in those days did do some outrageous things!*

Oh, yes, looking at that photograph in the bedroom can make me smile through my tears. But I would be less than honest if I didn't admit that, even now, eighteen months after Eamonn's death, I still miss him terribly. I miss his playful leg-pulling. I miss his clever verbal banter. And I miss him not being there to tell me off for the little things that used to irritate him – like my sniffing!

I miss the romantic touches, too; not only the physical ones – Eamonn couldn't seem to pass by me in a room without kissing me or touching me affectionately – but all those love notes and cards and telegrams sent from various parts of the world to mark a birthday or anniversary, or simply to tell me he loved me. Like many wives, I'm sure, I have kept nearly all my husband's letters and I'll treasure them forever.

As anyone who had written communication with Eamonn knows, he had a trademark: his handwritten letters were always in green ink. They were to me, too; but I'll remember them more for what they said than the colour of the ink. If ever I need convincing of how much I was loved, which I don't, all I need to do is read through the thousands of words he penned to me throughout our long relationship. One day, maybe I will. But not yet. The pain of him not being around is still too strong for me to read his beautiful words without getting upset that he will never write to me again.

Sometimes, when I'm making my bed, and adjust the side he slept on, I can see him lying there. I desperately want to see him and remember him as he was before he became ill, but those last days were so bad that his frail body and gaunt face seem indelibly and graphically imprinted in my mind's eye and I cannot shift the image. Hopefully, time will ease this torment and I will be able to see him clearly as he was before that sad decline.

In the meantime, I look at the picture in my bedroom and draw my inspiration and energy from it, trying, as Eamonn always did, to think constructively: to try to turn a negative into a positive. One of the more positive thoughts that often crosses my mind is the amazing media coverage Eamonn's death received. Throughout our marriage, we never once talked about his fame or the adulation he received; but I can assure you that he would have been astonished at the way the newspapers and television acknowledged his passing. And even more amazed at the unbelievable turnout of famous personalities at the Westminster Abbey memorial service.

I cannot imagine Eamonn thinking for a moment that The Times *would carry an obituary; but it did – three columns, in fact – in which the writer observed:*

It was possible to watch Eamonn Andrews carefully for a long time without noticing the professional skill with which he worked, guiding a conversation, drawing none of the limelight to himself. It is not to do him justice simply to say that he had the 'gift of the gab'; what he did was to imbue his guests with a confidence which allowed them to shine through. In this, he showed an unobtrusive professionalism, which seemed to belong to his character and to the world of television, so that it would be entirely meaningless in any other world. The remarkable affection which television viewers felt for Eamonn Andrews was based, however, not only on the skill of his work. It grew, too, from his genuine interest in, and friendliness for, people. These qualities made it easy for his audience to identify with him, and to feel that he had taken them with him to meet and share the world of gorgeous actresses, brilliant comedians and cheerfully ebullient politicians.

That tribute would most certainly have brought a pleasing smile from Eamonn, because he took his work very seriously and believed, most passionately, in This is Your Life. *He once put his feelings about the programme into words:*

All of us have, I'm sure, an in-built desire for surprises from the first Christmas stocking we ever hung. There is hardly a person in these islands who, at one time or another, hasn't crept down to the end of the bed on Christmas morning and experienced the thrilled surprise of delving into the Christmas stocking.

I'm sure that desire for surprise stays with all of us and that is why, on *This is Your Life*, we keep the contents of the stocking a surprise for the guest of honour. We do it not to shock, not to pry, but to give them that moment of joy . . . to excite the reaction: 'What, it's for ME, this gift?'

I think viewers share this. We continue the theme of surprise by picking out of the stocking, out of the parcel, more and more 'gifts' . . . And as we try to enchant our guests, we hope, at the same time, to tell viewers a story worth telling.

In Ireland, of course, Eamonn was far more than just the presenter of This is Your Life, *and after his death the RTE commissioned a memorial to him to stand in the entrance hall at Donnybrook. The seven feet ten inch bronze statue, sculptured by Marjorie Fitzgibbon, was unveiled in September 1988.*

Now, a seven feet ten inch memorial is what my darling lover of surprises would have called the biggest surprise of all. While millions did look on him as larger than life, his view of himself was simply that of a fiercely determined man, who knew what he wanted out of life and persevered, sometimes against all odds, until he got it. Certainly he would never have imagined, in his wildest dreams – and he had many! – anyone thinking his devotion to work warranted such a towering tribute. In all honesty, he probably would have been embarrassed by it.

The family view of him was summed up, simply but poignantly, by Emma at the unveiling of the memorial. Her father's expressive literary talent has rubbed off on her and she told the Taoiseach, Charles Haughey, and other guests:

Speaking for my mother and the family, we're very proud. Proud and happy that Dad should be honoured in this way. We'd like to pay tribute to RTE and to the artistry of Marjorie Fitzgibbon. This isn't a photograph. Nor should it be. And she's certainly spot on in depicting a big man – big in so many ways. There were so many facets to Eamonn Andrews, and few portraits, whether in oils, bronze, on videotape or sound recording, can be expected to do justice to all of these facets.

People have spoken of his warmth, his popularity, his dedication to work, and his broadcasting professionalism. These are all true. But to those who knew him closely, and most particularly to Grainne, to Fergal, to Niamh and to me, he was more. He was everything.

* * *

Although it has been hard for me, I do hope that after reading this book, this very personal memoir, you will have a good idea of what Emma meant. And what Eamonn meant to us.

POSTSCRIPT

Only Mummy really knew just how deeply Daddy was stitched into the fabric of her existence.

We children had some idea. We saw her suffer, and felt some of her pain as she committed these memories to paper. It was so soon after Daddy's death that she said the pain was like re-opening a wound. And so much pain took its toll.

Mummy died shortly after finishing this book, less than eighteen months after Daddy.

There are so many things to remember: so much love, so much fun. As a family I think we had the best fun in the world.

But at the moment it is difficult to feel anything but sadness. I remember Mummy in the dark winter after Daddy's death. I see her sitting at the round table in the family-room, going through piles of photographs for this book. Suddenly, holding up one very old black and white shot of Daddy as a young man, she spoke in a voice I had never heard before, a voice sad and full of longing. 'I wish,' she said, 'I wish I could have him back . . . *all over again.*'

It was at that moment, in that warm room at home, that the extent of her loss – the depth and breadth and height of it – struck me with unbearable force. For Mummy was brave, as Daddy had been. But she was braver than we had ever imagined, as we watched her going to bed, or go shopping in Malahide, or face an audience, or write this book, or comfort us – or do all the little things she used to do with Daddy. This time she was doing them alone. She was brave and kind and funny and generous.

But she was also lost: lost for the touch of his hand, for the sound of his voice. Lost for her great love. Lost for her big fellow.

As Fergal says, Mummy and Daddy were made for each other; to view them separately would be like taking the day without the night.

Now we have lost them.

But what was lost is found.

Sursum corda.

Emma Andrews
June 1989

INDEX